# The Grammar of
# Identity

*Transnational Fiction and the Nature of*
*the Boundary*

STEPHEN CLINGMAN

OXFORD
UNIVERSITY PRESS

# OXFORD

**UNIVERSITY PRESS**

Great Clarendon Street, Oxford OX2 6DP
United Kingdom

Oxford University Press is a department of the University of Oxford.
It furthers the University's objective of excellence in research, scholarship,
and education by publishing worldwide.
Oxford is a registered trade mark of Oxford University Press
in the UK and in certain other countries

British Library Cataloguing in Publication Data

Data available

Library of Congress Cataloging in Publication Data

Data available

ISBN 978–0–19–927849–7 (Hbk)
ISBN 978–0–19–965381–2 (Pbk)

Printed and bound by
CPI Group (UK) Ltd., Croydon, CR0 4YY

For Moira, on this journey

# *Permissions*

The early beginnings of Chapter 2, on Caryl Phillips, were published in an essay in *Salmagundi*; I am also grateful to the editors of *Moving Worlds*, for permission to rework material from an article on Phillips published there. Selections from Ovid's *Metamorphoses*, translated by A. D. Melville (Oxford and New York: Oxford University Press, 1998), are used by kind permission of Oxford University Press. Selections from Virgil's *Aeneid*, translated by Robert Fitzgerald (translation copyright © 1980, 1982, 1983 by Robert Fitzgerald), are used by permission of Random House, Inc.

# Contents

# *Preface*

This book has, from the very start, been the expression of a search or a journey. In other words, it has taken on the inner form of its topic, an exploration whose own grammar of identity has unfolded through its navigations.

All writing is autobiographical: that may be nothing more than a truism. But it takes on a deeper resonance if we think of it this way: the autobiography emerges (as the word suggests) in nothing less than the writing. One has to write it to find it. And so, while it seems I can only say too much or too little, I would like to reflect on that aspect quite briefly. While the book that follows is not overtly personal, nonetheless it has personal origins and dimensions, and always a deep personal investment.

First, the impulse. I think back to a place of birth, another world, far from here. I won't do it the injustice of describing it, but it is still part of the archaeology of a life. Because I grew up in South Africa, under apartheid, privileged but still subject to a system of oppression and division, it seems I keep coming back to the question of identity. Apartheid was not all, or only, about identity, but identity formed a large part of its definition. Because of this experience, there is both compulsion and obligation: to address the issue, to find other ways of constructing the self in relation to others, other ways of defining ourselves in the places we inhabit. And of course, South Africa provides an example which never leaves my mind: how people committed to the morality of their undertakings can fashion identities which are connective, not divisive, unfolding within a closed system to change the nature of the system itself, altering its own inner grammar, topology.

These questions have appeared in my work before. First, indirectly, on the South African novelist Nadine Gordimer, where I explored her developing sense of self and place, the identities of the world around her. Then, more overtly, in the life of Bram Fischer, the Afrikaner lawyer and political figure who revolutionized his sense of self and country in identifying with the struggle of the majority of South Africa's people— and paid the highest price for it. Now, I am back to a study of fiction, most of it not about South Africa, but these are the underlying impulses and shapes. If that is a particular kind of fate, because of the particulars of birth to follow through its logic in various ways, then it is not one I mind. Indeed, it feels both a responsibility and a strangely happy privilege to undertake it.

And there is that other sense too: that an unfolding, transitive identity can be liberating within the self as well as in relation to others. As a form of thinking about location, my hope is that it may be a key to a view of our world.

* * *

Three moments, three motifs from the life of this book, inseparable from its journey.

First, I am in Amsterdam, on my way to a conference on the work of Caryl Phillips. I have, among other things, visited the Jewish museum and the Anne Frank house, which has meant so much to Phillips himself. On the way back to my hotel, I hear a voice singing, and before seeing anyone know it is an African man, because of the music, because of its sound. Then I see the man walking, singing himself from one place to another. Here are the collocations Phillips writes about: the new migrant in old Europe, with its own deeply compromised history, the link between one migrant and another, the question of navigation, solitude. Not least, there is music, which in this case seems the very form of distance, transition, connection.

Then, on the way back from the conference in Liège, the train to Amsterdam goes by a different route from the one I took to get there, because of maintenance work on the lines. I, however, am deep in concentration, reading a draft of my chapter on Sebald, trying to work out what it needs. The train slows and pulls into a station, and when I look up, I realize with sudden amazement where we are. We are in Antwerp's Centraal Station, where Sebald opens *Austerlitz*. For some reason I cannot explain, it seems familiar, as if I had seen it before, as if Sebald had photographed it. I jump up, agitated, take a photograph through the window, when the woman across from me says that if I turn around I can see the big Imperial clock at the other end of the station—part of the ethos Sebald describes. I photograph everything—photograph Sebald's description, take 'his' photograph, as it were. I feel as if I am in his book, experiencing one of his moments of uncanny linkage. The book has created the journey as much as the journey the book. It tells me in a strange way that, no matter the 'route', somehow I am on the right track. As the train leaves the station I go back to my chapter.

And a third motif. In *Austerlitz*, the eponymously named character gives the narrator a book by the South African writer Dan Jacobson, entitled *Heshel's Kingdom*. It tells the story of Jacobson's visit to Lithuania in search of his roots, of a grandfather who died, and by dying, saved his family from death at the hands of the Nazis, because they emigrated to South Africa. Jacobson's book tells of his visit to Kaunas (Kovno) and other villages and towns in the district, and when I read it, I feel he has made the journey for me, because that is exactly where my mother's parents and grandparents came from. In those towns and villages, or in unmarked graves nearby them, we have no doubt there are the remains of more distant family we never knew, who did not escape the fate that Jacobson's more immediate family, like ours, did.

So, link is added to link, urgency to urgency, question to question. Again, some of the impulses of this book may be apparent. And again there is something about the links and journeys of literature itself, for here is a book by a white South African Jewish writer in the pages of a book by a German writer confronting the endless resonance of the Holocaust. I don't mind being triangulated between them, because these are among the metonymies, linkages, transitions and navigations I want to explore. There is something here about the transitive and connective identities invoked by writing which carries at least the hint of a form of hope, the work to be done.

And despite the subject matter, it is positive work. This book took as much as I could give, and sometimes, it felt, more. But, whatever its faults, it never ceased to challenge, engage and enliven me as a form of discovery, and for that I am grateful.

\* \* \*

A line from Salman Rushdie, which has more than incidental relevance for this book: 'Begin all over again.' And one from Walter Benjamin: 'Important thoughts must be put to sleep for a long time.' Benjamin may have been under the influence of hashish when he made the remark, but the line is still striking. As for this book, it is not for me to say whether its ideas are important, but they have certainly had to form and transform, whether in sleep or waking life, over quite a long time.

For this reason, I am immensely grateful for the help, support, and friendship of others, and would like to record my thanks here. At the University of Massachusetts, a Samuel F. Conti Faculty Fellowship gave me a precious year in which to write the bulk of a first draft. Lee Edwards, former Dean of the College of Humanities and Fine Arts, was never less than enthusiastic and supportive as I undertook this project. Two successive chairs of the English Department, Anne Herrington and Joseph Bartolomeo, have offered all the support I could have wished. Randall Knoper and Suzanne Daly gave invaluable help in reading my work, on occasion when they could least afford the time; I am grateful for their wonderful friendship, encouragement, and generosity. Further afield, Linda Slakey, then Dean of Commonwealth College at the University of Massachusetts, was quite prepared to discuss with me the difference between a combination and a blend in genetics and biology. John Kingston and Peggy Speas in Linguistics lent an ear or gave me pointers, but cannot be held responsible for what I made of them. Jon Machta, in the Department of Physics and Astronomy was able to find me a key article that helped open up the basic frame of this book. David Mednicoff was always encouraging. James Kelly, Humanities Bibliographer at the University of Massachusetts, has been the epitome of tireless energy and willingness to help. Colleagues and friends at other institutions gave attentive readings and the most generous support: Barbara Harlow, Michael Gorra, and Lawrence Douglas. Eva Paus, at Mount Holyoke College, helped with translations from the German. I have to mention especially James Simpson, whose friendship and example of intellectual clarity and spirit have inspired me since both of us were just starting out.

In some ways, this book emerged from my teaching, and I am grateful to two wonderful graduate classes for their input, their enthusiasm, and their responsiveness as we undertook a collective venture on the topic of 'Transnational Fiction'. In this regard, I want to mention a few people in particular. Mazen Naous has been part of this work from the beginning; his friendship, and the music we have played together, represent the kind of connections this book is about. David Odhiambo,

Leni Zumas, Nicole Matos, Shehryar Fazli, Jacob Dyer-Spiegel, Amanda Carr have made me feel the book was their project too. And there are other former students, who (so long as they do not mind) are part of the book as well: Laura Wright, Renée Schatteman, Maureen Fielding, Alessandra Di Maio, Michael Reder, Josna Rege, Lloren Foster. I am grateful for all they have given.

At Oxford University Press, Andrew McNeillie was immensely encouraging from the start, yet patient enough to give me time when I needed it; Jacqueline Baker took over gracefully and graciously towards the end. In other practical matters, Sarah D'Stair in Amherst took charge of checking permissions for the book; Rhiannon Elinevsky checked references at a crucial stage. It may be quite rare for booksellers to be cited in acknowledgements, but Nat Herold and Mark Wootton have made Amherst Books a quite rare resource. I am also grateful to Yisrael Espinoza, the online editor of the HiRISE website, who generously provided printable images for the cover of this book. A nice coincidence that he shares an historic surname with Baruch Spinoza, who appears in my Chapter 2; from the philosopher who was also a lens polisher to twenty-first century images from space, there is a pleasing resonance.

I owe especial thanks to two of the writers in this book. When it comes to matters of identity, Caryl Phillips has been nothing less than a model of how to proceed. More than that, he has been a remarkable friend, who understood from the start what this book was about and gave me every encouragement. Yet he did not read anything I wrote about him—a model in a different way of how not to interfere! Nadine Gordimer, too, has known how to walk the fine line between being an object of study and a tremendous friend. I think back to those years ago when I ventured into her house for the first time to ask her questions about her life and work. She too has never interfered with anything I have written, but gave her encouragement when (but not simply because) it was needed.

There have been very special friends who have sustained me all along. Yehudit Heller offered interest, energy, and insight, ranging from biblical matters to questions of mythology, translation, and etymology. She and Eric Heller have been part of our lives in Amherst all these years; friendship such as theirs begins to define what life can be about. I have already mentioned Mazen Naous and Suzanne Daly in other contexts, but let me say again how much their friendship has meant to me. Nancy Pick, together with Lawrence Douglas, provided conviviality, support, and always good humour. And then there is my cousin, the writer and poet Denis Hirson in Paris, who has been my companion throughout, at the beginning, middle, and now at the end. Denis kept me going when I might have given up, always believing in the book, while at the same time—with an honesty to match his compassion and encouragement—holding me to the highest standards. If I have not lived up to those standards, the fault is mine, not his; the same goes for all the others who have helped me as I wrote this book.

I have to end by thanking particular members of my family. My uncle Stanley Clingman may recognize the seeds of one part of the project for which I am grateful. My brother Paul, together with his family in Johannesburg, has always given unconditional support. The same is true of my mother, Madge Clingman, and the memory of my father, who once trained as a navigator, is implicit in the movements of this book. Amelia and Rebecca, our daughters have—yet again—provided remarkable tolerance regarding the strange and obsessive marathons that seem to occupy the person called their father. Moira, my first reader always, has been my partner and more than that on the journey, and gratitude seems an inadequate word to express everything I feel.

Amherst
May 2008

# Introduction
# The Grammar of Identity

When we think of the world's future, we always mean the destination it will reach if it keeps going in the direction we can see it
going in now; it does not occur to us that its path is not a straight
line but a curve, constantly changing direction.

Ludwig Wittgenstein, *Culture and Value*

Language...is not intrinsically a system of communication, nor
is it the only system used for communication.

Noam Chomsky, 'Linguistics and Cognitive Science:
Problems and Mysteries'

Language is the main instrument of man's refusal to accept the
world as it is.

George Steiner, *After Babel*

An image appears in a novel written some eighty years ago, of the earth
suspended in space. It comes as two of the main characters, who have
decided not to marry one another, undergo an unnerving accident on
a strange road which brings them together again. Their hands touch
and we are told that 'a spurious unity' descended on them—as spurious
as the night that encircles them, which seems absolute, but is 'being
modified by gleams of day that leaked up round the edges of the earth,
and by the stars'. The moment is full of crossings: an accident brings
unity, but a unity that is only spurious; the context of the accident—
the night—is itself only a false unity, being modified already by light.
What happens to these two individuals cannot be separated from their
location—the road, the night, the planet. But it is a location that is
far from being one thing, and we may ask the question, is it day or

night on earth? It depends where you are, might be the answer. But
'where' are you? If you are in India, it might be the night of a spurious
unity. But if you are 'on earth', the question makes no sense, for light
and dark continually edge into one another—touch one another, leak
into one another's space, in continual movement across the surface of
the globe. If you were at the outer edges of the solar system—also in
a sense our 'home'—you could ask the question again, and come up
with an even more complicated answer. And then there are the stars of
the passage: points of light in the dark which we often see connected
as constellations, though there may be millions of light years between
them.

It is a small moment, but an emblematic one. It comes from
E. M. Forster's *A Passage to India*—a title that 'travelled' from a poem
by Walt Whitman.[1] It is a novel mostly read with suspicion nowa-
days, because of its orientalism, because of its sense of 'great Asiatic
mystery', because it may rehearse (even if only by deflection) themes
of the threatening Asian repressed.[2] And yet it is a novel which has
its own wisdoms, as in the image of the earth in this passage. These
are the notions such a moment puts into question: location; identity;
perspective; connection; unity; division; symmetry and asymmetry; the
nature of a boundary which is itself nothing other than movement,
perpetually dissolving as it shifts. It marks a fitting motif for this
book, therefore, which is concerned with precisely these issues: what
a grammar of identity might mean as a grammar of the transitive; how
that redefines our sense of location; how we might rethink the nature
of boundaries, whether within or between individuals, within or across
nations, or as a defining characteristic of the transnational. Accordingly,
I want to hold this image of the earth turning and moving in space:

---

[1] For the episode above, see E. M. Forster, *A Passage to India* (San Diego, New York
and London: Harcourt, Brace, Jovanovich, 1924; repr., 1984), 94. (Note that pagination
in a number of Harcourt editions varies.)

[2] Edward Said, *Orientalism* (New York: Vintage, 1979), 99, 244; also Salman
Rushdie, 'Outside the Whale', in *Imaginary Homelands* (London: Granta, 1991), 89.
For the event in the caves as the 'extinction of the recognisable object of culture . . . at
the edge of experience', see Homi Bhabha, 'Articulating the Archaic: Cultural Difference
and Colonial Nonsense', in *The Location of Culture* (London and New York: Routledge,
1994), 126. A larger consideration of the novel would show how it not only subjects
India but allows itself to be Indianized in its formal philosophy—the kind of 'grammar'
suggested in this study.

as a reality; as a problem; and potentially as the key to a form of understanding.

## IMAGINING THE TRANSNATIONAL

This book is premised on the idea that there is a phenomenon called transnational fiction which is of great importance as an 'inner' map of the world we have inherited and currently inhabit. Yet, what is 'transnational fiction', what characterizes it, and why is it significant? These are questions it will be the task of this book to address and, if not solve, then at least resolve into a series of fitting and—always the hope—searching explorations.

But where to begin? If we wish to explore transnational fiction, it might be appropriate to start with the idea—in the widest sense— of 'national fiction', and here the opening point has to be Benedict Anderson's *Imagined Communities*, which a quarter of a century ago set out the principal features and mechanisms whereby nations 'imagined' themselves into being. Anderson's book was seminal and inspirational, and changed a whole framework of thinking. Here were some of the historical processes and markers underlying a sense of boundaried containment in the national imagination: the rise of print culture, in the form of novel and newspaper; the census, map, and museum in establishing a sense both of connection with the past and of territorial cohesion. Anderson explored the peregrinations of those who 'invented' forms of nationalism, the migration of the concept back and forth between the old and new worlds, the way in which nations across those spaces were not necessarily 'isomorphic' with the languages or the print cultures in which they were propagated. In fascinating terms he explored the time of the nation as embodying Walter Benjamin's 'homogeneous, empty time', where simultaneity was 'transverse, cross-time, marked not by prefiguring and fulfilment, but by temporal coincidence, and measured by clock and calendar'.[3]

As significant as Anderson's account was, since then it has come under explicit and implicit critique, as others have explored both within

---

[3] Benedict Anderson, *Imagined Communities: Reflections on the Origin and Spread of Nationalism*, rev. edn (London and New York: Verso, 1991), 24. For the question of 'isomorphism', see p. 46.

and beyond the frame of his model. Some of these later perspectives, whether responding directly to Anderson or not, are important for this study. Partha Chatterjee, reconsidering issues of European tutelage in the history and possibilities of nationalism, questioned 'whose imagined community' was under discussion. Paul Gilroy, taking up oceanography rather than territory, explored the unfolding of identity through space and time in the transnational environment of the 'Black Atlantic'. Arjun Appadurai has offered ideas of postnational cartography and 'ethnoscapes' in the conceptual mapping of a postmodern and post-colonial world. In a different frame—but one very important for this book—James Clifford has set out the idea of 'traveling cultures' founded on movement, mediation, asymmetry, and unevenness rather than any self-contained location, whether national or ethnographic. In such a formulation the nature of the boundary, even the imagined boundary, becomes something much less than solid or impermeable, but equally it becomes intriguingly problematic.[4] Even *within* the imagined community (as we shall see most sharply in Caryl Phillips's *A Distant Shore*), the time and space of the contemporary nation are gapped, divided, and incoherent in ways Anderson's model could not fully conceive.

The fact is, however the world looked when Anderson's book was first published, we live in an even more complex setting now. Our planet seems at one and the same time to be unbounded, globalized, and accessible—and yet massively divided. To popular 'sages' such as Thomas Friedman, the world is 'flat'; to others it is extraordinarily uneven.[5] In this setting the fundamental question is not whether boundaries exist—because they do, they always do—but what kind of

    [4] For references here, see the following: Partha Chatterjee, *The Nation and its Fragments: Colonial and Postcolonial Histories* (Princeton, NJ: Princeton University Press, 1993), ch. 1; Paul Gilroy, *The Black Atlantic: Modernity and Double Consciousness* (Cambridge, MA: Harvard, 1993); Arjun Appadurai, 'Sovereignty without Territoriality: Notes for a Postnational Geography', in *The Anthropology of Space and Place*, ed. Setha M. Low and Denise Lawrence-Zúñiga (Oxford: Blackwell, 2003); Arjun Appadurai, 'Global Ethnoscapes: Notes and Queries for a Transnational Anthropology', in *Recapturing Anthropology: Working in the Present*, ed. Richard Fox (Santa Fe: School of American Research Press, 1991); James Clifford, 'Traveling Cultures', in *Cultural Studies*, ed. Lawrence Grossberg, Cary Nelson, and Paula A. Treichler (New York and London: Routledge, 1992).
    [5] See Thomas L. Friedman, *The World is Flat: A Brief History of the Twenty-First Century* (New York: Farrar, Straus, and Giroux, 2005). For a contrasting view, the work of R. Radhakrishnan, *Theory in an Uneven World* (Oxford: Blackwell, 2003).

boundaries they are. It is one of the key questions at the centre of this study.

Let us approach this from a different direction. A way of thinking about the contemporary world is to see it under two competing descriptions and tendencies, of the *many* and the *one*. From a certain point of view, the world of the many is the global itself—of multiplicity, merging, and confusion in all its guises. This is the world of flow—of power, money, markets, and people around the earth—or a particular kind of structuring (far from neutral) of that flow. This is the context in which critics and theorists discuss Empires (old and new), migration, diaspora, exile, the cosmopolitan, as well as the identities that go with them, whether postmodern or postcolonial, hybrid, nomadic, or multicultural. There are serious questions as to whether the national has lost its legitimacy in this new–old context, or whether its inspirational capacities are still required. Conversely, there is discussion of whether the end of national sovereignty in a global context is all that new, or, as Neil Lazarus points out, has been a fact of life for centuries for most of the world's population.[6]

From another angle, however, and possibly in response, there is a countervailing reality, governed by the *one* or *singularity* when it comes to questions of location, identity, and identification, whether considered in terms of ethnicity, nationality, or religion. Around the world we witness its pathology: raging battles over territory and boundaries; the call to 'purity', or religious orthodoxy or fundamentalism; walls which go up and are (inevitably) pulled down; the ritual of sacrifice, whether of self or others, to enforce or reinforce that singularity. This is not just a question of suicide bombers, who blow up themselves and others as a form of political *statement*; there is the larger question of how many possibilities of 'self' are sacrificed for the sake of singular identities. Of course the landscape is confused and cross-cutting: religious identities override national boundaries, while national, religious, and ethnic identities are seldom coterminous. But that tendency to the *one* or *singular* is consistent in its orientation: a way of ruling out transition, change, interaction, modulation, morphology, transformation.

---

[6] Neil Lazarus, 'Transnationalism and the Alleged Death of the Nation State', in *Cultural Readings of Imperialism: Edward Said and the Gravity of History*, ed. Keith Ansell-Pearson, Benita Parry, and Judith Squires (New York: St Martin's, 1997).

Yet, think again: which is the *many*, which is the *one*? In a different light the global world—with all its confusion, its clashing array—is the one: one world. And those who subscribe to the *one* are trying to create a new collectivity—of the many, who somehow will all look and behave the same way. For Jean-Luc Nancy, coming at this from an ontological perspective, the 'one' and the 'many' already invoke each other, co-created, *being with*.[7] Some have attempted to modulate these principles through versions of reconciliation: often, naive celebrations of hybridity or the multicultural. There are also melancholic views of the hybrid as a space of the perpetual 'in-between'. But it seems we need a new form of negotiation in the face of this complexity: one that will recognize difference without assuming anything like hard and fast boundaries, which will cater to the reality of differentiation without cutting off the possibility of connection. Such a form would be able to account for the many without assuming that difference is all, or that all is simply one and the 'same'. It would allow for the possibility of linkage and movement without opting for either simplistic celebration or perpetual alienation.

In short, we need a new way to understand the complexities of identity and location, for how they might be reconceived—something even like a *mechanism* for rethinking their interactions. Is there an alternative way of constructing versions of self, self and other, individual and collectivity, collectivity and (other) collectivity, position and (other) position? How do we negotiate the differences among and between us? What can fiction tell us in this context?

This book proceeds from three concepts: the idea of transnational fiction; the grammar of identity; the nature of the boundary. Linking them all is the idea of navigation. It is worth exploring each in turn.

## TRANSNATIONAL FICTION

One names the object as if it were well understood, but what exactly is it? Or, if we are unable to define it in some singular way, what features and characteristics does transnational fiction exhibit? There are various possibilities.

---

[7] Jean-Luc Nancy, *Being Singular Plural*, trans. Robert D. Richardson and Anne E. O'Byrne (Stanford: Stanford University Press, 2000), 28 ff.

On one level, the ubiquity of transnational fiction is obvious, in that now, more than ever, the literary world is replete with writers who have *travelled*, often more than once across national boundaries. Salman Rushdie, born in Bombay (a city which itself has 'travelled' into a new/old incarnation as Mumbai), goes to school in England, then lives in London and moves to New York—and later on is knighted in Britain. Caryl Phillips, born in St Kitts, moves to Leeds at the age of three months, then also lives in London before moving to New York. W. G. Sebald, born in Germany, lived in England, though he wrote in German. The first of the writers in this study, Joseph Conrad, was born in a country not yet Poland, under the Russian Empire, before moving to France, and later to England, travelling the world as a sailor. Under what 'national' description, therefore, do we place such writers? Perhaps this, in and of itself, might be a definition of transnational fiction: the fiction of writers who have crossed national boundaries. But then, what do we make of a Nadine Gordimer, someone who has always lived in South Africa, yet who, in *The Pickup*, writes a novel which enters transnational territory? Even Charlotte Brontë, the most culturally 'homebound' of figures, managed to write a novel featuring a West Indian character who threatened the very rationality of the national—albeit as a problem and not a solution. Perhaps, then, the physical location of the writer, whether travelled or not, is not adequate to describe the transnational.

These last examples prompt the question from a reverse angle: if describing the transnational is difficult, is there such a thing as 'national fiction' to counterpose against it? The more closely we inspect the idea, however, the more it dissolves in front of our eyes. While governments construct national fictions all the time, it is not so clear that literature does. Shakespeare may be on the postage stamps, but his central characters include the Prince of Denmark, Cleopatra, Othello, and the Merchant of Venice, and he set one of his plays on what might pass for an early-colonial Caribbean island. If anyone is *the* Italian poet it is surely Dante, yet look what he said (too easily, but nonetheless): 'To me ... the whole world is a homeland, like the sea to fish'.[8] Chinua Achebe may in a sense have written the history of his nation—yet he was Igbo and a supporter of Biafra, and had to go into exile during

---

[8] Quoted by Wai Chee Dimock, 'Literature for the Planet', *PMLA*, 116/1 (2001): 178.

the Nigerian Civil War; he also wrote in English, which he—justly—claimed to have 'Africanized'.[9] There may well have been—there surely are—writers who have written 'for the nation', especially in conditions of national resistance to colonialism or oppression; but, even under the pressure of apartheid in South Africa in the 1980s, Njabulo Ndebele pointed out that writers should not conflate the national or liberatory with the literary, because the literary had its own unpredictable yet intrinsically democratic effects which do not conform to preordained lineaments.[10]

Perhaps, then, *all* writing has an element of the 'transnational'—a case made compellingly by Wai Chee Dimock in her study of Mandelstam's affiliation with Dante in the context of a Soviet Union that tried to police both time and space. As Dimock remarks, 'There is a morphological mismatch between literature and the nation, between the dynamic expanse of a linguistic continuum and the finite borders of a territorial regime.'[11] Here, by definition, literature overflows national borders, but if all writing is transnational in this sense, then it too might disappear as a separable phenomenon. To make it the totality is also to negate it; and in general, the question of boundaries—ultimately *intrinsic* to the transnational—will not disappear so easily.[12] A different tack would be to suggest that transnational fiction is written by, and directed towards, migrant and multi-lingual communities, who exist in multiple and in-between spaces. It is, in essence, a migrant and migrating literature. But even then we have to consider what the *migrating* element in such fiction means, making it transnational fiction.[13]

---

[9] Chinua Achebe, 'The African Writer and the English Language', in *Morning Yet on Creation Day* (Garden City: Anchor Press, 1975).

[10] 'Turkish Tales and Some Thoughts on South African Fiction', reprinted in Njabulo Ndebele, *South African Literature and Culture: Rediscovery of the Ordinary* (Manchester: Manchester University Press; New York: St Martin's, 1994). See also 'The Rediscovery of the Ordinary: Some New Writings in South Africa' in the same volume.

[11] Dimock, 'Literature', 177.

[12] In this regard see Wai Chee Dimock's more recent work, *Through Other Continents: American Literature Across Deep Time* (Princeton and Oxford: Princeton University Press, 2006) for a textured sense of transition and connection across a wider literary landscape.

[13] Azade Seyhan provides some further specification in this regard in her study of Turkish-German writers in Germany and Chicano/a writers in the United States. For her, transnational literature concerns those who write in second or third languages, who have crossed borders, and address issues facing 'deterritorialized cultures'. These are, as she puts it, 'the voices of transplanted and translated subjects'. Azade Seyhan, *Writing Outside the Nation* (Princeton and Oxford: Princeton University Press, 2001), 9, 10.

Along these lines, we might take a different approach: if transnational fiction is not simply a matter of writers who travel, its key feature may be *works* that travel, no matter the provenance or trajectories of their authors. Here we should distinguish between books that travel as objects—imported across borders, circulating as texts—and those that travel in the way they are *written*. This, too, is a proposition we can test, perhaps no more illuminatingly than in the case of V. S. Naipaul, an author who, ever since leaving Trinidad for Oxford and later settling in England, has journeyed widely, and whose books, in some senses, also cross boundaries. Yet when he writes about India—his ancestral home—or about Africa in a novel such as *A Bend in the River*, we might ask whether there is anything truly transnational about it. Rather than verities being overturned or challenged, or a sense of space or time opening up, instead we feel them closing down. In the Africa of *A Bend in the River*, the central character and narrator, Salim, talks of the motto inscribed on ruins at the dock gates of his new domicile on the Congo River: *Miscerique probat populos et foedera iungi*: 'He approves of the mingling of the peoples and their bonds of union'[14]—an apparent invitation to the transnational. But he also discovers (from a Father Huismans—for Salim is uneducated in the legacy of Europe, and in the logic of this book has to be schooled by a white man) that the motto is a corruption of the original in the *Aeneid*, where Venus, addressing Juno, tries to prevent Aeneas from staying with Dido in Libya by suggesting that Jupiter might *not* approve 'the blending of peoples and the bonds of union'.[15] Salim is horrified at the distortion: 'Rome was Rome. What was this place?' (*BIR*, 63). The moment is emblematic in so many ways: Rome is Rome; Africa will always be Africa. Tautologies rule, and there can be no 'commingling', no 'bonds of union', no connection, no combination, no transition, no transformation, no transnational perspective. Naipaul finds what he wants in Virgil, whose own poem of an apparently 'transnational' voyage has but one paradoxical and predestined legacy: the founding of a nation and of Empire.

---

[14] V. S. Naipaul, *A Bend in the River* (New York: Vintage, 1989), 62. Henceforth referenced as *BIR*.

[15] My translation (partly 'combined' from various others): see *Aeneid*, Book 4, 110–12. Fitzgerald's version is provocatively rendered: 'Does he approve/ A union and a mingling of these races?' See Virgil, *The Aeneid*, trans. Robert Fitzgerald (New York: Vintage, 1990), Bk 4, 156–9.

But when Naipaul writes a book of settlement and of 'home'—of his own, in Wiltshire, in England, in *The Enigma of Arrival*—then (in another paradox) what a difference there is! For here are fewer of the verities, and this is an extraordinary inspection of the self in its various phases and transitions, from Trinidad to England and beyond, across various routes in Naipaul's life, in his work, in his understanding of his subject. Tracking his habitual path across the downs near his home in Wiltshire, he muses on the writing he is doing on Africa—the book within the memoir of this narrative—itself a reimagined combination of experiences in Kenya, Uganda, the Congo, Rwanda, and Trinidad. This is where he imagines a story emerging from Giorgio de Chirico's *The Enigma of Arrival*—a story he never writes except in its hidden archaeology in this book, of the self who does not want the journey to end. It is in this account that Naipaul realizes the inward transformations accompanying the outer: 'To be what I wanted to be, I had to cease to be or grow out of what I was.'[16] The book—is it novel, autobiography, essay?—becomes a work in absorbing and almost literal terms of *revision, research, review*. We get the syntax of a writing life, how it is composed across and between its journeys, how in a sense it never 'arrives', how Naipaul's 'placement' in his rural cottage is a perpetual form of displacement: how arrival can only be 'the enigma of arrival'. Through time and space we get a sense of transitivities and boundaries, of transitivities that exist only and *because of* the boundaries. This looks more like a version worth exploring as transnational fiction.

Transnational fiction, then, does not necessarily come from writers who travel or books that do; on the other hand, it can be undertaken by a writer who never leaves home. Given these realities, this study is founded on a specific view: what makes fiction transnational are questions of *form*. This is true in two senses and at two levels, though they are connected. On one level it has to do with recognizable formal characteristics in the novels: their structures of time and space, and a set of figurations and properties whose logic will become clear, of metonymy, chiasmus, constellation, and much else besides. On another, and perhaps deeper, level, we should understand form as what *informs*

---

[16] V. S. Naipaul, *The Enigma of Arrival* (New York: Vintage, 1988), 245. For other passages alluded to here, see pp. 170–4.

these novels and produces their more visible patterns. At this level form becomes content—a way of being and seeing. Novels working in this manner become not only a mode of exploring the world but also a *kind* of world to be explored.

What these informing characteristics are also become evident. They concern the grammar of identity and location; the nature of boundaries, both transitive and intransitive; and navigation as a modality of existence in, and as defining, both the transitive self and transnational space. Let us consider further how this works.

## SYNTAX OF THE SELF

In approaching the idea of a grammar of identity, it is worth distinguishing between 'narrow' and 'wide' senses, though we might as well say 'proximate' and 'deep'. The narrow or proximate sense is concerned more immediately with a 'grammar' within the self, and the wide or deep with structures that prompt yet also give expression to those narrower versions. To say this is to recognize that these distinctions are only terms of convenience: narrow and wide, deep and proximate are intricately connected, and are simply different ways of considering grammars that are both active within the self and enacted in larger settings. The aim is to keep a whole series of contexts in view: all the way from processes and possibilities within the individual, to relations between self and other, to larger questions of location and navigation in a wider world. The premise here is that there is a correlation between how the self is put together and how we navigate ourselves through space and time. It is this *how* that we can understand as a form of grammar, and movement is intrinsic to its constitution.

Let us begin in the 'narrower' frame, with the idea of a syntax of the self. If we are to take the idea of a 'grammar' seriously, we should explore it in grammatical terms, and part of this rests on concepts which are quite familiar, yet also complex and quite illuminating—the two key figurations in human language of metaphor and metonymy. My aim here is to clarify some ideas, clear away some misconceptions, and see the relevance of these terms in thinking about identity in a new way, particularly in relation to transnational fiction, the nature of boundaries, and issues of navigation.

Of the two terms, metaphor is if anything the more accustomed and 'easier', certainly the one closer to us most of the time. We say 'He was a lion in battle' and understand that part of the resonance of 'lion' carries over to 'he', lending its attributes, as it were. This is the etymological source of the word 'metaphor', from the Greek, meaning to 'carry across', the Latin equivalent of which comes from *transferro, -e, -tuli, -latum*, so that 'translation' has some of the same meaning as metaphor. This is the correspondence that Salman Rushdie first seized on in saying that migrants were 'people who had been translated, who had, so to speak, entered the condition of metaphor'.[17] On its face, this would seem to be a version highly suited to a transnational mode of writing—and indeed, the idea has been taken up by scholars and critics in that way. But we should note (as we shall see in Chapter 3) that when Rushdie's characters enter that condition, say by growing horns, or developing cracks, they are, in a sense becoming composite—a *combination*, just as Kafka's Gregor Samsa does not simply become a cockroach but retains the memories and faculties of a human being. Metaphor may not always have this composite aspect (though it probably does), but it is important to see that it can sustain difference as well as similarity.

We also understand how metonymy works—though it can be the more difficult concept. When the road sign says 'Left lane must turn left' we know it is not telling us the lane will suddenly veer leftwards, but that objects attached to the lane—namely, cars—must go left; and that it is drivers attached to (or inside) the cars who must turn the wheel. So the reference works by contiguity or association. When it comes to questions of identity, however, metonymy has been understood in ways that are, if not misleading, then frequently one-dimensional. Thus Arjun Appadurai remarks on how often anthropologists work by what he calls 'metonymic freezing'. In such a version one feature of a group—attached to the group, so to speak—may come to represent the group as its quintessence. This is metonymy as a form of synecdoche—the part standing for the whole. In this way, ideas can become 'metonymic prisons' for particular places—not a good

---

[17] Salman Rushdie and Günter Grass, 'Fictions are Lies that Tell the Truth: Salman Rushdie and Günter Grass in Conversation', in *Conversations with Salman Rushdie*, ed. Michael Reder (Jackson: University Press of Mississippi, 2000), 77.

version of anthropology. By contrast, Appadurai calls for a 'polythetic' approach in which 'multiple chains of family resemblance between places would blur any single set of cultural boundaries between them.'[18] Others have taken a similar line in assuming the limiting power of metonymy.[19]

But it is not true that metonymy always involves 'freezing'. To understand this, it is worth returning to one of the major sources of this discussion, Roman Jakobson's essay 'Two Aspects of Language and Two Types of Aphasic Disturbances', written in the mid-1950s.[20] This was where Jakobson took up the idea that any form of linguistic expression involved two axes: the axis of selection (or substitution) and the axis of combination. The former enables us to select or substitute a word ('cat' or 'dog') to put in a sentence, the second to form the sentence 'The cat sat on the mat.' In the forms of aphasia he was exploring, Jakobson also distinguished two corresponding types. In the selective or substitutive disorder, aphasics lost the capacity for comprehending or expressing similarity—words that could be substituted for one another. In the contiguity disorder, they lost the capacity for combination, being reduced ultimately to one-word sentences or even less. As Jakobson put it, 'The relation of similarity is suppressed in the former, the relation of contiguity in the latter type of aphasia.'[21] At the same time, Jakobson assigned two 'semantic lines' as corresponding to these two axes: the metaphoric for the axis of similarity (substitution), and the metonymic for the axis of combination (contiguity). In a suggestive move, he also speculated on equivalent literary genres: romanticism was aligned with the metaphoric/substitutive axis, and realism with the metonymic/combinatory. Poetry was metaphoric/substitutive, prose was metonymic/combinatory.

But there is a contradiction at the heart of Jakobson's formulation—and part of it depends on what he means by 'similarity'. In what sense

---

[18] Arjun Appadurai, 'Putting Hierarchy in its Place', *Cultural Anthropology*, 3/1 (1988): 36, 40, 46. Appadurai is following Needham in calling for the 'polythetic'.

[19] For instance, even one of the inspirations of this study, Clifford, in 'Traveling Cultures', 100.

[20] Roman Jakobson, 'Two Aspects of Language and Two Types of Aphasic Disturbances', in *Selected Writings*, vol. 2: *Word and Language* (The Hague and Paris: Mouton, 1971). The essay was written in 1954 and first published in 1956.

[21] Jakobson, 'Two Aspects', 254.

is 'cat' *similar* to 'dog', even though they can perform 'similar' roles in a sentence, or be substituted for one another? More delicately—yet more to the point—we have already seen that metaphor can work through *difference* as well as similarity, so that something meaningful happens in the figure of speech (without difference nothing meaningful would occur). The whole point of a metaphor, especially a good one, is that it dislodges us from what we already know, perhaps setting up an oscillation between two meanings. A metaphor, that is to say, can be a 'combination' even if it works by substitution, and even if it operates on the vertical axis of selection. Conversely, metonymy can be used as a form of substitution, or representation in the way that Appadurai describes. 'The pen is mightier than the sword': here the pen represents (or substitutes for) the hand that holds the pen, which in turn represents the person attached to the hand. This potential crossflow between the metaphoric and metonymic is something that Jakobson elsewhere commented on himself.[22]

Is this contradiction fatal? Not at all, because it helps us to get closer to our subject. The key may be not the axes but the *function*. Is what we see combinatory or substitutive? Or which dominates in any given formulation? What matters as much as axis is orientation, tendency, transition. And tendencies remain: where metaphor will incline more to the substitutive, the intrinsic capacities of metonymy for combination admit unfolding and sometimes unexpected results. We can see this again in the proverb, 'The pen is mightier than the sword.' We have seen already how both 'pen' and 'sword' operate in terms of *representation*: they represent, along a chain of associations, the individuals who wield them. That is the *product*—the meaning we come to. But if we think of the *process,* we see how the meaning was arrived at through a series of associations taking us along a metonymic chain of *difference* in,

---

[22] 'In poetry, where similarity is superinduced upon contiguity, any metonymy is slightly metaphoric and any metaphor has a metonymic tint.' Roman Jakobson, 'Linguistics and Poetics', in *Selected Writings*, vol. 3, ed. Stephen Rudy (The Hague, Paris and New York: Mouton, 1981), 42. This crossflow is also noted in Barbara Johnson, 'Metaphor, Metonymy, and Voice in *Their Eyes Were Watching God*', in *A World of Difference* (Baltimore and London: Johns Hopkins University Press, 1987)—an essay which would merit further consideration not only because of its remarkably clear and suggestive qualities but also because a syntactic and transitive view might help unlock some of the otherwise more absolute polarities of utterance (inside/outside) and identity (singular/universal) in Johnson's model.

through, and because of contiguity. Ultimately this chain might suggest even other associations, such as pen–hand–person–*peace*, and sword–hand–person–*war*. Or—as another way of making the point—if *pen* and *sword* are trying to achieve the same purpose, they do so by different means, which may come to mean different ends. All this happens in the unfolding syntax of a sentence in which pen and sword are compared and found to be different as much as they are similar. There may be a family resemblance between the two terms, but only one in which the offspring turn out to be quite different.

This, then, is what metonymy allows: transition, navigation, mutation, alteration, a whole morphology of meanings. (This is true even of the metonymic element in metaphor.) When it comes to matters of identity, the implications are crucial, for a metonymic version of identity allows exactly for such combinations and transitions. If there is a subtext to this argument, it is worth making it overt: a formulation such as this guards against definitions of identity which are *substitutive*, especially where such substitutions flatten out and congeal all difference into singularity. This means it also guards against *representation* in specific senses, where the definition of identity claims to represent the sole and absolute possibilities of the self, whether our own or that of others. Any version of identity, 'I am $x$', where '$x$' equals the sole and total definition of the 'I', is inimical to transition, possibility, change. It prevents combination *within* the self, and also any combination with others *beyond* the self. (That is, except with others who, through some act of collective substitution, are similarly supposed to be '$x$'; but then that does not allow for any 'combination'.) Similarly, any formula 'You are $y$' leads to closures and exclusions in relation to others—and, when there is assumed to be no connection between '$x$' and '$y$', to some of the worst crimes of our histories. The idea, rather, is to develop a sense of the '$x$–$y$' within ourselves, which might connect with the '$y$–$x$' in others, or even the '$y$–$z$'. Such a version does not override or negate difference within the self or in relation to others—indeed, as we shall see, in an important sense it *depends* on it. But it does hold out the possibility of connection. And this is why so many of the writers in this study follow the metonymic, the syntactic, the *space* (direct or more distant) of encounter and combination within and between selves—because this is where the protocols and problems of a transitive version of identity are enacted.

Moreover, as much as the metonymic or syntactic in this sense encodes a spatial possibility of combination, it also does so in *time*—inevitably of great significance. Even in as archetypal a formulation of the self as Descartes's *cogito* we can see this at work. *Cogito ergo sum*, I think, therefore I am: the self that thinks is the self that exists. The account seems absolute as a definition both of singular identity and existence—and yet there is still room for shift. Is this self *exactly* the same self, we might ask, identical beginning and end in every respect? Is the self that exists not *changed* by the act of thinking? Perhaps the process of thinking (not to mention engaging with the world) alters the inner lineaments of the self, even in the most subtle ways, so that the 'I' that says the '*cogito*' may not be exactly the same—in time, in space—as the 'I' that gets to the '*sum*'.[23] Along the journey of the sentence something may have happened to the identity, precisely because of what syntax both enjoins and, in this instance, defines: the *self-thinking*, the *thinking-self*. Or, as Nietzsche averred, rather than the 'I' creating thought, the 'I' is 'a synthesis *produced* by thinking'.[24] And this happens not only in specific moments, but over the course of a lifetime, involving emotions and other subtle tremors of the self as much as it does conscious thought.

The self is therefore capable of many phases, possibilities, connected elements, both within itself and in relation to others, in time as well as space. The syntax of the self—its combinatory, unfolding possibilities—is a transitive syntax. It is a function of, and permits, *navigation*.

---

[23] One might raise this question on purely grammatical grounds, for, in Descartes's Latin formulation, there is no 'I'-word (*ego*) as there is in the English, and how would we know that the 'I' that thinks in the *cogito* is exactly the same 'I' that exists in the *sum*? The account here is obviously different from Lacan's psychoanalytic destabilization, 'I think where I am not, therefore I am where I do not think', as well as his reading of the metaphoric and metonymic, where 'the symptom is a metaphor . . . as desire is a metonymy', the former linked to the question of being, the latter to its lack. See Jacques Lacan, 'The Agency of the Letter in the Unconscious or Reason Since Freud', in *Écrits: A Selection* (New York and London: Norton, 1977), esp. 166, 171–2, 175.

[24] 'For in the past one believed in "the soul" as one believed in grammar and the grammatical subject: one said "I" is the condition, "think" is the predicate and conditioned—thinking is an activity to which a subject *must* be thought of as the cause. Then one tried with admirable artfulness to fathom whether one could not get out of this net—whether the reverse was not perhaps true: "think" the condition, "I" conditioned; "I" thus being only a synthesis *produced* by thinking.' Friedrich Nietzsche, Aphorism 54, *Beyond Good and Evil*, trans. R. J. Hollingdale (Harmondsworth: Penguin, 1973), 62–3.

## NAVIGATION

This is where we can turn to a grammar of identity in the 'wide' sense—what it means in broader contexts and at some deeper level of human orientation and expression.

Here the fundamental insight derives from the Chomskyan revolution in linguistics: that grammar must be understood as *generative*. For, as Chomsky showed, a grammar is not a surface description of a language, nor a static corpus underlying a language, but a mechanism with a set of rules we can understand as *generating* a language—ultimately all language and languages. This is what Chomsky called 'universal grammar', and it is responsible for the fact that we are all capable of speech, enabling us to convert the components of language into living communication. The inspiration in this regard was Wilhelm von Humboldt, the father of modern linguistics, who saw language as a process rather than a result. It was also Humboldt who specified the central paradox underlying the endless renewability of language, in that it 'provides for infinite use of finite means'.[25] Steven Pinker, who has written cogently on this aspect, provides an excellent gloss. Language is a 'discrete combinatorial system': the elements of language are limited and discrete, but in combination can make up almost any sentence imaginable, precisely because of the generative capacity.[26] Particular aspects of language govern this remarkable attribute. Some of these suggest structure, in that not all combinations are possible in any given instance: 'A sentence is not a chain but a tree', as Pinker points out (*TLI*, 90). Yet within these structures language can undergo infinite elaboration, through a principle of *recursion*: one can add elements on to, or within, sentences infinitely, so that 'The dog ate my homework' can take on endlessly variable forms simply by inserting or adding other words (before school, after school, name, size, shape, history of the dog, etc).

---

[25] Noam Chomsky, 'Linguistics and Adjacent Fields: A Personal View', in *The Chomskyan Turn*, ed. Asa Kasher (Oxford and Cambridge, MA: Blackwell, 1991), 7. For the original, see Wilhelm von Humboldt, *On Language*, ed. Michael Losonsky, trans. Peter Heath (Cambridge: Cambridge University Press, 1999), 91. It is worth pointing out that while the specifics of Chomsky's linguistic account have changed a number of times, the generative aspect remains central.

[26] Steven Pinker, *The Language Instinct: How The Mind Creates Language* (New York: Perennial Classics, 2000), 75. Henceforth referenced as *TLI*.

Pinker indicates that, in this respect, language is unlike most other complex systems, which involve *blends*, where more and more additions (one can think of paint) involve tinier and tinier differences. Rather, he suggests, language is like DNA, where four kinds of nucleotides can be combined into sixty-four kinds of codons, and the codons into an unlimited number of genes. For Pinker, the grammatical analogy is compelling, even breathtaking: 'It may not be a coincidence that the two systems in the universe that most impress us with their open-ended complex design—life and mind—are based on discrete combinatorial systems' (*TLI*, 76). All this convinces Pinker that syntax—the combinatory capacity to organize these structured and infinite variables—is a Darwinian 'organ of extreme perfection and complication' (*TLI*, 117). He also follows Chomsky's rationalist impulses in arguing that learning is caused by 'complexity in the mind' rather than the other way round.

Yet it is another of Pinker's observations that may be more suggestive for our purposes: in human beings the capacity for speech and the capacity for walking come at the same developmental stage. Indeed, it is well known that the arrival of speech in children is explosive and exponential: by eighteen months a minimum of a new word every two hours, and thousands of syntactic structures by the age of three (*TLI*, 271, 273). But it begins earlier than this, and Pinker follows interpretations in social and evolutionary biology in indicating it may have to do with survival—that children who are learning to walk must be able to understand warnings, words, directions. As he proposes, it may be no coincidence that the vocabulary spurt and the beginnings of grammar 'follow closely on the heels of the baby, quite literally—the ability to walk unaccompanied appears around fifteen months' (*TLI*, 295). But what if, besides survival, there is another, more positive and more constructive, correlation? Here I must launch out in directions with which Pinker would probably not agree. What if the correspondence has to do with *navigation?* Think of it this way: you begin the sentence, and when you begin you are not quite sure how it will end. You navigate your way through its recursive and combinatory possibilities, looking for landmarks, safe havens, and new vistas—just as you might navigate through a landscape half-known and unknown. Some of this may be conscious, some of it by no means. Not all options are possible in the sentence, precisely because unfolding structures govern options, but then these structures too must be negotiated, chosen, become an aspect of the pathway.[27] From a different perspective, Tom Roeper points out the intriguing pattern that in many languages the word 'to' conjoins infinitive forms (*to* run) with the directional (the preposition, *to* school).[28] Speculative this may be, but what if 'to' is one marker of how the verbal (in a doubled sense in the infinitive, the very concept of action without limit) and the navigational are linked? Syntax and the capacity for navigation may in other words be intrinsically connected, at some deep level within the human psyche.

It is this idea which is suggested by Noam Chomsky and his colleagues Marc Hauser and Tecumseh Fitch in an article that caused a stir in the linguistic and cognitive science communities some years ago concerning the evolution of language. The key step in their discussion is based on the distinction between the faculty of language in the broad sense (FLB), a set of conceptual-intentional and sensory-motor capacities which is for the most part common to all animals, and the faculty of language in the narrow sense (FLN), which is confined to humans. The core property of FLN is recursion, which 'takes a finite set of elements and yields a potentially infinite array of discrete expressions'.[29] According to Chomsky and his colleagues, FLN is 'recently evolved and unique to our species', and unlikely to have developed through minor modifications of FLB (1573–4). Yet the question remains whether recursion—itself an adaptive capacity allowing an endless variety of thoughts—evolved 'for reasons other than communication' (1574). And this is where their contribution is so suggestive, for Chomsky and his colleagues speculate that it might have, and that one of the computational problems it might have solved was precisely that of 'navigation'. They entertain the possibility that recursion in animals was a closed modular system 'designed for a particular function (e.g., navigation)'

---

[27] On this question see Noam Chomsky, *Syntactic Structures* (The Hague: Mouton, 1975), 20. Also, Noam Chomsky, *Aspects of the Theory of Syntax* (Cambridge, MA: MIT Press, 1965), ch. 2, and *passim*.

[28] Tom Roeper, *The Prism of Grammar: How Child Language Illuminates Humanism* (Cambridge, MA and London: MIT Press, 2007), 15. I should stress that my speculation is not Roeper's, whose focus is on how grammar helps us understand the very mechanisms of the human.

[29] Marc D. Hauser, Noam Chomsky, and W. Tecumseh Fitch, 'The Faculty of Language: What Is It, Who Has It, and How Did It Evolve?' *Science*, 298 (2002): 1571. Further page references in this paragraph are to this article.

(1578), and that at some point in evolutionary history it became accessible to humans for other purposes—specifically, language and communication.[30] If Chomsky and his colleagues are correct, this would be one more reason to consider the line between animals and humans as itself metonymic rather than divided across an impermeable species boundary—transition intrinsic to the evolutionary story, and navigation common to all as the transitive as well as differentiating element.

It has to be said immediately that this theory has aroused controversy. Steven Pinker, together with his colleague Ray Jackendoff, has rejected the idea that 'recursion evolved for navigation' or that language is 'not an adaptation for communication'.[31] Daniel Everett, exploring the extraordinarily limited language of the Pirahã in Brazil, has argued that the way culture constrains grammar in their case undermines the notion of a universal grammar.[32] Much of the debate is minutely detailed, forensic, disputatious. Amongst this is some evidence that these capacities are bio-neurological: the fact, for instance, that London cab-drivers who have 'the Knowledge'—that is, the map of London lodged in their minds—develop enlarged hippocampi, a part of the brain associated

[30] Hauser *et al.* suggest other possible original functions for recursion in animals, such as number quantification or social relationships. But both the latter involve forms of navigation; and navigation appears to be the underlying and unifying idea the authors favour.

[31] Steven Pinker and Ray Jackendoff, 'The Faculty of Language: What's Special About It?,' *Cognition* 95/2 (2005): esp. 229–31. Also Steven Pinker and Ray Jackendoff, 'The Nature of the Language Faculty and its Implications for Evolution of Language (Reply to Fitch, Hauser, and Chomsky),' *Cognition* 97/2 (2005): 211–25. It is worth saying that there are many disagreements between Chomsky and Pinker, this among them.

[32] Daniel L. Everett, 'Cultural Constraints on Grammar and Cognition in Pirahã,' *Current Anthropology*, 46/4 (2005): 621–46. I am not equipped to comment with any authority on Everett's discussion, but note some features in passing: (a) the Pirahã may have limited language, but they are extremely good navigators in their physical environment; (b) both in their language and spatial orientation they are fascinated by liminal situations (transitional boundaries): e.g. match flames flickering into/out of life, or arrival/disappearance in the landscape; (c) the Pirahã may have limited grammar in some respects, but they also whistle, hum, and sing to communicate, and have multiple tonal inflections and prosodic complexity—which may involve grammar or syntax of a different kind; (d) if culture constrains grammar, that does not mean grammar does not operate; (e) the Pirahã are concerned with ethnic/language boundaries: the 'straight heads' who speak their language, and the 'crooked heads'—all those who do not; (f) if the Pirahã lack a highly developed syntactic capacity, they also have no fiction, and no myths of origin. In all these features, variably, we see familiar concerns: syntax, navigation, fiction, boundaries, liminality, identity—perhaps a 'grammar' mixed in specific (cultural) ratios.

with navigation in birds and animals.[33] Since the jury is out on these discussions, and may be so for a very long time, my case is a looser and simpler one. Opening up navigation as a syntactic capacity (and vice versa) provides extraordinarily rich possibilities for the idea of transnational fiction. Doing so links syntax within the self to syntax beyond the self, as navigation. It allows us to think the transnational as intrinsically navigational. The novels themselves become evidence for the navigational as a syntactic capacity embedded deeply within language and in fiction. And all this would appear to be connected with some of our deepest promptings as human beings.

Yet, to return to one of our opening questions, does this imply that all fiction is equally and openly transnational? Not necessarily, though all fiction may respond at some deep level to this navigational prompting. It would go against the grain of a study such as this to set up hard boundaries between one kind of fictional work and another; and in a certain radical sense it may be possible to apply the lens of the transnational—its categories and codes—to any work of fiction. But, as we saw in the case of Naipaul, some works will respond to these promptings more directly, turn to them, address them, seek out their complexities. The seeds of this may lie in fiction from any and every era, which is part of the reason for drawing on writing from other periods in this study. In our time, however, we can call such works transnational fiction, and one reason they become transnational is because of their concern with the nature of the boundary.


## THE NATURE OF THE BOUNDARY

Navigation, whether internal, external, or linking the two, cannot be thought or conceived without the boundary. This is the central paradox at the heart of a transitive imagination: *navigation occurs not despite but because of the boundary*. This is not a bad thing, because boundaries

---

[33] Alluded to in Valentina Bambini, Claudio Gentili, and Pietro Pietrini, 'On Cultural Constraints on Pirahã' Grammar, *Current Anthropology*, 47/1 (2006): 143. For the original research, see Eleanor A. Maguire *et al.*, 'Navigation-Related Structural Change in the Hippocampi of Taxi Drivers', *Proceedings of the National Academy of Sciences, USA* 97/8 (2000): 4398–403. Among other things, Maguire *et al.* comment: 'The need to navigate is a basic cross-species behavior' (4402).

exist everywhere and in every way. But what matters just as much as the existence of the boundary is the nature of the boundary navigation invokes: how navigation can, in effect, *transform* the nature of the boundary—the effect becoming a cause. Because navigation conjoins meaning and movement, the self and the world outside the self, these principles are linked through all these dimensions.

We can see this, for instance, in questions of syntax, which not only has to *confront* division but *requires* division—in the elements of language and meaning, in morphologies, in sequencing. There is no meaning without *space*, or the gap between meanings, or the elements involving difference in the sentence. But out of these gaps and differences, according to the generative capacities of syntax, a form of navigation takes place, allowing the miracle of utterance and expression. It is the transition across these boundaries that produces meaning, and where meaning is not complete, or is deferred, then further navigations are both invited and required. It is when we fall into singularity—assuming the 'substitutions' of complete and whole meanings—that both our navigations and utterances fall into negation. And so the boundary is also a horizon, a destination never quite reached, like the boundary of the world. The boundary of meaning, then, is a transitive boundary; the transitive is intrinsically connected with meaning; navigation depends on, and creates, the transitive boundary which itself may undergo change. In all these ways the boundary is not a limit but the space of transition.

This is true for grammars of identity as well. As we have seen, the self can be a combinatory reality both in space and time, and what provides its transitive form is the capacity for navigation. Differences within the self or between the self and other selves are not overridden or transcended in such a formulation. Rather, they become the foundation of *identity as a kind of meaning*—but meaning considered always as navigation, exploration, transition. Jean-Luc Nancy remarks that '[f]rom one singular to another, there is contiguity but not continuity', a formulation that captures the sense of space in the boundary between beings.[34] But where Nancy sees singularity and (apparently) intransitive boundaries, in the view suggested here the boundary—both within the

---

[34] Nancy, *Being*, 5. Note that while Nancy also talks of '*is being* in a transitive sense of the verb' (6), his image of the intransitive boundary generally appears to be irreducible: 'a singularity is always a body, and all bodies are singularities' (18).

self and beyond—becomes the positive invocation if not obligation to the transitive. In this sense, difference is not the barrier to navigation, but the very *ground* of its possibility and necessity. Does recognizing this make our navigations in the realm of identity easy? As we shall see many times over, that is far from the case. Recognizing and accepting different modalities within the self—its different elements, its different possibilities—is not simple; what Freud recognized as repression is one result when it does not occur. Similarly, recognizing points of contact between one self and another can be immensely difficult—especially when internal differentiation is not accepted. And there is the fundamental reality that people approach one another on massively uneven terms, of power, resources, authority. Yet at the least—as we shall see—these points of encounter, differentiation, refusal, repression, combination—can be inspected. This is the territory of (among other things) transnational fiction: a navigational space.

If identity is often connected with location, then we can put location, too, under the same lens. The fact is that landscape itself is intrinsically metonymic, as one feature literally leads to another. Transition and transitivity are of the essence in the physical world around us as contiguity, difference, modulation, and transformation unfold. Very few boundaries are impermeable—and if they are impermeable to *us* they are not for that reason intransitive in themselves. The oceans may be barriers to land, but connect one landmass and another. Even the space that surrounds the earth is the connective (transitive) medium of a differentiated universe. By the same token, nothing in and of itself occupies absolute and complete space. If it did we would live inside one of Zeno's paradoxes, where movement itself becomes impossible.[35] Human boundaries, therefore, when they become 'hard' boundaries of enclosure and exclusion, militate against this transitive notion. Asserting singularities of ownership, identity, location, they refuse any connective syntax of difference. But we do not have to romanticize too much—the self open to change navigating a landscape in transition—to see that a notion of transitive boundaries helps us reformulate our sense of location as well as identity. Indeed, it might help us see location as environment, rather than fixed 'place'.

[35] It is not accidental that a novel such as Zadie Smith's *White Teeth* (New York: Vintage, 2001), 384–5, draws attention to Zeno; note also that at issue in this sequence are questions of the 'one' and the 'many'.

This has implications in various settings. With regard to the national, for instance, we can see that what matters is not whether boundaries exist, either within the nation or around it, but what kind of boundaries they *are*. Within the nation, strange as it may seem, boundaries may be necessary, even crucial, so long as they are transitive. For without a sense of internal differentiation and transition, the result may be the singular claim: the entire nation as '*x*'—the formula which has had such disastrous results. From this point of view, we should be able to think *the transnational in the national*; and if the external boundaries of the nation are transitive, we can think *the national in the transnational* as well. Along these lines, we should also be able to distinguish between different versions of the transnational. Religious fundamentalisms, for instance, often extend beyond national boundaries, but only in the form of a 'bad transnationalism', precisely because of their claims to singularity in the realm of identity, their intransitive versions of space and time, their absolute decrees on meaning and truth.[36] By the same token, such a perspective would allow us to question the claims of the 'global' as a solution to problems of the 'one' and the 'many'. For the global has not solved the problem of boundaries. In the global, boundaries are both hard and fast, and yet infinitely receding, intangible. Paradoxically, the global might, in Walter Benjamin's sense, be 'homogeneous, empty' because it is also (in a word that will become important later on in this study) 'indifferent'—incapable of meaningful navigation. But one way to think about the transnational is to see it as a way of making the global *meaningful* insofar as the nature of the boundary is conceived and navigated differently. If the national and the transnational exist in one another's gravitational fields, it is the transitive boundary that explains the movement from one to the other.

This no doubt has ramifications in spheres from the political to the geographical. Yet this is not a study in political or geographical philosophy, but primarily in the *grammar* underlying them. From that point of view, we can still ask, what *exactly* does navigation mean in this space, the space and boundary of the transnational? In that respect, we should be clear. Whether it concerns language, fiction, identity, or location, navigation does not mean crossing or having crossed, but *being in the*

---

[36] I owe the phrase 'bad transnationalism' to Mazen Naous.

*space of crossing.*[37] It means *being prepared to be* in the space of crossing, in transition, in movement, in journey. It means accepting placement as *displacement*, position as *disposition*, not through coercion of others or by others of ourselves, but through 'disposition' as an affect of the self, as a kind of approach.[38] To those who might object that this has little connection with the world of *realpolitik*, shifting our orientations in this way might on the contrary have significant effects on the 'real': how we see the world, and our places in it, the forms in which the world is constructed. And so the 'grammar' of identity might be political after all.

If this is so, however, it also means recognizing the painful side of displacement, pre-eminently as it affects those for whom the 'transnational' is not a matter of choice.[39] For coercion, injustice, disruption have been part of human history as we know it, and we can see the effects everywhere. But that, too, allows us to see something important in terms of our approach. In a fitting way, we can see it as a question of language—specifically as a matter of etymology. In recent years, partly following on the work of James Clifford and Paul Gilroy, much has been made of the opposition between 'roots' and 'routes'—the supposition being that the idea of 'routes' is much more conducive to a transnational vision.[40] But there is an antinomy in the very term itself which has not been sufficiently recognized, and which etymology clarifies. For the 'root' of the word 'route' is the Latin *rupta*, 'broken'; and, as the dictionary informs us, the adjective has to be accompanied by the implied noun *via*, so that the full phrase is *rupta via*: broken road.[41]

---

[37] Such a notion seems intrinsic to landscapes of the transnational. Compare Brent Hayes Edwards's concept of *décalage* in *The Practice of Diaspora: Literature, Translation, and the Rise of Black Internationalism* (Cambridge, MA and London: Harvard University Press, 2003), which invokes ideas of gap, interval, and articulation; as Edwards remarks, 'it is *only* difference . . . that allows movement' (15).

[38] Again, consider Nancy's ontological account: 'every position is dis-position'; and ' "To be" . . . is the verb of dis-position.' See *Being*, 12, 96.

[39] On this doubleness, see in particular R. Radhakrishnan, *Diasporic Mediations: Between Home and Location* (Minneapolis and London: University of Minnesota Press, 1996), especially ch. 8, 'Postcoloniality and the Boundaries of Identity'.

[40] See, e.g., Gilroy, *Black Atlantic*, 19. For a searching account of these concepts, see Elizabeth M. DeLoughrey, *Routes and Roots: Navigating Caribbean and Pacific Island Literatures* (Honolulu: University of Hawai'i Press, 2007).

[41] *The Oxford English Dictionary*, 2nd edn, 1989, *s.v.* 'Route, n.', *OED Online.* Oxford University Press, University of Massachusetts, Amherst, <http://dictionary.oed.com.silk.library.umass.edu:2048/cgi/entry/50209577> (accessed 30 November 2006).

Routes are not simply continuous; they are broken, and disruption is built into the term. Unevenness and disparity are part of our history, part of the very definition of our routes and boundaries. To be in the place of transition, in the disposition of crossing, is to encounter this reality as well, an intrinsic part of the transnational.

This is the space the fictions in this study inhabit—the transitive boundary as the complex space of navigation. The novels work all the way from the small to the large scale, from intricate matters of identity, to location, to the national and transnational. In that space, they consider both navigation and disruption, the doubled nature of our routes; often what they find is a record of horror and atrocity, in which they are sometimes (like ourselves) complicit. This is not easy territory, therefore, and yet it is crucial territory to explore. And it is also significant space for our times, for we are ourselves in transition, with very few secure coordinates. We have left one shore—perhaps many shores—without reaching any safe haven. We are in provisional, transitional space, still trying to work out its protocols. This is why these novels speak to us with a degree of urgency. If the transnational is not something they achieve, then it is something they invoke, even by way of its absence. Here navigation does not have a message to communicate but is the very *form* of the message—a message we still have to understand. Differentially, unevenly, symptomatically, hopefully, we are in the space of navigation. It is the space of our history at this time.

## DEEP STRUCTURE/DEEP BACKGROUND

Yet if the novels in this study have a particular currency, the sources go far back—perhaps as far back as we can imagine. For we can also think of the promptings of navigation as a deep structure—a generative element within the bedrock or, more accurately, fluid core of human culture. This dimension also provides a form of deep background to the idea of fictional navigation, suggesting the profound promptings from which these novels arise, and the areas of resonance into which they enter. The lineaments here can only be sketched, but we can trace them in realms of myth, evolution, psychology, and ethics. In a strange way, the background also emerges as foreground.

For instance, a view of navigation as foundational in human culture lends a different perspective to the mythic foundations of language and the human. So, where the Tower of Babel story purports to tell the origins of human dispersal, we can see it in a different light. Instead of God's edict and decree, pre-empting humankind's attempt to build a tower up to heaven and 'make us a name', resulting in the proliferation of languages and the great scattering across the face of the earth—here we can see that scattering as part of the inner navigational promptings of human language itself. Instead of multiple languages causing dispersal, it might be the navigational prompting towards dispersal ('language' in the deep sense) that causes the proliferation of languages in a continuing process through time.[42] In this regard, language in human evolution may have been profoundly recursive—reproducing the conditions of its own (re)generation in multiple and varied forms. There would be a transitivity in such a process belying any questions of mutual intelligibility as defining the nature of linguistic boundaries; indeed, the very idea of a boundary in linguistic terms would be altered in such an understanding. But equally important, for our purposes, is what accepting this view might mean for our 'orientations', our dispositions in the world. Instead of attempting to reach up to heaven, achieving the power of the 'One' and the 'Name', we might accept meaning as a matter of how we *proceed*. Instead of the ramparts of the vertical, we might accept the pathway of the horizontal, finding the transcendent in the transitive rather than the tower.[43] It is this world of the transitive—complicated, troubling, illuminated, on one level mythic, archetypal, existential—that the novels in this study explore in our time.

[42] Of course, there are many views on the Tower of Babel and language. For Derrida, it reflects the jealousy of a God who asserts his own name, scatters the human lineage, and at one and the same time 'imposes and forbids translation'. For Pinker, the proliferation of languages is akin to an evolutionary process: 'To understand why there is more than one language . . . we must understand the effects of innovation, learning, and migration.' For George Steiner, language is both a prime resource of human innovation and survival ('*Language is the main instrument of man's refusal to accept the world as it is*') and profoundly connected with the ethnos: '[A] language builds a wall around the "middle kingdom" of the group's identity.' [Steiner's italics] See respectively, Jacques Derrida, 'Des Tours de Babel', in *Difference in Translation*, ed. Joseph F. Graham (Ithaca and London: Cornell University Press, 1985), 170; Pinker, *TLI*, 243; George Steiner, *After Babel: Aspects of Language and Translation*, 2nd edn (Oxford and New York: Oxford University Press, 1992), 228, 242–4.

[43] This discussion is prompted in part by Bruce Chatwin's *The Songlines*, to which I will return in the Conclusion.

But what if this very notion of the transitive is rejected—or if rejection is part of the story of transition? In this regard, it is as important to understand the implications of a 'negative' grammar of identity and location as it is of the positive. For instance, among the most ordinary and yet deepest forms of human experience we can think of contiguity and transitivity as a question of *touch*. For this is what touch is: contiguity realized, made *tangible*.[44] Touch is the archetypal gesture of healing and consolation; it is the embodiment of a solidarity that goes beneath language to another 'language': of what this form of contact means. But touch can also repel, push away, push down. Or it can be refused altogether, the boundary between one part of the self and another, or one self and another, constructed as intransitive, impermeable. Then the rejected element takes on a 'substitute' meaning—for how can we know what it means if we will not combine with it or allow it to act in combination? It becomes the unwanted '*y*' or '*z*'—the element with which (or the person with whom) we wish to have no contact. In this form the boundary becomes the impossibility of navigation.

And the effects? In Freudian terms, one result has already been suggested: within the psyche, repression of the internal element of 'difference' (desire, fear, an aspect of the self) that cannot be accepted. But such an effect also draws on and gives expression to realities beyond the self. Along these lines, in *Totem and Taboo* Freud saw both neurosis and taboo as revolving around a central prohibition of touching (neurosis was termed the 'touching phobia' or '*délire du toucher*').[45] By definition, such a prohibition invokes an intransitive boundary, and the patterns it produces are quite remarkable. Not only does the alien object become untouchable, but by that very token it also becomes contagious, contaminating any other object with which it comes into contact—whether in fact, or conceptually. In this way, a chain of prohibition results, running from object to object, until 'at last the whole world lies under an embargo of "impossibility" '.[46] In grammatical terms this is quite fascinating. For one thing, we can see here a negative metonymy

---

[44] For an inspiring moment defining what he calls 'tangibility', see Edwin Cameron, *Witness to Aids* (Cape Town: Tafelberg, 2005), 61–2.

[45] Sigmund Freud, *Totem and Taboo*, trans. James Strachey (New York and London: Norton, 1950), 35.

[46] Freud, *Totem*, 35. 'Impossible' was the word used by one of Freud's patients to describe untouchable objects.

at work, in the series of restricted objects held at bay by the intransitive boundary. In this respect the boundary is constructed to hold off objects which threaten *precisely because of their mutual transitivity*: a transitivity in which 'I', by this definition, cannot and must not participate. Here is a different angle on the Freudian perspective: not only the dynamics of the unconscious provoking the intransitive boundary but the intransitive boundary—in and of itself—provoking and even *constructing* the unconscious. All this is at stake when we fashion the grammars of our identity—especially since identities are often managed through verdicts on what can and cannot be touched. The transitivities we are prepared to admit incline us to the specific forms of our unconscious.

Some of the ramifications of this will be apparent in various ways in this study—for instance, in the work of Charlotte Brontë, Jean Rhys, and (in a different form) Anne Michaels. Here we shall see how a horizontal dynamic of refusal converts into a vertical dynamic of the unconscious—but also how the *acceptance* of contact can heal both repression and trauma. Within this matrix we can also understand a central proposition: that repression of elements *within* the self is the counterpart of repression of others *beyond* the self, and vice versa. In itself this suggests an intrinsic metonymy between individual selves and others across a transitive boundary, even if registered only in a reverse and repressive form. We will also enter the complex territory of sacrifice—a grammar of sacrifice. For sacrifice involves transitivity: the sacrificial object takes on and carries my sins away. But it also involves substitution in that the sacrifice *substitutes* for me. And where death is involved, that substitution becomes absolute: death marks the absolutely intransitive boundary, with perhaps only shadows and traces remaining—a kind of haunting we can sense but not 'touch'. For Freud, sacrifice was linked with taboo, in that the vertical offering created a bond of complicity within the horizontal community, another way of fashioning its boundaries. Here we shall see how sacrifice is used to 'cleanse' difference and anneal the connective (but less than fully combinatory) bonds that remain. By the same token, where some are sacrificed by others and left in a world without connection, haunting and the uncanny become the only kind of 'map' they can follow—the fate of Sebald's Austerlitz. All this is enacted across the transnational boundaries these novels confront.

The responsibilities and protocols of touch and navigation: sooner or later we encounter questions of ethics in these settings. How do the implications of the journey—whether one moves in fact or only as a matter of 'disposition'—affect the territory one 'journeys' through? How do these models affect the fundamentals of human relationships? As suggested earlier, and as Levinas reminds us, there are differences in 'height' among us—asymmetries in power, authority, access to resources.[47] Nor are our relations simply binary—between one 'self' and an 'other'. Levinas talks of what he calls 'proximity', of the presence of the third 'alongside the neighbor approached', and the need: 'There must be justice among incomparable ones.'[48] In this setting he proposes a model of 'substitution' that is both radical and absolutely demanding: 'No one can substitute himself for me, who substitutes myself for all.'[49] Yet Primo Levi, who saw something like the end of the world in Auschwitz, saw things this way: '[O]ne is never in another's place.'[50]

Perhaps it is *because* 'one is never in another's place' that the question of ethics arises to begin with—but also because one life touches on others. This is complex territory, therefore, and it has wider implications. At the least, any notion of transitivity has to take into account what is at stake in inequality, unevenness, the difference in 'height' among individuals and peoples. Nor can we romanticize versions of displacement or disposition when these realities are the hard experience of life for many. But these are also elements in a transnational setting the novels

---

[47] Emmanuel Levinas, 'Martin Buber and the Theory of Knowledge', in *The Levinas Reader*, ed. Seán Hand (Oxford: Blackwell, 1989), 72–3.

[48] Emmanuel Levinas, 'Substitution', in *Basic Philosophical Writings*, ed. Adriann T. Peperzak, Simon Critchley, and Robert Bernasconi (Bloomington: Indiana University Press, 1996), 122. For Levinas, proximity was not merely 'the indifference of spatial contiguity': see 'Substitution', ed. Peperzak *et al.*, 81. This essay appears in different forms in different collections; see notes above and below.

[49] Levinas, 'Substitution', in *The Levinas Reader*, ed. Hand, 115. For Levinas, 'substitution' is a substitution of responsibility rather than person, but nonetheless many questions arise from it, not least that of sacrifice in the form of self-sacrifice (see Levinas, 'Enigma and Phenomenon', 76; and 'Substitution', 94, both in *Basic Philosophical Writings*, ed. Peperzak *et al.*). Levinas is also intriguing to consider by way of a 'grammar', including his ideas that substitution frees one from the 'tautological way of identity' and that it does not fit into 'the categories of noun or verb', but can only exist 'in the accusative', as a matter of perpetual accusation, even persecution: 'it is accusation which I cannot answer, but for which I cannot decline responsibility' (Levinas, ed. Hand, 'Substitution', 107, 114, 116, 117).

[50] Primo Levi, *The Drowned and The Saved*, trans. Raymond Rosenthal (New York: Vintage, 1989), 60.

in this study explore. We will see unevenness in various manifestations and ramifications, but also chains of responsibility, deferral, complicity. Not least, the novels investigate the protocols of *encounter*, where touch, contiguity, gap, transitivity, become an essential part of the story. In the case of W. G. Sebald it becomes a space submitted to exquisite examination as the locus of transmission, engagement, narration—an aesthetic as well as ethic in his writing.

This too is part of the deep structure of these novels: the protocols of navigation become a central aspect of the transnational work of fiction.

## THE WORK OF FICTION

The ideas suggested here should be thought of as a set of conceptual and theoretical explorations. What they establish is a frame for thinking about the novels in this study, and they give us a language in which to do so. What follows in the succeeding chapters should also be thought of, primarily, as *exploration*—essays in a specific sense as forays, travels, ventures, navigations, so that the form of this book is in keeping with its subject matter. Primarily, they are meditations on aspects of the transnational, conducted in and through the novels. What we discover on the journey may affect our view of the frame, as the novels both reflect on and extend our thinking.

From this perspective, an idea quite deeply embedded here is that the novels are not merely documents for some pre-existing theory; they are, in a quite profound sense, *guides* to our very forms of understanding. They become an inner map of our world where the transnational is still a space of crossing, and a horizon to be reached. This means allowing ourselves to work with them, to contemplate, for each, their particular contours and approach. But there is also a dimension where their mapping emerges from their combination, and that too is an aspect of this book. For instance, in recent decades our prevailing categories of analysis have been the modern and postmodern, the colonial and postcolonial. But what logic of transitivity do these boundaries exclude? Often the categories seem both too wide and too narrow, so that we have to think of both Chinua Achebe and Zadie Smith as 'postcolonial' but cannot allow a Sebald to speak to a Rushdie. Here the idea is to set both Sebald and Rushdie together, and to put them both in relation to

Conrad, as well as the other writers in this study. This is a different kind of syntax, a different kind of navigation, a different kind of mapping. The idea is to see if it can tell a different kind of story, in its different kind of routes—with everything we now understand by the term.

One exploration may lead only indirectly to another, therefore; there will be degrees of overlap, but (to modify an image of Benjamin's to which we shall return), the fragments of the vessel will not fit together perfectly or absolutely: always there is the space of the boundary. The chapters which follow will, to varying extents, reflect different *styles* as well as subject matter—a formal complement to the navigational approach. Some focus on one author, others on two or more; some are more widely researched, others based more directly on an interpretive hermeneutics. As for the selection of novels and other works (Sebald resisted the term 'novel'), this is not meant to be exclusive; it is not in any way a curriculum. From that point of view, what I am suggesting are ways of reading: a set of perspectives, concepts, topics, and methods that can be applied to other texts, in other ways, as we approach the transnational imaginary.

But, precisely because of the contiguities, certain features will recur among these works. Empire, which Conrad introduces, remains a containing if transforming horizon of our world.[51] The spectral and uncanny emerge where other kinds of syntax are unavailable or suppressed. We shall see transactions between the vertical and horizontal in a variety of contexts. There will be versions of what James Clifford calls 'traveling-in-dwelling, dwelling-in-traveling'—and frequently their impossibility.[52] Formally, these works invoke figurations of gap and transitivity across time and space: constellation, or metonymy itself as the sign of the journey.[53] Metamorphosis—not least in Rushdie—enters as theme and form, chiasmus as a motif both of connection and reversal. The route as *rupta via* will be a consistent presence. The topographies of the earth—sand, desert, waterways—become emblematic locales for

[51] I am retaining the capitalized version of 'Empire' in the book, partly in the light of Coetzee's usage in *Waiting for the Barbarians*, but also because it seems enough of a conceptual presence more generally to merit it; the adjectival form, 'imperial', will be in lower-case except where dictated by the immediate context.

[52] See Clifford, 'Traveling Cultures', 108.

[53] See Michael Gorra, *The Bells in Their Silence* (Princeton and Oxford: Princeton University Press, 2004), 63–6. Gorra's understanding is in some ways similar to my own, with somewhat different inflections on the metonymic and metaphoric.

exploring a transitive syntax, and they are also figured as *topologies*—a concept which will take on a specific kind of meaning. Often we will see a transnational dimension in the lives as well as work of the writers. Always there is the nature of the boundary—between elements of the self, between the self and others, in our grammars of identity, location, and narration.

Paul Gilroy, setting out to explore the oceanic world of identity formation he calls the Black Atlantic, offers an invocation: 'I have settled on the image of ships in motion across the spaces between Europe, America, Africa, and the Caribbean'.[54] This is not a bad place to begin to think—by way of sounding, reversal, connection, routes, navigation—of Joseph Conrad.

[54] Gilroy, *Black Atlantic*, 4.

# 1

# Waterways of the Earth

*Joseph Conrad*

Nel mezzo del cammin di nostra vita
mi ritrovai per una selva oscura
ché la diritta via era smarrita.

Dante, *Inferno* I, 1–3

During those weeks when his father was dying, Konrad would sit
at a little table lit by a green lamp in a windowless cabinet to do his
homework in the late afternoon after school. The ink stains in his
exercise book and on his hands came from the fear in his heart.

W. G. Sebald, *The Rings of Saturn*

There may be no paragraph, no sentence, no word of Joseph Conrad's
*Heart of Darkness* that has escaped attention or not been mined for
critical meaning over the course of the hundred years and more since
it was first published. Is it possible to say anything new or relevant
about a work of such fabulous density and resonance that has not at
least been intimated before? But, if the words have been scrutinized, the
perspectives and paradigms, as Benita Parry has noted, will shift; newness will come into the world, even on the foundations of a text that—
apparently—does not shift or change.[1] Yet that 'apparently' should be
questioned too: perhaps the novel's forms of reach and connection make
it a transitive text: a work dealing overtly with linkages through space
and time which becomes the kind of territory it describes, extending
itself as we read it. Its effects, that is to say, may be linked to its form,

---

[1] Benita Parry, *Conrad and Imperialism: Ideological Boundaries and Visionary Frontiers*
(London: Macmillan, 1983), 17–18.

which is also a form of approaching the world. In what way, to rephrase the question, does *Heart of Darkness* include us, not only constituting a horizon for us across more than a century but doing so precisely because of its approach to a differentiated world without any final horizon?

From this perspective I would like to contemplate a well-traversed but nonetheless intriguing paragraph near the beginning of the novel. The sentence which anticipates it is well known enough: Marlow, waiting for the tide on board the *Nellie* at dusk on the Thames in London suddenly announces, 'And this also . . . has been one of the dark places of the earth.'[2] This is the declaration preceding his narrative regarding the Congo and Kurtz and his own bemusing experiences; it is a great equation of a sentence, displacing the opposition between Congo and London, between one place and another, between one time and another, linked as they are, we might say—as Conrad might say—by waterways leading to the 'uttermost ends of the earth' (*HOD*, 8). But it is the succeeding lines that begin to present their own specific puzzle. This is where the unnamed frame-narrator—one of Marlow's companions (if one can call them that) on board the ship—opens his description of Marlow:

He was the only man of us who still 'followed the sea.' The worst that could be said of him was that he did not represent his class. He was a seaman, but he was a wanderer too, while most seamen lead, if one may so express it, a sedentary life. Their minds are of the stay-at-home order, and their home is always with them—the ship—and so is their country—the sea. One ship is very much like another and the sea is always the same.   (*HOD*, 9)

A number of questions arise here. Seamen, we find paradoxically, are 'sedentary' and 'stay-at-home' types, in mind if not in body. Then there is the idea that 'their country is the sea', which is alluring because it immediately poses questions of belonging or identity. If these sailors' home is the ship and their country the sea, then where on earth— to ask a question invited by the word 'country'—do they belong? Or, to put it differently, what is their 'nationality'? The thought here, we might suppose, is that water—suggesting an oceanography rather than geography—represents an alternative country, a transnational rather

[2] Joseph Conrad, *Heart of Darkness*, ed. Robert Kimbrough, 3rd edn, Norton Critical Edition (New York: Norton, 1988), 9. Henceforth referenced as *HOD*.

than national space. But even as we raise that possibility we learn, in typical Conradian fashion, that Marlow is *different* from these and other sailors; that he does *not* represent his class; that he is a wanderer, where other seamen are stay-at-home types. What then, we might ask, is *Marlow's* country or nationality? If he is displaced even from the ship as 'home' or the sea as 'country', then he appears somehow to be suspended in space, displaced entirely, neither grounded by land nor affiliated by water—in essence not belonging anywhere. In his version of the transnational, if we grant the term for a moment, in the underlying grammar of this displacement, there is yet a further degree of shift or oscillation, away from both land and water into some space of non-definition and, perhaps, transition. This is certainly the feeling we get about him in the novel—Marlow the 'enigmatic', 'Buddhic' figure who seems to understand everything and nothing, whose place seems to be 'everywhere' and 'nowhere'.

The paragraph continues to be intriguing, as we learn why most seamen are not much interested in land, for 'there is nothing mysterious to a seaman unless it be the sea itself'; as to the rest, '[A] casual spree on shore suffices to unfold for him the secret of a whole continent, and generally he finds the secret not worth knowing.' Here is the margin as synecdoche, the part representing the whole, and for most seamen perhaps entire continents can be known in that way. Yet for Marlow, so the implication would run, this cannot be an adequate form of knowledge, and the secret a continent holds is bound to be more mysterious. For Marlow, the land, we might say, takes on something of the form of the sea, which is why he is no ordinary seaman. Why should this be the case? We might surmise that it is because of Marlow's experience—perhaps of sea, perhaps of sea/land—that he has become this kind of narrator of his world. And it is in fact at this point in the paragraph that we get the frame-narrator's famous description of Marlow's narrative method, again in contrast to the more standard versions of seamen:

The yarns of seamen have a direct simplicity, the whole meaning of which lies within the shell of a cracked nut. But Marlow was not typical (if his propensity to spin yarns be excepted) and to him the meaning of an episode was not inside like a kernel but outside, enveloping the tale which brought it out only as a glow brings out a haze, in the likeness of one of those misty halos that, sometimes, are made visible by the spectral illumination of moonshine.

The lines, proceeding in syntactic chains of mimicry, yet difference (not inside like…as a glow…in the likeness…), are a study in themselves, and so is the paragraph, which in typical Conradian form has proceeded from considerations of Marlow in relation to other seamen, to the nature of mystery and knowledge in relation to the sea and land, to questions of adequate narration. Both the lines and the paragraph take on metonymic form, where, like a syntactic progression of linkage and association, one thing leads to another. Here form is suited to content; the novel becomes travelling or transnational fiction, and it has no interest in fixed identities, whether of names or people or things.

## SEA-WRITING

How did Conrad come to be the kind of person who would write this way, of whom the adjective *Conradian* means among other things this combination of features and characteristics? A significant part of the answer might well lie in his own past, his own experience of location and identity. Here is Conrad's father, Apollo Korzeniowski, writing to him on the occasion of his christening as Jósef Teodor Konrad Nałecz Korzeniowski in December 1857:

Baby son, sleep…let Holy Water flow
On your soul, on your forehead;
*Heaven* and *Godliness* surround you…
Bless you, my little son:
Be a *Pole!* Though foes
May spread before you
A web of happiness,
Renounce it—love your poverty.
     Hushaby, my baby son!
[…]
Baby son, tell yourself
You are without land, without love,
Without country, without people,
While *Poland—your Mother* is entombed.[3]

---

[3] 'To My Son Born in the 85th Year of Muscovite Oppression, A Song for the Day of his Christening', from Zdzisław Najder, *Joseph Conrad: A Chronicle* (New Brunswick:

When Apollo wrote those words he was already a Polish patriot, committed to the liberation of a divided country from the Russian Empire, and within a few years both he and his wife Ewa Bobrowska were involved in clandestine activity to that end. Their early life together involved peregrinations, and the young boy moved with them: from Berdyczów in the Ukraine, where he was born, to Derebczynka, where Apollo was an estate manager, to Zytomierz, and thence to Warsaw, where the Korzeniowskis were actively engaged in preparing the way for the uprising of 1863. Apollo's arrest in 1861, followed by his trial together with Ewa before a military tribunal in 1862, produced further moves: the family's exile first to Vologda, three hundred miles north-east of Moscow, then to Chernikhov, near Kiev. Their story is a well-known one: these journeys and domiciles in the harshest conditions caused first one and then the other parent to become seriously ill, and by April 1865, when the boy (habitually called Konrad or Konradek) was seven, his mother was dead. Four years later so was his father, and the eleven year old, who had suffered illness of his own during this time, was shunted back and forth, placed temporarily in boarding school under the care of a family friend, then passed to the official guardianship of his maternal grandmother in Cracow. Ultimately he came under the mentorship and tutelage of his uncle, Tadeusz Bobrowski.

Instability and displacement must have been the watchwords of his youth, perpetual movement part of his developing yet fugitive sense of self, the security of parents and belonging a fragile illusion. His father had written that his '*Mother—Poland*' was entombed; but the graphic reality for the young boy was that his real mother was dead, lost to the cause of national identity which, he may have felt, had both betrayed her and led her to betray him. His own first name was Jósef, in honour of his maternal grandfather, but for the child there may have been that other Joseph in the background, betrayed by his brothers and sold into slavery in a different Empire, that of Egypt. But what redemption from Russia, or from Poland? What personal illumination could there be, what safety from the reality of solitude and loss? His father had called on

Rutgers University Press, 1983), 11–12. See also Apollo's desire for his son (alongside his concern for his health) after Ewa's death, as written to his friend Buszczynski: 'My second, if not my first, object is to bring up Konradek not as a democrat, aristocrat, demagogue, republican, monarchist, nor as a servant and a flunky of those parties—but only as a Pole' (Najder, *Conrad*, 25).

him to have a singular notion of himself, resolved entirely into a matter of nationality—'be a *Pole*'—but everything about Conrad's experience might have transformed this into a question of intimate pain, if not the severest deception. His own successive illnesses, both then and later in his life, may have had something to do with it.

Who was Conrad? He was all these incarnations of himself as he moved from place to place finding what anchorage he could. No surprise then that at the age of seventeen, under his Uncle Tadeusz's benign protection, he announced his desire to leave for Marseilles, to further his journey and displacement, to find a home in continual movement, ultimately to take to the sea. Later his shift of name—the same but not the same as the original—and of language was of a piece with the rest. Indeed, Conrad was a language-chameleon, adept in French as well as English and *au courant* with words and phrases from around the globe.

He wrote about his life in his memoir, *A Personal Record*, which he began publishing under the title *Some Reminiscences* in serial form in 1908. Interestingly, it may have been prompted by a review written by the critic Robert Lynd of Conrad's recently published collection of short stories, *A Set of Six*. In his review, Lynd found it 'a very regrettable thing, even from the point of view of English literature', that Conrad had chosen to write in English. For, he argued, a writer who ceases to see the world coloured by his own language is apt to lose the concentration and intensity of vision required by the greatest literature: 'Mr Conrad, without either country or language, may be thought to have found a new patriotism for himself in the sea. His vision of men, however, is the vision of a cosmopolitan, of a homeless person.'[4] What interesting terms! Here is that idea again, only this time regarding Conrad himself, and levelled as an accusation: his 'country is the sea', and this is equivalent to being cosmopolitan, homeless. Conrad, whose private response was one of dejection, did his best not to show this in public, yet eleven years later, in his 'Author's Note' to a reprint of *A Personal Record*, still felt the need to address the question, insisting he had by no means made a choice to write in English, or had chosen that language rather than French. The truth of the matter, he insisted, was that his faculty to write

[4] Joseph Conrad, *The Mirror of the Sea and A Personal Record*, ed. Zdzisław Najder (Oxford: Oxford University Press, 1988), xiv–xv.

in English was as natural as any other with which he might have been born. English for him had been a matter neither of choice nor adoption, unless that meant being adopted by 'the genius of the language'. All he could claim, he wrote, was 'the right to be believed when I say that if I had not written in English I would not have written at all'.[5]

*A Personal Record* remains a fascinating account to this day, not only for its content and themes but even more for the way it is written. As an address to the question of identity, its form is one of perpetual displacement, a chain of memory and narrative associations that disperse themselves across time and space and the various aspects of Conrad's life as writer, sailor, and reader. His idea, as he remarked to his agent, J. B. Pinker, was '[t]o make Polish life enter English letters';[6] but the truth is that the book *travels* in every possible way, and finds its only kind of dwelling in this travelling. We are with Conrad in the Far East, Australia, Marseilles, on a visit back to his Uncle Tadeusz (an account which, as we shall see, W. G. Sebald takes up and develops in *The Rings of Saturn*). Through his uncle we learn of his mother and her writing table, which leads to his uncle's uncle Mr Nicholas B, *Chevalier de la Légion d'Honneur* and captain in Napoleon's army who, starving during the Russian campaign, had been obliged to eat Lithuanian dog. Why? '*Pro patria!*' remarks Conrad, which then produces a consideration of what some might take to be his own 'desertion' from nationality and Poland, and equally the defence of an unseen entelechy within a life: 'The inner voice may remain true enough in its secret counsel. The fidelity to a special tradition may last through the events of an unrelated existence, following faithfully, too, the traced way of an inexplicable impulse' (*PR*, 45). Yet we also learn later that Conrad is not interested in confession à la Rousseau, nor in any attempt to justify his existence— which would be 'not only needless and absurd, but almost inconceivable in a purely spectacular universe, where no such disagreeable necessity can possibly arise' (*PR*, 91). In such a universe, whether national, transnational or cosmic, what you see is not what you get, and the trajectory of a life is not something you can easily see on a map.

---

[5] Joseph Conrad, *A Personal Record and The Mirror of the Sea*, ed. Mara Kalnins (Harmondsworth: Penguin, 1998), 5–6. For convenience I have in general used the Kalnins edition for references to *A Personal Record* as well as *The Mirror of the Sea*, both cited in the text and below as *PR*.
[6] Kalnins, Introduction, Conrad, *PR*, xxii.

From this perspective it makes perfect sense that central to *A Personal Record* is a doubled kind of journey, where writing parallels sailing. The book is woven with an account of how Conrad wrote his first novel, *Almayer's Folly*, the slowly accumulating manuscript of which accompanied him on many of his journeys. The link becomes even more intimate when he muses on how he is now 'unconsciously compelled' to write volume after volume as in previous years he was compelled to go to sea 'voyage after voyage'. As Conrad puts it, '[l]eaves must follow upon each other as leagues used to follow in days gone by' (*PR*, 31). In that as well as the other sense of the word, *A Personal Record* is itself a kind of perpetual 'leaving' as it pursues questions of belonging, continuity, and disjunction through the many landscapes and phases of the self. Writing *is* travelling in such a form, and to this extent Conrad announces a major motif for the twentieth century. It is true that for its end the book turns towards resolution, as Conrad tells how he met his first English ship and his first English sailor, heard the English language for the first time, and saw the flag, the Red Ensign, 'destined for so many years to be the only roof over my head' (*PR*, 126). This may be his answer to Robert Lynd, and it may, for a moment, be reminiscent of Conrad's other volume of memoirs, *The Mirror of the Sea*, first published in 1906, and with which *A Personal Record* is often paired. There, in an essay entitled 'The Heroic Age', Conrad is prepared to complete the volume by saying that 'we must turn to the national spirit, which, superior in its force and continuity to good and evil fortune, can alone give us the feeling of an enduring existence and of an invincible power against the fates' (*PR*, 299). Yet *The Mirror of the Sea*, proffered to the reader 'with the unreserve of a last hour's confession' (*PR*, 133) and written in a rather bland authoritative form, turns out to be intractably less searching or revelatory than *A Personal Record*, which rejects confession as a superficial mode of writing.

Which of these texts is more *Conradian* in the sense we have been following? Edward Said has noted how Conrad possesses two voices: the urbane, wry, confident voice of his public commentaries (not least in the Prefaces to his own books) and the 'rich, confusing' voice of his private writing.[7] These two texts mirror that duality in every way, and

---

[7] Edward Said, *Beginnings: Intention and Method* (New York: Basic Books, 1975), 131.

*A Personal Record*, shifting and metonymic in the very grammar of its form, is much closer to the voice of the writer who called himself a 'homo duplex',[8] who had, as he said, taken a 'standing jump out of his racial surrounding and associations' (*PR*, 113). Doubled in every way, this is a writer who knows that nationality gives, in the end, only superficial cover against the otherwise 'invincible power of the fates'— the fates whose power Conrad was always ready to register in his fiction. As he wrote in *A Personal Record*, what drew him towards England, and what he had in view 'was not a naval career but the sea' (*PR*, 113): the sea, whose nationality and modes of being are unknown. Moved on the tides, swells, and currents of associative memory, *A Personal Record* is a kind of sea-writing in that way, its geography of identity one of shifting registration, journeying and dispersal. It is quite literally the writing of navigation.

It is early in *A Personal Record* that Conrad recalls the moment when the quest for exploration in the wider sense first crystallized for him:

It was in 1868, when nine years old or thereabouts, that while looking at a map of Africa of the time and putting my finger on the blank space then representing the unsolved mystery of that continent, I said to myself with absolute assurance and an amazing audacity which are no longer in my character now:
       When I grow up I shall go *there*.   (*PR*, 27)

'There', as Conrad informs us, was the region of Stanley Falls, in what later became the Congo Free State. The significance of the 'blank space' at its heart was something Conrad later elaborated in an essay of 1926, where he remarked on how when he was a child 'the honest maps of the nineteenth century' had nourished in him a passionate interest in the truth of geographical facts. For the maps of prior ages had been cleared, as he put it, of their 'dull imaginary wonders' and replaced with 'exciting spaces of white paper', where knowledge and conquest were still lacking. This was the map as metaphor, where honest truth was substituted for myth: 'My imagination could depict to itself there worthy, adventurous and devoted men, nibbling at the edges, attacking from north and south and east and west, conquering a bit of truth here and a bit of truth there, and sometimes swallowed up by the mystery their hearts

---

[8] Najder, *Conrad*, 295.

were so set on unveiling.'[9] Yet, even in the cause of 'truth', this form of substitution had its own way of being misleading. Mapping here is epistemological as much as cartographical, representing the progressive colonizations of reason, a knowledge of the world based on secure foundations of authority, perspective, and the self.

But perhaps one reason the later Conrad no longer had the audacity that had once driven him was because he no longer believed in such a version of 'there'. By the time he reached Africa in 1890 and, more importantly, by the time he returned, what kind of writing, travelling, mapping, knowledge would be adequate to describe what he had seen and experienced? And what sort of person could write it? Not Conrad himself, or not alone. It was possible only through an intermediary, Marlow; a different voice, a figure who still 'followed the sea' but who was no ordinary seaman.

## THE CONGO RIVER

Sometimes when Conrad was ill and raving, he would speak Polish;[10] he certainly returned from Africa ill. According to his chronicler, Zdzisław Najder, the idea of working in Africa came about almost for want of something better to do—though Conrad's interest was kindled by the sensational news of the American journalist Henry Morton Stanley's expedition in search of Emin Pasha. He found his way to Albert Thys, director of the Société Belge pour le Commerce du Haut Congo, who appointed him to his new post, by a chain of accidental connections. Then followed a trip to the Ukraine to visit his uncle, Tadeusz Bobrowski, which included a stop in Brussels, where he met his distant (and dying) relative Aleksander Poradowski and his wife, the woman Conrad came to refer to as his 'Aunt' Marguerite Poradowska, with whom for some years he kept up a correspondence suffused with romantic inflections. In the Ukraine he appears not to have fitted in, indeed to have alienated some of his relatives and family friends by his lack of interest in Polish identity or affairs; so it may have been with a sense of

---

[9] Joseph Conrad, 'Geography and Some Explorers', in *Last Essays* (Garden City: Doubleday, Page and Co., 1926), 13–14.

[10] Najder, *Conrad*, 198.

belonging neither 'here' nor 'there' that Conrad stepped on board ship from Brussels for the Congo on 10 May 1890.[11]

Conrad expected to stay in Africa for three years. On board, approaching Boma, he was impatient to arrive—even though he knew the alarming statistics regarding company (Société) employees in the Congo.[12] What did he expect to find there? If the official pronouncements of the time were anything to go by, this was a great and civilizing mission. After the Berlin Conference of 1884–5 had parcelled out the territories of Africa to the colonial powers of Europe, the Congo Free State was ceded to Leopold II, King of Belgium, to come under his direct property and rule. Belgium itself was a relative backwater, but this did not prevent its monarch from presenting his interests in the Congo in the most resplendent terms: 'To bring civilization to the only part of this globe where it has not yet penetrated, to pierce the darkness which envelops entire populations—is, I dare say, a crusade worthy of this age of progress.' Henry Morton Stanley, who became Leopold's agent in the Congo, was prepared to pay homage to him this way: 'if royal greatness consists in the wisdom and goodness of a sovereign leading his people with the solicitude of a shepherd watching over his flock, then the greatest sovereign is your own'.[13] The truth was otherwise, and metaphors of civilization and the light of progress penetrating the darkness of Africa concealed a most rapacious and abysmal campaign to maximize profit. It was an enterprise that took no account of the human suffering and cost, the lives and communities ruined, the numbers of dead and dying, the people with their hands cut off.[14] Conrad came to understand this only too well. As he put it in a letter of 1903 to Roger Casement, then producing a report on the situation in the Congo (and later both knighted and executed by the British): 'It is an extraordinary thing that the conscience of Europe which seventy years ago has put

[11] For some of the developments mentioned here, see Najder, *Conrad*, 117–22.

[12] For instance, that only 7 per cent of the company's employees managed to complete their full terms of service, and that some were sent home at the end of a year so as not to die in the Congo and ruin the figures. Conrad to Karol Zagórski, 22 May 1890, in Frederick R. Karl and Laurence Davies, eds, *The Collected Letters of Joseph Conrad*, vol. 1 (Cambridge: Cambridge University Press, 1983), 52.

[13] For both Leopold's and Stanley's views, see Najder, *Conrad*, 123.

[14] For some details on this, see Adam Hochschild, *King Leopold's Ghost* (Boston: Houghton Mifflin, 1998).

down the slave trade on humanitarian grounds tolerates the Congo State to day. It is as if the moral clock had been put back many hours.... [I]n 1903...there exists in Africa a Congo State, created by the act of European powers where ruthless systematic cruelty to the blacks is the basis of administration...'.[15]

Conrad met Casement in Matadi on the lower reaches of the Congo River soon after he arrived there in June 1890. That event, as well as his progress in a foot-caravan upriver to Kinshasa was noted in his *Congo River Diary*—a document which records in fairly dispassionate terms the progress of his disillusionment, as well as his fairly casual assumptions. '[S]aw at a camp[in]g place the dead body of a Backongo. Shot? Horrid smell'; 'Water effects very beautiful this morning. Mists generally raising before sky clears'; 'Saw another dead body lying by the path in an attitude of meditative repose'; 'Today fell into a muddy puddle. Beastly, The fault of the man that carried me'; 'Night miserably cold. No sleep. Mosquitoes'; 'On the road today passed a skeleton tied up to a post. Also white man's grave—no name. Heap of stones in the form of a cross. Health good now.' An albino woman he came across produced another, perhaps typical Conradian response: 'Horrid chalky white with pink blotches...Features very Negroid and ugly.'[16] At Kinshasa Conrad found that the steamer he had been meant to command was damaged, so he continued upriver to Stanleyville on the *Roi des Belges*, serving as first mate and logging notes in his 'Up-River Book'—mostly a compilation of geographic and nautical details to be of practical use in later navigations of the river.[17] It is intriguing that in the only equivalent to this text in *Heart of Darkness*, the nautical handbook written by Towser (or Towson), Marlow finds marginal comments in what he takes to be cypher, but which turn out to have been written by the Harlequin in Russian. The practical details of Conrad's upriver ambitions turn into mirror-code in the novel, while nautical exactitude—a form of sea-writing by no means adequate to the kind of reality he now faced—becomes interlaced with the enigmatic tracings of

---

[15] Owen Knowles and Gene M. Moore, *Oxford Reader's Companion to Conrad* (Oxford: Oxford University Press, 2000), 67.

[16] For these entries, among many others, see Joseph Conrad, *Congo Diary and Other Uncollected Pieces*, ed. Zdzisław Najder (Garden City: Doubleday, 1978), 7–13.

[17] For the 'Up-River Book', see Conrad, *Congo Diary*.

Empire. No navigation, even (perhaps especially) of a river in the heart of Africa, was beyond its margins.

The *Roi des Belges*—a tramp of a boat, given its royal name—reached Stanley Falls in September 1890, and Conrad realized he had reached 'the very spot' of his boyish boast. But by this stage his experiences had left him a physically sickened and spiritually disenchanted man. 'A great melancholy descended on me,' he later wrote. 'Yes, this was the very spot. But there was no shadowy friend to stand by my side in the night of the enormous wilderness, no great haunting memory, but only the unholy recollection of a prosaic newspaper "stunt" and the distasteful knowledge of the vilest scramble for loot that ever disfigured the history of human conscience and geographical exploration.'[18] The newspaper stunt, appropriately at Stanley Falls, was Stanley's 'discovery' of the missionary David Livingstone in 'darkest' Africa, which had first gained him his fame; but by now Conrad was not sure where the true darkness lay. 'Everything here is repellent to me,' he wrote to his 'Aunt' Marguerite in his last letter from the Congo on 26 September. 'Men and things, but men above all. And I am repellent to them, also.'[19] Conrad detailed the scabrous carping and intrigue of the white community, particularly his conflict with the manager, Alexandre Delcommune, and asked Marguerite to conceal the fact that he had been ill from fever as well as dysentery. In the grip of a new kind of alienation, he expressed what he longed for: 'I believe that I feel homesick for the sea.' Conrad wrote almost nothing about his last months in Africa, though we do know that, sick and unable to walk, he was carried almost the whole two-hundred miles back from Kinshasa to Matadi before leaving the Congo in December 1890. It was from this African experience, remarks Najder, that Conrad's distinction derived between the comradely, purer duties of the sea and the corrupt affairs of the land.[20] But if the sea was a kind of country for which one could feel homesick, we may also question the topography of too exact an opposition. In the heart of a continent Conrad had been on a waterway that flowed into the sea. What threaded or surrounded what may have been uncertain, how to differentiate water from earth an open question, and notions of

---

[18] Conrad, 'Geography', 17.
[19] This and the following quotation: Conrad to Poradowska, 26 September 1890, in Karl and Davies, eds, *Conrad Letters*, vol. 1, 62.
[20] Najder, *Conrad*, 141.

purity or escape adulterated for ever. The river was a transitive medium, connecting ocean and land.

When Conrad returned to Europe he was deeply ill, not only physically but mentally. 'I see everything with such despondency—all in black. My nerves are completely frayed,' he wrote to Marguerite in April 1891, and the following month he wrote again: 'I am still plunged in densest night and my dreams are only nightmares.'[21] He was hospitalized in London, and travelled to Champel-les-Bains in Switzerland to convalesce, but seven months after he returned from Africa he was ill again: 'An attack of malaria in the form of dyspepsia. It is disheartening.'[22] When Conrad was serving on the *Roi des Belges*, an agent named Georges Antoine Klein had been taken on board; he was ill and had later died. In some circuitous fashion this probably provided a spur to the creation of Kurtz in *Heart of Darkness*. Of course, the novel was not autobiography, though it is worth considering the possibility that fact and fiction created their own metonymies of infusion and adjacency in Conrad's writing, their own mutually permeable boundaries. Interestingly, Marlow, who also becomes seriously ill in the novel, comments that in contrast to Kurtz his experience of illness was one of 'greyness'. Facing death, he found that he probably 'would have nothing to say' (*HOD*, 69).

Is it conceivable that Conrad's own illness, precipitated by the horror of his experience in Africa, had to do with this reality, in narrative terms as much as psychologically? Instead of mapping Africa, as he had intended when he was a boy, he had become thoroughly *unmapped* by what he found at the heart and horizon of human progress. He had seen there was no outside to Empire, no place of escape at even the remotest place on earth, that corruption ran to the ends of its furthest waterways, which also meant the furthest reaches of the self. What knowledge was adequate there or anywhere else, given that knowledge itself—even any knowledge *about* such knowledge—was infected by this reality? And how could one express all this? It was not so much that he had 'nothing to say' but no way to say it. For that he needed a new form. He was

---

[21] Respectively, Conrad to Poradowska, 14 April 1891 and 10 May 1891, Karl and Davies, eds, *Conrad Letters*, vol. 1, 75, 79.

[22] Conrad to Poradowska, 30 July 1891, Karl and Davies, eds., *Conrad Letters*, vol. 1, 88.

ill because he could not find it, and until he did would have 'nothing'
worth saying.[23]


## KAMUDI


When Conrad went to the Congo, he took with him, as on his other
journeys, the manuscript of *Almayer's Folly*. It was a novel he eventually
submitted to his publishers under a pseudonym, Kamudi—loosely,
Malay for 'rudder', a navigational term, another shift of identity. Yet,
notwithstanding his experiences, it was a book that was completed
for the most part in the 'old' form. True enough, certain aspects are
distinctively Conrad's: the sense of a rather dispassionate universe gazing
down on the absurd affairs of men; a description of Lakamba, the Rajah
of Sambir in Borneo, listening in the middle of the night to Verdi on
the gramophone as the music floats '[t]hrough the open shutter . . . out
on the great silence over the river and forest'.[24] In this early novel of
globalization, the tables are turned interestingly on Europe: we see a
form of white madness in Almayer, whose pathetic hopes in a landscape
he finds demoralizing rest on an impossible European future both for
himself and for his daughter Nina; we see it, too, in his panic over racial
purity when Nina elopes with Dain. Here the Malays, both well-born
and not, are allowed their own perspective on white foolishness and
ease of deception, and even Taminah, the lowest of the low as a female
slave, is allowed hints of an interior life ('all feelings and all passions, all
hopes and all fears'), though Conrad also writes dismissively of her 'half-
formed, savage mind' (*AF*, 92, 95). There is already a Conradian 'event
obscurity', so that sequences of time, space, and causality are unclear, or
the detail that matters happens at some other level entirely. Yet for all
this, and for all the cosmopolitanism of the work's array of characters, it

---

[23] On this compare Batchelor who, following Najder, sees Conrad as suffering from
intense bouts of depression, but also adds his own gloss, that artist and depressive were in
a productive kind of war with one another: 'When the artist felt blocked the depressive
expressed himself in epistolary screams of rage': John Batchelor, *The Life of Joseph Conrad:
A Critical Biography* (Oxford: Blackwell, 1994), 58. In my view, artistry and illness were
not alternating modes of being but intimately connected in their own kind of syntax.

[24] Joseph Conrad, *Almayer's Folly* (Harmondsworth: Penguin, 1976), 74. Henceforth
referenced as *AF*.

is still a novel mainly Manichean in cast, in which white and non-white are incorrigibly separate, and sometimes at war with one another even within a single character, as in the case of Nina herself, who is of 'mixed' blood. Rather than any syntactic or metonymic view, this is the logic of divided identity.

H. G. Wells, who wrote a brief review of the work, also offered an unsigned response to Conrad's second novel, *An Outcast of the Islands*. His assessment of the latter was mostly adulatory, but pointed to what he saw as a weakness: 'His style is like a river-mist; for a space things are seen clearly, and then comes a great grey bank of printed matter...creeping round the reader, swallowing him up.'[25] It was perhaps no accident that in Conrad's Preface to his following novel, *The Nigger of the 'Narcissus'*, he gave his most vatic formulation of the role of the artist: 'My task which I am trying to achieve is, by the power of the written word, to make you hear, to make you feel—it is before all, to make you *see*.'[26] But see *what?* The opening of the Preface spoke of the attempt to render a kind of justice to the 'visible universe' by bringing to light the truth 'underlying its every aspect'.[27] The truth was *underlying*, that is, not available for mapping from the visible topography of the seen—yet it seems Conrad himself had not fully lived up to his own formulation, certainly not in the novel he was describing. Perhaps in response to Wells, *The Nigger of the 'Narcissus'* turns out to be both authoritative and reductive in style and vision, its singularity almost literally rendered in the name of Singleton, the character on whom it pins its moral hopes, steering a heavily laden symbolic ship with gravity and care. On questions of race the novel has moments of the almost unspeakable, as in the description of James Wait: 'a face pathetic and brutal: the tragic, the mysterious, the repulsive mask of a nigger's soul' (*NON*, 12). Here it is not clear whether the mask is repulsive because it conceals or reveals the soul; either way the logic of substitution, mask for soul, soul for mask, will produce only one result. Unsurprisingly, singularity of this kind is in league with a binary view of the world, not least in the novel's politics where the morally enervated seamen in

---

[25] Quoted in Batchelor, *Life of Joseph Conrad*, 54–5.
[26] Joseph Conrad, 'Preface', *The Nigger of the 'Narcissus'*, ed. Cedric Watts (Harmondsworth: 1988), xlix. Henceforth referenced as *NON*.
[27] Conrad, 'Preface', *NON*, xlvii.

their collective disorder are ranged against Singleton.[28] Ultimately, as the ship returns to London after Wait's death, England herself is seen as both ship and home: '[t]he great flagship of the race; stronger than the storms! and anchored in the open sea' (*NON*, 121).

The image is a complex one: the national ship is afloat on the sea, yet in this version race, home, and identity are anchored together against it. It is reminiscent of the ending of *The Mirror of the Sea*, in which national identity provided the only bastion against the fates. But more attuned with a different kind of sea-writing in the novel is another image, describing the *Narcissus*: 'the ship, a fragment detached from the earth, went on lonely and swift like a small planet' (*NON*, 21). It is a fabulous image, and here the vista opens up: the ship is on the sea as the earth is in space; the earth itself is a ship on this voyage, except that it is not the earth but only a 'small planet'. Who, in such a view, can think of *location* or *anchorage*? Sea around the land, space around the earth, and all in movement; this had to be the real advance in Conrad's writing, the aspect that he most meaningfully bequeathed. Race, nation, identity: none could be fixed in this transitive and transitional view. A new truth to find and a form to find it. As Stein says in *Lord Jim*, 'In the destructive element immerse', and he is of course talking of the sea.[29]

## SEA-CHANGE

Full fathom five thy father lies,
Of his bones are coral made;
Those are pearls that were his eyes;
Nothing of him that doth fade,
But doth suffer a sea-change
Into something rich and strange...[30]

Because of topography, oceanography, there are resonances across space and time. Three hundred years before Conrad, in an England (island) just beginning its rise to imperial power by conquering the sea,

---

[28] See Frederic Jameson, *The Political Unconscious: Narrative as a Socially Symbolic Act* (London: Methuen, 1981), 216, for a paired pattern of '*ressentiment* and existentializing metaphysics' in the novel.

[29] Joseph Conrad, *Lord Jim*, ed. Cedric Watts and Robert Hampson (Harmondsworth: Penguin, 1986), 200. Henceforth referenced as *LJ*.

[30] William Shakespeare, *The Tempest*, ed. Stephen Orgel (Oxford: Oxford University Press, 1987), 1.2. 397–401.

Shakespeare set his own water-story on an unnamed island in an unnamed ocean, to exercise questions of fidelity, identity, art, and power. The multiple stages of the theatre—Prospero controlling Ariel controlling the Neapolitan and Milanese aristocracy, roiling them in tempests and fading dreams, the banquet prepared by Juno which disappears at a word as nymphs and reapers heavily vanish—these plays within the play within the play mirror the surrounding circles of sea and land connecting both old world and new in a dawning age of exploration. Distance in this regard is complicated, and illusion is part of it too: none of these platforms is real, all dissolve into watery elements of continuity and shift. Meaning transforms as it travels, undergoes its own versions of sea-change.[31]

Here we find that old and new are not simply opposites. Prospero to Caliban is Sycorax to Ariel: these are not binaries but diagonal relationships, sounding across one another's wavelengths. And what of Prospero's recognitions? 'This thing of darkness I / Acknowledge mine.' He must acknowledge that the darkness is in him, is him, here at the furthest reaches of his power, here in his Empire—an island, a world, a theatre—surrounded by water. At the end Prospero will bury his staff 'certain fathoms in the earth' and drown his book 'deeper than did ever plummet sound'. He surrenders power and art, and may in doing so discover other forms. In one sense hierarchy is recovered as Prospero is given his due, Miranda married off, and all find 'ourselves / When no man was his own.' And Caliban is—what—left alone, bereft, free/unfree? Perhaps the old world has immersed itself in the new only in order to recover its authority. Yet we have also seen something else: an oceanography of exile, danger, journey, and the syntactic possibilities of transformation. The waters connect, the waters divide, across the imagined boundaries of the earth. The movement is navigational, transitional, transitive.

## NOSTROMO, LORD JIM, MARLOW

Conrad's vast novels lay before him: immediately, *Heart of Darkness* and *Lord Jim*—both written in a remarkable period of creativity from

---

[31] I owe at least something in this analysis to the images and insights of Peter Greenaway's magnificent film *Prospero's Books*.

1899 to 1900—and *Nostromo*, completed under exacting strain in 1903 to 1904. Of these *Nostromo* is perhaps the least inventive in terms of transnational form, though it helps create our sense of transnational territory, both in Conradian and wider perspectives. In its subtitle it is *A Tale of the Seaboard*, and where the novel's Republic of Costaguana reaches the sea in Sulaco (the opening pages of the novel observe the shoreline and mountains from the haze of the sea) there is again that classic juxtaposition, for Conrad, of water and earth. This not so much, in Said's remark, 'as if they represented opposing values',[32] but more as if they merge, transfuse, sift into, question one another. For the most dedicated republican of all the novel's characters, Giorgio Viola, '[a]ll the earth made by God is holy; but the sea, which knows nothing of kings and priests and tyrants, is the holiest of all.'[33] There is also that breathtaking mode of suspension (to invoke *time* or *sequence* or *moment* would be to grasp at what Conrad deliberately abandons) with Nostromo and Martin Decoud on the still lighter in the black night of the Golfo Placido as all their intentions come up against the surrounding impenetrable infinity of sea, sky, and space. Here *location*, *movement*, *self*, all come into question—and in this deeper sense it is no accident that Decoud later commits suicide in the waters of the gulf, an act which no one else sees or can decode. Decoud is involved in his own 'national' project, to win independence for Sulaco from Costaguana, and later might be considered by some as one of its visionaries. But his vision cannot delve this deeper, unmapped reality, and against its underlying truth any 'national' foundation or ambition seems pointless if not wholly absurd.

The Republic of Costaguana, of course, comprises varied forms of identity, indigenous, Hispanic, African, English, Italian, and is searching for its own 'nationality', but on the question of the national Conrad is particularly scathing. All its versions in the novel are farcical, and it is indicative that Conrad leaves it to a parrot ('very human') in the Gould household to shriek '*Viva Costaguana!*' while puffing itself up and ruffling its feathers (*N*, 99). In this respect as well as others, nationalism is linked to mimicry, a thematic conjunction of tremendous, though intrinsically ambivalent, significance in a transnational landscape.[34] Decoud, whose own nationalist motives are somewhat suspect, speaks 'like a patriot' (*N*, 170)—never the real thing—and patriot/parrot are words which mimic one another homophonically, their shifting morphology a kind of internal syntax. In the figure of the insurrectionist Pedro Montero ('following the example of the Duc de Morny') Conrad creates a mimic almost Naipaulian in his idiocy, and this must raise the question as to whether Costaguanan nationalism is presented as cretinous only because it is non-Western. The question of race further complicates this issue: Pedro, like his brother the General, probably has 'Negro blood'; no need to explain then his 'ape-like faculty for imitating all the outward signs of refinement and distinction, and . . . parrot-like talent for languages' (*N*, 328). Also no accident that the patrician class in Sulaco are called 'Blancos', or that their support for a 'President-Dictator' is presented by Conrad in relatively benign terms; or that the Monterist rebellion is considered to be the expression of 'Negro Liberalism'. As Chinua Achebe would observe many years later, although Conrad was open to the humanity of various peoples in the world, he did seem to have a problem with Africans.[35]

Yet if third-world nationalism is presented in racially-weighted and farcical terms, this does not mean that the novel's scepticism is single-minded. Garibaldi, Giorgio Viola's hero, was a kind of transnational-nationalist, fighting for liberty not only in Italy but also in South America. As for the world of Empire, like the nationalism which ostensibly opposes it, this does not come off lightly either: the San Tomé mine is regarded as an 'Imperium in Imperio' and its moral cost is part of the novel's accounting. In the figure of Gould's American backer, Holroyd, the encompassing power of a United States Empire is also evident. Like Kurtz, with Holroyd's German, 'Scotch', English, Danish, and French parentage, all of Europe is in him, and as he puts it prophetically to Gould, 'Time itself has got to wait on the greatest country in the whole of God's universe . . . We shall run the world's business whether the

---

[34] For the seminal essay on mimicry, see Homi Bhabha, 'Of Mimicry and Man: The Ambivalence of Colonial Discourse', in *The Location of Culture* (London and New York: Routledge, 1994).

[35] For a revealing and, in its own way, complicated encounter with Achebe on this theme by a writer who—as we shall see in the next chapter—has taken much from Conrad, see Caryl Phillips, 'Out of Africa', *Guardian*, 22 February 2003, <http://books.guardian.co.uk/departments/classics/story/0,,900335,00.html> (accessed 10 January 2004).

world likes it or not' (*N*, 94–95). That is a serious act of presumption in a Conrad novel—the notion that time can be controlled by an imperial synchrony—as all his narrative gestures work at undermining 'flat' notions of time as well as space. Yet such hubris does not limit the power of Empire to control the mappable globe. At the end of the novel the secessionist occidental province of Sulaco fits in very nicely as a kind of 'outpost of progress' within the broader global reach of an Anglo-European imperial power, and it is appropriate that the public story of its history is given to the pony-narrator Captain Mitchell, surely one of the literary world's great burlesques. In this regard we see something important: Empire, the global, and the national are not opposed but part of a (mal)functioning system whose elements (including public narrative and memory) comprise a landscape of mutual reference and deception, out of touch with any kind of transnational truth.

Does this mean that Conrad has all the answers in *Nostromo*? No it does not, and not only because of the novel's voicings on race. Two additional features in the novel move in the direction of resolution and reduction, and both of them seem to mark particular limits. One of them is thematic: at the end of the novel, Giorgio and his remaining daughter, Linda, return to the lighthouse—the lighthouse which penetrates (as much as it can) the dark of the Golfo Placido. That, the novel seems to say, is all there is or can be: a commitment to duty and light in the darkness. The other key is a narrative one, and it comes when Conrad as narrator tells us—because there is no one else who can—how Decoud died and what it meant: 'the truth was that he died from solitude, the enemy known but to few on this earth, and whom only the simplest of us are fit to withstand' (*N*, 412). Light in the darkness and narrative authority, the former provided by the latter beyond any single or particular image: these are precisely the features displaced in *Lord Jim* and *Heart of Darkness*, which pursue shifting metonymies of perspective in much more radical style. In that respect these novels tell us more about the form we think of as transnational fiction—at least in Conrad's hands.

The difference, to a significant extent, is the presence of Marlow, Conrad's 'non-ordinary' seaman as narrator. While Najder is perceptive in seeing Marlow as mediating between Conrad's sense of Englishness and non-Englishness, to understand him as representing an 'integrating point of view' and thereby solving Conrad's perennial crisis around writing may be to approach this from the wrong angle.[36] Marlow may have resolved Conrad's writing crises not so much because he permitted 'integration' but because his narrative presence allowed the formal registration of *displacement* that was Conrad's inner topic. If *Lord Jim* is, as Fredric Jameson observes, 'one of the most breathtaking exercises in nonstop textual production that our literature has to show',[37] it may have a great deal to do with this fact.

Think, in *Lord Jim*, what Marlow's presence introduces. Immediately, authorial perspective becomes variable: Marlow could never comment on Decoud in *Nostromo* the way that Conrad does, or if he did, the fact of his narration would mean diverting, suspending, or displacing his authority in other ways. In *Lord Jim* his presence is of a piece with so much else: the cuts in time and space in the novel; the 'keyhole' form of quotation in which Marlow specializes, rendering only parts of what others have said; the rotating narration in which Marlow's account—often hearsay—will be supplemented by others or interpolated by him from other sources, whether Gentleman Brown or Jim. Towards the end of the novel the 'privileged man' receives a letter from Marlow which further complicates the transmission of the story, as well as any notion of a fixed or steady perspective. In essence, what Marlow's presence both permits and invites is a metonymic form, where one account leads to or is braided with another, where the narrative becomes an assemblage by adjacency, where the locus of enunciation moves as much as its object. One emblematic moment of this occurs when Marlow, peripatetic as always, comes across a travelling story regarding Jim. He meets a French lieutenant in a café in Sydney, who tells him some of the missing details on the discovery of the abandoned *Patna*—the ship from which Jim had jumped on the way to Mecca. Everything here, including the narration, is in motion—through space and time, through navigation and displacement, through and across transitive boundaries.

Thematic details in the novel underscore this pattern, for instance the fact that although Jim is described by Marlow as 'one of us', he also cannot see or understand him clearly: 'He was very far away from me,' comments Marlow, 'who watched him across three feet of space' (*LJ*, 104). Here time and space are distended in the very closest observation,

[36] Najder, *Conrad*, 231.
[37] Jameson, *Political Unconscious*, 219, refers to the first half of *Lord Jim* in this way.

and auditory perception is unclear, too: did Jim say to Marlow that he would hear 'of' him or 'from' him? (*LJ*, 221). Marlow remarks, 'I affirm nothing. . . . It is impossible to see him clearly' (*LJ*, 293). Truth itself undergoes a kind of doubling in the novel, sometimes in a negative form: concerning the story made up by the other European officers as to why they had abandoned the *Patna*—and reflecting to some extent on his own version—Jim observes, 'It was not a lie—but it wasn't truth all the same. It was something . . .' (*LJ*, 138). For this reason, among others, the attempt by the official enquiry into the *Patna* fiasco to establish the facts can only approach a certain level of understanding, and Brierly, who wants a fixed kind of truth and morality from English officers, will end, like Decoud, committing suicide by jumping into the ocean, weighted in his case not by four ingots of incorruptible silver but by four belaying pins. He also leaves his gold chronometer hanging from the rail—the very measure of time.

In Jim's jump from the *Patna* (and we remember Conrad's own 'standing jump out of his racial surrounding and associations' when he left Poland) time and space are frozen. As Jameson observes, there is a before and after, but not the actual moment.[38] And in a sense the wrong person has leaped: the others in the lifeboat below were calling for George, who has 'acted' third engineer and is now in fact dead of a heart attack. Jim leaps by a kind of metonymic contiguity in place of someone who was filling a place—the apparently definitive moment of identity an inherently transitive affair. And after that? His search for an inner truth is founded on an earlier moment of what he took to be inner falsity. There is a puzzle here worth reflecting on. For Jim wants to 'get out . . . stay out' (*LJ*, 217); his quest is absolute. But in those terms, the absolute is like a prison: there is no 'outside' to self or geography, and the horizon of the self is the horizon of how far Jim can travel. From another point of view, the fact that there is no 'outside' should mean there is no absolute boundary, allowing for a transitive view of both self and world—the truth, in fact, of Jim's jump in the first place.

But this is what Jim cannot allow, and both self and geography close in. Only Marlow, as narrator, is left 'outside', or at least straddling the line between outside and 'in'. But this is different in *Heart of Darkness,* where there is no outside at all.

---

[38] Jameson, *Political Unconscious,* 264.

## THE BUTTERFLY AND THE RING

There are two key images in *Lord Jim*, the butterfly and the ring; and they are key for what they tell us about metonymy and metaphor, the grammar of the self and the transnational. Both are connected with Stein, Jim's German father figure (the mimic, the oblique, the travelled) living in Java, whose insights are of course offered in a foreign (displaced) syntax. It is Stein who, commenting on the need to 'immerse' in the destructive element, provides a classic Conradian topos: 'A man that is born falls into a dream like a man who falls into the sea. If he tries to climb out into the air as inexperienced people endeavour to do, he drowns' (*LJ*, 200). Here is Conrad's oceanography of identity and existence: the clarity of consciousness or the stability of land will delude us; we drown in air rather than in water. Stein is also a collector of butterflies, and as he and Marlow discuss Jim the idea of the butterfly becomes a metaphor representing the romantic quest—to capture beauty and truth, the rare specimen that Stein once caught, the moment of luminous integrity that has eluded Jim. But when Marlow points out this difference, that Jim let his opportunity escape, Stein says, 'And do you know how many opportunities I let escape; how many dreams I had lost that had come in my way?' (*LJ*, 202–3) Here the butterfly is no longer metaphor but metonym, a point of adjacency linking Stein and Jim. It is why Stein can feel for him, empathize with him. Metaphor gives identity: the butterfly is opportunity, graspable. But the metonym gives connection through displacement: it is what we have lost that links us.

The ring inhabits similar territory, but differently. A silver ring given by Stein to Jim, it opens up his pathway in Patusan, the sign of his identity and credentials. Later, when Jim sends it as a token of his authority and good faith to Dain Waris in the battle against Gentleman Brown which leads to Dain's death, it seals his fate. In that form it becomes doubled. As attachment to Jim, it is metonym, but in these circumstances metonym as representation, where its resonance is also metaphoric.[39] To Doramin, Dain's father, it is the absolute image of Jim's identity as a white man, whose inexorable unreliability has now

---

[39] On this question, regarding the mutual inflections of metaphor and metonym, see the Introduction, pp. 13–15.

come to light, and he kills Jim for it. To Jim it is the absolute sign of his fate and he dies for it, a version of sacrifice. But on another level the ring considered as an object is a circle which leads only to itself. Its pathway out is the path of return; there is no final destination or origin. The circle represents nothing more than itself, it is the ultimate syntax of displacement and rotation. Though it may seek identity, or meaning, or attachment, in this guise it also is an embodiment: of a metonymic path continuing eternally through time and space, which cannot wholly be known. This is navigation in the abstract, absolute, without beginning, end, or transition in any meaningful sense. No one can navigate according to that regime. The beginning of the path is fated to be its end; the circle of perfection has no escape.

## STEVIE

In *The Secret Agent*, which Conrad published in 1907, Stevie draws circles in calm yet compulsive concentration: 'circles, circles; innumerable circles, concentric, eccentric; a coruscating whirl of circles that by their tangled multitude of repeated curves, uniformity of form, and confusion of intersecting lines suggested a rendering of cosmic chaos, the symbolism of a mad art attempting the inconceivable'.[40] It is Stevie who becomes the sacrificial figure, blown up in Greenwich Park not quite according to the plan of Verloc, not quite the first suicide bomber in literature, but nearly so.[41] Greenwich is where time and space are anchored, rendered into lines, meridians, and circles by which the world, along its waterways and pathways, is organized, made real and practicable for humankind. But Stevie follows a different kind of mapping. Perhaps not accidentally, he is aphasic, 'robbed...of the power of connected speech' (*SA*, 132). Incapable of the normal flow of syntax, it takes him four pages to form a verbless sentence that nonetheless seems wholly accurate in its observation: 'Bad world for poor people' (*SA*, 139–43). Apt to lose his way in London, Stevie can

---

[40] Joseph Conrad, *The Secret Agent* (Harmondsworth: Penguin, 1963), 45–6. Henceforth referenced as *SA*.

[41] For the anarchist 'Professor' in the novel as literature's first suicide bomber, see Terry Eagleton, *After Theory* (New York: Basic Books, 2003), 215.

navigate neither in speech nor on foot, and so it is he who must be labelled, in a very literal form. His sister Winnie attaches a label with his name and address to his coat, the only means whereby he is identified after his death. Through that attachment the whole subterranean (and transnational) maze of the bombing is then laid bare by Inspector Heat and the Assistant Commissioner—a different kind of navigation.

This is Stevie as far as we know him. Adoptive son to Verloc, who '[m]ight have been' his father (*SA*, 198), he cannot find his place except as sacrificial figure used for the violence of others. After the explosion, the disaggregated elements of his body mix with the earth, a cosmic merging (or chaos) of another kind. Lost on land as Jim and Marlow are lost on the waterways of the earth, his circles do not match the circles of this world.

## HEART OF DARKNESS

'[S]ometimes it takes all my resolution and power of self-control,' Conrad wrote to Edward Garnett in March 1898, some months before he began *Heart of Darkness*, 'to refrain from butting my head against the wall. I want to howl and foam at the mouth...After such crises of despair I doze for hours till half conscious that there is that story I am unable to write...'. He pointed to the way his writing was connected to a visceral self-consciousness: 'I seem to have lost all *sense* of style and yet I am haunted, mercilessly haunted by the *necessity* of style. And that story I can't write weaves itself into all I see, into all I speak, into all I think, into the lines of every book I try to read....You know how bad it is when one *feels* one's liver, or lungs. Well I feel my brain. I am distinc[t]ly conscious of the contents of my head. My story is there in a fluid—in an evading shape. I can't get hold of it. It is all there—to bursting, yet I Can't get hold of it no more than you can grasp a handful of water.'[42] Clearly, Conrad's torments around writing had not abated, but by the time he came to write *Heart of Darkness*, the novel's form must have been available to him. Rather than clutching for the narrative, Conrad

---

[42]  Conrad to Garnett, 29 March [1898], in Frederick R. Karl and Laurence Davies, eds, *The Collected Letters of Joseph Conrad*, vol. 2 (Cambridge: Cambridge University Press, 1986), 49–50.

felt himself gripped. 'The story I told you of holds me. It grows like the genii out of the bottle in the Tale,' he wrote to Ford Madox Ford.[43]

It was a novel that, more than seventy years later, seriously undermined Conrad's reputation, not least in Chinua Achebe's accusation that the work showed Conrad to be 'a thoroughgoing racist'.[44] It is intriguing that Achebe and Conrad had some things in common: both came to write in English rather than their 'home' languages (though Achebe was more concerned to Africanize English than Conrad was to make it Polish); Achebe also experienced exile (initially because of his support for a 'national' state in Biafra rather than in flight from nationalism). Both, that is, knew the hazards of the transnational in their lives as well as their writing, although while Conrad took to the waters to write, Achebe was much more 'grounded' in every respect in the history, territory, and culture of his beloved Igboland. On the question of Africa, however, they could not be more divided. Achebe pointed to the image of Africa in *Heart of Darkness*, highlighting the fact that so few Africans speak (or when they do make only scarcely intelligible or cannibalistic remarks), the way that Conrad makes Africa a 'setting and backdrop which eliminates the African as human factor'.[45] In Conrad's formulation, we might say, knowledge and 'truth' about Africa are defined as European, while Africa represents the screen upon which racially biased images of African primitivity and savagery are projected. As Patrick Brantlinger suggests, some of the novel's motifs step straight out of the repertory of imperial or colonial iconography; Africa is the site of unreason and madness, of a thoroughly primeval time.[46] Though Achebe does not quite put it this way, it is arguable that in *Heart of Darkness* Africa becomes *the* archetypal site of the European unconscious, the natural setting in which the return of the repressed, in the form of Kurtz, finds its fitting home or location. It is a form of cultural imperialism in grave contrast to the promise of Marlow's early

---

[43] Conrad to Ford [3 January 1899], Karl and Davies, eds., *Conrad Letters*, vol. 2, 146.

[44] Chinua Achebe, 'An Image of Africa', in Conrad, *Heart of Darkness*, ed. Kimbrough, 257.

[45] Achebe, 'An Image of Africa', 257.

[46] See Patrick Brantlinger, 'Heart of Darkness: Anti-Imperialism, Racism or Impressionism?', in Joseph Conrad, *Heart of Darkness*, ed. Ross C. Murfin (Boston and New York: Bedford, 1996), 285.

introduction as narrator, who, we were told, was not satisfied with that kind of approach.

One of the remarkable things about Achebe's case, is that it took so long after the publication of Conrad's novel for someone even to raise the issue. It is perhaps an index of the problem he was addressing that he had to be the first to do so. Certainly, the debate raised by his observations has continued to resonate; but the question is, what are we to make of it in 'transnational' terms? One immediate suggestion is to recognize that even culturally the novel is complex. For instance, regarding its habits of representation, Achebe is accurate: to put it mildly, we do not get anything like an 'enlightened' picture of Africa in *Heart of Darkness*, even taking into account the inevitable limits of Conrad's time and perspective. Yet at the same time, in terms of genre, the novel undermines many of the standard patterns of the African adventure romance in the hands of European writers. Not least, in this novel we have no young white man who earns his masculinity and adulthood taming the dark continent's seduction and threat. Here is no white boy turned into a man through his experiences while African men are tamed and turned into 'boys'. Rather, Marlow is thoroughly displaced by what he discovers, while African men are driven not into boyhood but, because of evident European rapacity, to death. Where Marlow, like Conrad, mentions his own boyhood avocation for maps— and in almost exactly the same terms of a pursuit for truth—his rite of passage to a deeper or firmer understanding never occurs. We might say, by contrast, that he is *unmanned* as well as *unmapped* by his experience; and this is to a significant extent because of what he has seen of the reality of *Europe* in Africa. Jameson points out, in relation to Conrad, that we have to be able to think the reactionary with the progressive;[47] but, as in this profound 'unsettlement', it also means we should be able to think the progressive, or at least the subversive, with the reactionary.

Bearing that in mind, the novel's grammar of identity and vision also takes on an intriguingly doubled form. The point is difficult unless we maintain a distinction—as in the butterfly or the ring in *Lord Jim*— between forms of representation and substitution on the one hand, and versions of conceptual and almost physical syntax on the other. At the

---

[47] Jameson, *Political Unconscious*, 235, n. 30.

level of representation Conrad's images (and often his concepts) tend to the fixed and hierarchical: Africa is 'primitive', 'savage', 'mad', and so on. Along a metaphoric axis, each of these terms can be 'substituted' for the continent.[48] Moreover, metonymy in the novel is not its simple or bipolar opposite, at least at the level of representation. As Arjun Appadurai might point out, the 'savage and superb' (*HOD*, 60) African woman Marlow sees at the edge of the river represents the continent through a form of synecdoche, the part for the whole. She also provides 'representative' linkages between nature and native, as well as Africa's awful compulsion for Marlow.

But if metonymy in that form is unreliable and even untenable, Conrad also allows it to be unruly, uncontained. For in the extended reach of Marlow's imagination we get a different picture. Here we see not what *divides* Europe and Africa, but *what makes them contiguous*, linked as they are by the waterways of the earth. We see not what the visible margins of the earth *represent* but what its waterways *connect*. At this level a syntax of combination subverts the hierarchies of representation. So, if Africa is in some sense 'mad', this does not mean that Europe, in the novel's vision, is 'rational'. If Africa is 'savage', then so too, we know from the novel, is Europe. In this form the Thames is not, as Achebe suggests, a 'river emeritus' compared with the Congo, but its extension and equivalent. A metonymic linkage between the two displaces the putative opposition; they are literally connected by water. At the level of representation one could wish this had emerged in a more positive form, but it does not; that was Conrad, and that was, to some extent, his time and place. And strangely, Conrad may take an equally distended view of gender as he does of race.[49] But still the mode of metonymic combination is worth claiming and reclaiming, because it is capable of offering not a world of binary opposition but one of deeply unsettling connection.

The novel's most profound gestures emerge in relation to this form of recognition, down to the level of style, which so tormented Conrad.

[48] See Michael Gorra, *The Bells in Their Silence* (Princeton and Oxford: Princeton University Press, 2004), 64. For metaphor as intrinsically linked to a territorial imperative grounded in a division between the domestic and the foreign, see Eric Cheyfitz, *The Poetics of Imperialism: Translation and Colonization from The Tempest to Tarzan*, exp. edn (Philadelphia: University of Pennsylvania Press, 1997), 35–6.

[49] Johanna M. Smith, ' "Too Beautiful Altogether": Ideologies of Gender and Empire in *Heart of Darkness*', in Conrad, *Heart of Darkness*, ed. Murfin, 169–84.

Take one of his presiding words, 'gloom'. In the context of an imperial discourse whose key metaphors made much of bringing 'light' to a 'dark' continent caught in the 'sleep of ages', 'gloom' in its essence *combines* light and dark: the two become linked within a single word— an internal conceptual metonymy. As Marlow says of his experience in meeting Kurtz, the effect was 'sombre' (a similarly doubled word): '[I]t seemed to throw a kind of light' (*HOD*, 11). In this regard the very medium that enables vision becomes 'spectral'—ghostly or shaded, but also combining seemingly opposed points on the spectrum (an idea which returns in other forms in this book). No accident, then, that vision itself is paradoxical: Marlow will claim that his listeners on the *Nellie* can see Kurtz more clearly than he can, though in the dark they cannot even see him, three or four feet away, as he tells the story.[50] Here the narrator himself is invisible as well as unseeing, and the combination is emblematic, for as much as Marlow's story is obscure, he is also extremely hard to locate. Where tone usually lends perspective, one of the novel's key markers in this respect, as J. Hillis Miller suggests, is its tonal indeterminacy.[51] When Marlow calls the Accountant 'this miracle' (*HOD*, 21), or speaks of the need to have something one can sacrifice or bow down to, what *precisely* is his tone or attitude? In this way *Heart of Darkness* goes beyond irony or parody into another form of enunciation entirely. Like Conrad's *locus classicus* which opens the novel, the Turneresque 'offing' in the Thames where 'sea and sky are welded without a joint', there are no lines of difference or perspective in the novel—which is another way of saying that the nature of the boundary is by no means clear. The very *element* of the novel is fog, mist, blur. Dream or reality? These are not opposites to Marlow but they merge into one another in his narrative, a syntax of mutual infusion.

All this is reinforced thematically in the novel, not least through a sustained pattern of mimicry. In *Nostromo* it is only the inauthentic that 'mimics', but here it is impossible to tell what or who the real is. If Marlow's experiences throw 'a kind of light', then this is not light itself but only a form of *similitude* to light. Of the august Director of Companies at the novel's outset we learn that on the whole of the Thames there was 'nothing that looked half so nautical'. Marlow, for his

---

[50] See J. Hillis Miller, '*Heart of Darkness* Revisited', in Conrad, *Heart of Darkness*, ed. Murfin, 215–16.

[51] Hillis Miller, '*Heart of Darkness* Revisited', 219.

part, 'resemble[s] an idol', and about to set out for Africa he feels that he is 'an impostor' (*HOD*, 7, 16). As for Kurtz, to his followers he is anything and everything—poet, journalist, politician—but no one can say exactly what he is. When he is about to die—meet the absolute—we are told that '[t]he shade of the original Kurtz frequented the bedside of the hollow sham': a residue visiting a copy (*HOD*, 67). Even the African woman who so compels Marlow is described as an 'apparition' (*HOD*, 60): perhaps not the real thing after all. Very little, in short, seems identical with itself in the novel; everything stands beside itself in a principle of continuously self-displacing metonymy. Marlow is not even sure that the papers Kurtz gave him for safekeeping are 'the right bundle' (*HOD*, 74), and when Marlow tells the Intended that Kurtz's last word had been 'your name', language itself becomes doubled, as if there are two systems at work, in which the single phrase—'the horror'—can mean wholly different, yet still connected, things. Here the two meanings speak through one another, linking the Intended and her beliefs in Brussels with the nightmare of Kurtz's regime in Africa.

It is inevitable, in such a setting, that time will become similarly unanchored. On one level we see this directly as theme: Africa, England, and Rome are connected through time just as the waterways of the earth link them in space. Yet cross-cutting time is built into the very texture and structure of the book. Marlow sees 'little sticks' coming towards his boat and only later realizes they are arrows. This is not just Watts's 'delayed decoding', a form of narrative impressionism.[52] These are what Stephen Hawking might call *arrows of time*, and here, as far as the normal ratios of cause and effect are concerned (or before and after in perception), time is reversed: Marlow *understands*, and then he really 'sees'.[53] As for Marlow's narrative, its associative or metonymic form means, among other things, that it meanders in every direction in time as well as space, while his progress 'up river'—a kind of 'backwards' in time—is also the novel's progress forward in chronology. *Time in*, we might say, is *time out*, and in temporal terms it is hard to say what 'back' or 'forward' means in *Heart of Darkness*. If, in Benedict

---

[52] See Ian Watt, 'Impressionism and Symbolism in Heart of Darkness', in Conrad, *Heart of Darkness*, ed. Kimbrough, 317–19.

[53] For the arrow of time, see Stephen Hawking, *A Brief History of Time: From the Big Bang to Black Holes* (New York: Bantam, 1988).

Anderson's formulation, national time invokes perfect synchrony (or Empire a seamless narrative of sequence and progress) then in *Heart of Darkness* we have a profoundly transnational and counter-imperial form.

Moreover, everything from this point of view—perspective, perception, time, location—is undermined by the novel's narrative structure. There is room for debate about what the successive narrators in *Heart of Darkness* entail: the frame-narrator who hears (and retells) Marlow's story; any implied narrator beyond him; Conrad's narrative voice around that. Chinua Achebe, assessing this puzzle, saw distinction without a difference: no 'correction' to Marlow's perspective, and therefore a pervasive racism throughout the novel.[54] But we might draw a different conclusion, at least on the structural level. The point is that *it does not matter* how many narrators there are because they cannot provide any more clarity than Marlow can or any more fixed an observation point. In that light, the successive frames of the novel come across only as a hollow irony. The circles of narration are flattened, turned inside out, rendered nugatory. Marlow, whose narration is innermost in the structure of the novel, approaches its outer boundary, while the frame-narrator can provide no perspective on his lack of perspective. Again, there is no authoritative or located text.

Ultimately what this means is that there is no outside to the novel: the only outside is revealed at its inside, and what you see at the centre runs all the way through to the observing and observable horizon. It is a world whose implications are deeply unsettling. At the end of the novel we see all this quite graphically, where content becomes a kind of form. Here Marlow, in his famous betrayal, preserves belief or truth through telling his lie to Kurtz's Intended. The resonance is immense. In a morbid version of the liar's paradox—'everything I tell you is a lie', which can only be true if false and vice versa—the only way the truth of European 'progress' can be preserved is through the lie that runs from its core to its frame. The Brussels to which Marlow returns, the Thames on which the *Nellie* lies moored, the faith in a civilizing mission of the Intended—none has any uncompromised foundation. Inside is outside, veracity vicious in its illusions. For Marlow, the character-narrator who unlike Kurtz returns to life, there is only the thoroughgoing reality of

---

[54] Achebe, 'An Image of Africa', 256.

unsettlement in a world governed by Empire where there is no vision or possibility of truth. Marlow can no longer navigate according to any clear understanding.

This may be an essential point about *Heart of Darkness*. It is a book of unmapping or unknowing at the heart of European civilization. That means—for all its liabilities regarding race—it is also an extraordinarily courageous novel, for Conrad has looked into European modernity at the core of its beliefs, its vaunted imperial ambitions, and its truth, and found that there is nothing there. In *Lord Jim*, Marlow as narrator stood to some extent *outside* Jim's story. Here, in Conrad's most radical work, he is both subject and object, the internal narrator at its effective perimeter, the character who journeys in search of a centre, the one who finds both there and at the horizon that he has nowhere to go, no firm ground on which to stand, no home to which he can return. Unlike ordinary seamen whose 'country is the sea', he is displaced from this too, afloat and moored on the tide (temporary/transitive/in movement) of the Thames on the *Nellie*. He is on a river in the dark, between ocean and land.

Conrad, whose whole life had been one of displacement, whose journey to the Congo had left him sick in heart and mind and homesick for the sea, had found a form in which to register the fact that upon the waterways of the earth, a world without horizon, there is no final location, no outside, no beyond. As he understood, in that setting the reach of Empire is almost total. Yet also, because of that, he was able to understand the syntax of connection it entailed. There is a doubleness in *Heart of Darkness*, one which still sounds for us more than a hundred years later and will not let us rest in relation to the novel. The waters connect, the waters divide; *Heart of Darkness* explores the nature of that boundary.

# 2

# Route, Constellation, Faultline

*Caryl Phillips*

In order for a part of the past to be touched by the present instant, there must be no continuity between them.

Walter Benjamin, *The Arcades Project*

'I saw only one other black man in Venice. He looked nothing like Othello.'

So Caryl Phillips writes in the opening sentence of a short essay entitled 'A Black European Success', one of the many that make up the record of his travels through Europe in *The European Tribe*.[1] In this book, published in 1987, Phillips reverses the lens on a continent used to turning its ethnographical and cultural gaze on a world it has dominated. Phillips, whose personal history has been inseparable from the effects and after-effects of that domination, now looks back, travelling through Europe as a black man and recording the results of what Bruce Chatwin might have called his 'progress'—this circuit, this journey, this search. Even as he finds many of the key and continuing motifs of his writing—the presence of postcolonial immigrant populations in Europe, the mutually resonant history of blacks and Jews, the role of writers such as James Baldwin in a racially inflected transnational experience—the effects of the book are disruptive, both in content and form. Not accidentally, Phillips begins his survey in Casablanca, *adjacent* to Europe in North Africa, as if in implicit reminder that the two continents, supposedly distinct, are connected via the matrix of the Mediterranean, not to mention the complexities of their interlocking

---

[1] Caryl Phillips, *The European Tribe* (New York: Farrar, Straus, Giroux, 1987). Henceforth referenced as *ET*.

histories. The essays themselves take on a syntactic aspect, less a chronicle than a series of counterpointed juxtapositions leaving readers to thread their implicit narrative, working questions of transition and transmission, contiguity and difference, in the spaces between them. In this context, Phillips himself straddles various boundaries as both insider and outsider, not least that of race. 'Ultimately, the one certainty for Europe,' he writes, 'is that she knows a "nigger" when she sees one: she should—they were a figment of her imagination, a product of her creative mind' (*ET*, 121). To Europe he remarks 'Your eyesight is defective' (*ET*, 128). The book becomes an act of personal and experiential navigation through a hostile environment that is also in some sense 'home'—gapped, transitional, interstitial.

There is no doubt that Phillips's sense of home has been complicated, but it is not, for that reason, unrepresentative. He is best considered as part of the second generation of West Indians in Britain.[2] Born in St Kitts in the West Indies in 1958, his parents brought him with them to Britain when he was twelve weeks old—one of the youngest of 'migrants'. He grew up in Leeds, a northern industrial and working-class city which, after London and Birmingham, attracted a sizeable West Indian population, particularly from Jamaica and St Kitts. When Phillips was eight his parents divorced, and his mother moved with her children to a predominantly white working-class area—yet a further migration. Phillips's mother worked three jobs to bring up her children, while the children had to be on constant lookout in streets that harboured an ever-present sense of racial threat. At school Phillips faced the ignorance and jibes of teachers as well as pupils. When he was ten, the Conservative MP Enoch Powell gave his 'rivers of blood' speech about the 'menace' of continued immigration from the ex-colonies, which affected the atmosphere considerably.[3] Phillips cultivated the resources

---

[2] I have drawn on a range of sources for much of the information in these paragraphs: Caryl Phillips, personal communication, 23 November 2004; Phillips, Introduction to *ET*; Caryl Phillips, 'On "The Nature of Blood" and the Ghost of Anne Frank', *Common Quest* (Summer 1998), 4–7; Stephen Clingman, 'Other Voices: An Interview with Caryl Phillips', *Salmagundi*, 143 (2004): 113–40; C. Rosalind Bell, 'Worlds Within: An Interview with Caryl Phillips', *Callaloo* 14/3 (1991): 578–606.

[3] See Caryl Phillips, *A New World Order: Essays* (London: Secker and Warburg, 2001), 273–5. Henceforth referenced as *NWO*. Also, for Phillips's background, see the general introduction and several of the essays in the 'Britain' section of *NWO*.

that were required—a quick wit and quick feet—but for a young black boy growing up, the sense of dissonance was palpable. Along with the rest of his generation, he was black and British before that was a concept even recognized let alone welcomed by white society. Unlike his parents he was not 'from' the Caribbean, but nor, apparently, did he wholly 'belong' in England. His sense of self as well as location were matters of disjunction and perpetual negotiation.

'The key issue for me and my generation... growing up in the Britain of the late 1960s and 1970s,' Phillips has written, 'was identity' (*NWO*, 275). In this regard the most unsettling question of all may have been the direct challenge, 'where are you *really* from?'—a question which, in the circumstances, carried existential as well as geographical implications.[4] '[W]e grew up,' Phillips has commented, 'not quite knowing if this was home.'[5] These were among the frustrations and thwarted ambitions of a younger black generation that produced the Notting Hill riots of the 1970s, but it is intriguing and also characteristic that Phillips did not embrace an alternate version of race for his sense of identity. When Phillips was eighteen he went to Oxford University and on occasion would travel to London to wander around Ladbroke Grove and Notting Hill, testing out pubs, coffee bars, and reggae venues to see if he would fit in. But the idea of black solidarity had no convincing appeal, not least because Phillips had never been part of a black community, whether at school or university. In addition, he grew up in Leeds, aware that class was as strong a determinant of identity as race: 'I was working class; I knew that'.[6] And even from a young age he was aware of all those other outsiders whose lives intersected with his own. One was a history teacher at school, a Mr Stern (whose name reappears, perhaps coincidentally, in *The Nature of Blood*), an immigrant from Berlin who was drawn to Phillips by his precociousness and who, very likely, identified with *him*. Phillips's fiction is full of such marginal figures, who come together from vastly different directions yet find a glancing, and sometimes more than glancing, connection. Even from

---

[4] For one example see *NWO*, 303. Also see Clingman, 'Other Voices', 135; *NWO*, 296; *ET*, 125–6; and Phillips, 'On "The Nature of Blood" ', 6–7.

[5] Bell, 'Worlds Within', 599.

[6] For this and many of the details in this paragraph, see Clingman, 'Other Voices', 119–20.

an early age, his version of identity had more to do with the transitive space of intersection and crossing than fixed location or singularity.

In this regard, it makes sense that Phillips's experience of displacement found a particular resonance in Jewish history. The source of this rested on a reality hardly capable of articulation at the time, that Phillips could find no informed public discussion of his own situation, of how he came to be in England. Such an account would have involved the legacy of slavery, the era of colonization, the migrations and countermigrations that followed, the residue of British prejudice that remained. In Britain in the 1970s there was little concerning this except silence. But by that period the European world was at last returning to the question of the Holocaust, the incomprehensible crime at the core of its recent past. Given the lack of reference points for his own circumstances, Phillips fixed on that of the Jews, as if through the linkage he could make sense of his history and experience. Coming home from school one day he watched an episode from the television series The World at War, and the effect was overwhelming. As Phillips records it, he was 'terrified'. Prior to that, the world as he understood it had been divided into whites and blacks, and Jews were white people. Now he saw the divisions even within the 'white' community, and he was left with a forceful question: 'If white people could do that to white people, then what the hell would they do to me?'[7]

It was then that Phillips sat down to write his first short story, about a young Dutch-Jewish boy in occupied Holland who resists the decree that all Jews must wear the yellow star. Paradoxically, however, it is the very enforcement of the visible marker of exclusion that provides linkage and rescue. When the boy is knocked unconscious leaping from a cattle-truck to escape transportation to the concentration camps, a Dutch farmer sees sunlight glinting off his star, and saves him (*ET*, 67). Beyond the wish-fulfilment of a fourteen-year-old writer, even in such an early exploration one can see a profound recognition of the relationship between the black and Jewish experiences, triangulated against the background of white Europe—and all registered only one degree from the self. 'The Dutch boy was, of course, me,' Phillips has since remarked

---

[7] See *ET*, 66–7; also Phillips, 'On "The Nature of Blood"', 6. And Bell, 'Worlds Within', 601.

of the story.[8] Metonymy and transitive identity are built in, both for the young writer and his subject.

Perhaps it is no accident then that the black–Jewish collocation has remained an enduring investigation for Phillips. Growing up, he read *The Diary of Anne Frank*; as an adult writer he kept a poster of Anne Frank above his desk. In *The European Tribe* he writes of 'Anne Frank's Amsterdam', and also an essay entitled 'In the Ghetto', about Jewish history in Venice—a companion piece to his consideration of Othello. The 'Ghetto' essay records how, for Phillips, in the absence of any discussion of slavery and its legacy, 'I vicariously channeled a part of my hurt and frustration through the Jewish experience' (*ET*, 54). In the same essay he comments that 'the Jew is still Europe's nigger' (*ET*, 53). And in this context he mentions how, 'as a black man living in Europe', he always remembers Frantz Fanon writing in 1952 of his philosophy professor, a native of the Antilles who had said, 'Whenever you hear anyone abuse the Jews, pay attention, because he is talking about you' (*ET*, 54). While Phillips is not uncritical—he is also, in the 1980s, prepared to talk of Israel's relations with apartheid South Africa—the convergent, associative histories of blacks and Jews is an extremely powerful one for him.

It is also, in a strange way, a personal connection, for Phillips has revealed that he had a grandfather who was Jewish, a Portuguese man named Emmanuel de Fraites, who came to St Kitts by way of Madeira.[9] The grandfather, however, never acknowledged his grandchildren. In his collection of essays and reviews, *A New World Order*, Phillips recalls how he first saw him:

Back then I knew very little about my own Caribbean heritage. Some years later I saw a photograph of my father's mother and was shocked to discern traces of East India in her face. Soon after I was sitting in a bar in St Kitts with my brother and a friend told us that our grandfather had just walked in and taken a seat in the corner. My brother and I looked quizzically at each other, for we 'knew' that our grandfather, our mother's father, was dead. We had grown up in England with this 'knowledge'. But, sure enough, seated in the corner was Emmanuel de Fraites, a Jewish trader with Portuguese roots that reached back

---

[8] Phillips, 'On "The Nature of Blood" ', 6.

[9] Phillips, 'On "The Nature of Blood" ', 4; also, personal communication, 23 November 2004.

to the island of Madeira. I now understood that the cultural hybridity that is the quintessential Caribbean condition had certainly marked my person, and the quality of the blood that flowed through my veins was doggedly 'impure'.

(*NWO*, 130)

Contact, convergence, contiguity, rejection: the qualities of blood. These are direct for Phillips, by no means abstract but personal matters of continual complication and exploration. The linkage connects, the linkage divides, and the point of inspection concerns the nature of the boundary. This is the characteristic topography of Phillips's fiction.

These issues also go to the core of a European literary history— something of which Phillips is acutely aware. If he writes about Venice in *The European Tribe*, that is partly because two of Shakespeare's plays are set there, one about a black man, one about a Jew. Shylock and Othello: Phillips has recalled how personally he took *Othello* as a student, sometimes to the bemusement of his teachers,[10] and in *The European Tribe* he comments on both figures. Of Othello he remarks, 'I may be in danger of stating the obvious, but I shall state it anyhow. Othello was a black man' (*ET*, 46). And Shylock, he says, 'has always been my hero' (*ET*, 55). Othello and Shylock—each with his own broken path, crossing one another's paths—in Venice, European city of shimmerings, mirrorings, a ghetto, and water.

## ROUTE

If anyone knows about the 'route' as the *rupta via*, therefore, it is Caryl Phillips. If he grew up as a black child in the city of Leeds, always asked where he came 'from', then he knows about this version of the route. If his grandfather was Jewish, but the fact of it was always concealed, then this is another dimension of the route as disrupted. But if he knows this dimension, then he also knows its paradoxical corollary: how it can become a principle of recognition and correspondence among those whose routes are similarly broken. This is not the correspondence of an equation, but the correspondence of *communication*—the transmission

---

[10] Frank Birbalsingh, ed., *Frontiers of Caribbean Literatures in English* (New York: St Martin's, 1996), 191.

of meaning across difference, distance, time. As the transmission of meaning it is also a form of navigation in a transnational setting.

As such, this version of the route allows us to enter into the domain Paul Gilroy calls the Black Atlantic—a domain which has great relevance for Caryl Phillips—but to do so in a slightly different way, through a different inflection. For Gilroy the Black Atlantic is a place of 'an infinite process of identity construction', a 'webbed network', an area of 'transnational black Atlantic creativity'.[11] In his version of 'routes' rather than 'roots', it is a form of navigation through five hundred years of spatial history.[12] Intriguingly, in this setting Gilroy, like Phillips, draws inspiration from Jewish experience. Asking 'how black expressive cultures practice remembrance', he notes how the concept of 'diaspora' came to the black tradition from Jewish thought, and how the motif of slavery, as well as modes of journey and exile are common to both cultures.[13] In addressing the work of Toni Morrison, he announces a theme drawn obliquely from her novel *Beloved*, of setting the histories of blacks and Jews 'closer to each other'.[14] Such a conceptual alignment is itself a syntactic gesture—a mark of contiguity, adjacency, mutual invocation in the realm of identity.

In these terms as well as others, Phillips might well claim to be one of the latest inhabitants of the Black Atlantic. It is not just a question of his early migration, for as an adult, too, Phillips has been an inveterate traveller, subject to what he calls a 'compulsive itinerancy' (*NWO*, 305). In this regard, if any one area of the world has occupied his life and imagination, it is the triangular oceanic space between Africa, the Caribbean/North America, and Britain. Having moved to New York after leaving Britain in the late 1980s, Phillips still maintains a home in St Kitts, and visits Britain regularly. Most significantly, his writing—and it appears much of his sense of being— focuses intently on a black Atlantic geography and experience. His collection of essays, *A New World Order*, is divided into four sections, on the United States, Africa, the Caribbean, and Britain, and moves across

---

[11] Paul Gilroy, *The Black Atlantic: Modernity and Double Consciousness* (Cambridge, MA: Harvard University Press, 1993), 223, 29, 16.
[12] Gilroy, *Black Atlantic*, 19.
[13] See Gilroy, *Black Atlantic*, 205–23.
[14] Gilroy, *Black Atlantic*, 217. Consider Paul D's wish in relation to Sethe as a statement of contiguity: 'He wants to put his story next to hers'. Toni Morrison, *Beloved* (New York: Plume, 1988), 287.

all of them. In a companion piece to his novel *Crossing the River*, entitled 'Water', Phillips talks of '[r]ibbons of water which ineluctably bind us together'.[15]

How, though, does this version of the Black Atlantic space function in Phillips's imagination, in his own sense of belonging? This is a question that allows us to arrive at an acute sense of his *disposition* in every resonance of the term—something he measures in relation to both land and water. So, the Introduction to *A New World Order* announces a motif for each of its locations on land, whether in Europe, Africa, or the American world: 'I feel at home here, but I don't belong. I am of, and not of, this place' (*NWO*, 1). Yet in a later essay in the volume Phillips recalls telling his lawyer how he would like his body to be disposed of when he dies: 'I wish my ashes to be scattered in the middle of the Atlantic Ocean at a point equidistant between Britain, Africa, and North America' (*NWO*, 304). This is a point at the very centre of what Phillips thinks of as his 'Atlantic home', not a land burial at all. He tells of how, standing on the ramparts of Elmina Castle in Ghana, the slaving outpost where his own journey began so many centuries before, and 'probably the most beautiful building that I have ever seen', he can gaze out on the Atlantic Ocean and know exactly where he comes from, as well as where he will ultimately reside (*NWO*, 305, 309).

The moment is a poignant one, and it heightens the issues both emotionally and conceptually—making them more than simply conceptual. We can see it this way. On one level, there is an opposition: if land divides, then waters connect, and this is where Phillips will find his resting place, in the equidistant point of an oceanographic location and identity. But implicit here is also another truth. For the waters of the Atlantic were *themselves* the *rupta via*—the waters of slavery, the path of disruption, the road that divided, the continuous waters that separated. That perhaps is why there is another opposition here, between life and death: where life has divided, death may reconcile, in the very place which embodies that doubleness—and so it may be a kind of 'home'. But at some measure of depth here we get a sense of the full meaning of the route for someone such as Phillips. If his resting place is one of reconciliation, it is also one of incarnation, recognition. These are the waters of crossing, but also of partition; of continuity,

---

[15] Caryl Phillips, 'Water', *Agni*, 94 (1994): 30.

but also separation. This is the doubleness of the route, whether on the waterways of the earth or divided by land. Its version of the transitive involves absence as well as linkage, loss as well as finding, trauma as well as connection, receding horizons as well as approach. The equidistant point exists because of the broken route, and it also commemorates that brokenness.

In these circumstances, there is every sense for Phillips that *writing* is the appropriate and perhaps the only adequate form of navigation. A year after publishing *The Nature of Blood*, in a short essay entitled 'On "The Nature of Blood" and the Ghost of Anne Frank', Phillips reflected on the process of bringing the novel to conclusion.[16] That is where he talks of his Jewish grandfather—though he maintains that his sudden discovery did not prompt the novel or its title. But, more insistently, he records writing the novel as a form of *travel*, quite literally: how he worked on a draft in a hotel in Bangkok, how an element of the novel was missing, how he found it in a newspaper report of Ethiopian Jews in Israel whose donated blood was rejected by the government over fears of racial contamination. He also tells of completing the book in Amsterdam, in another hotel room, where he needed his writing to be 'in danger from my environment'. After working for two weeks he revisited Anne Frank's house, which he had first been to twenty years before. Now, as he puts it, he was run down by an 'emotional train', allowing himself to reflect on Anne Frank and the millions of lives lost. Nearby was a Caribbean restaurant, and sitting there Phillips was aware that another round of European madness could leave that too in rubble. But the emotion, as well as the writing, had left him strangely calmer, and that is where Phillips mentions the young Dutch boy of his story of twenty-five years before. Writing the novel had put him in touch with that boy, the boy who was one degree displaced from himself.

Writing then is navigation, both within the self and beyond. It works at a point equidistant from any safe shores where identity and location might be fixed. In the spaces and gaps, the divisions of a transnational world, it is a writing of the transitional and transitive. It explores the route as the *rupta via*; but it also becomes the *form* of the route, the route as the essence of the form.

---

[16] Phillips, 'On "The Nature of Blood" '; see n. 2 above.

## TRANSNATIONAL FORM

It is axiomatic to say that the limits of the national fall by the wayside of such a journey. To the extent that nationality has concerned Phillips, it has been in relation to Britain, but there it is Defoe's 'mongrel' nation composed by waves of migration that attracts him rather than Orwell's version of an organic continuity (Phillips has commented on how, seven years after Orwell wrote 'England Your England', the first postwar West Indian immigrants docked at Tilbury fully expecting to be received as British).[17] In interviews he has remarked that questions of nationality as such never interested him, and that it is important to get beyond 'fixed' notions of identity.[18] But what are the implications for the *kind* of writing one does? What is the connection between a transnational perspective and questions of form? Phillips has addressed the issue directly.

'Eventually *every* writer discovers that his or her main struggle is with this one word: form' (*NWO*, 293). So Phillips remarks in an essay entitled 'Extravagant Strangers', a meditation both on the nature of British identity, and on the literature produced by immigrant writers within Britain. The title of the essay comes again (almost inevitably) from Othello, for he is the original 'wheeling and extravagant stranger', the European immigrant at the heart of the English literary canon. As Phillips points out in the essay, many of Britain's most prominent writers were born in various elsewheres, from Ignatius Sancho and Olaudah Equiano to Thackeray, Kipling, Orwell, T. S. Eliot, Selvon, Conrad, Harris, Rushdie, and Naipaul among many others.[19] Here what counts primarily to Phillips, as his listing suggests, is not so much race but the condition of being an outsider. If race has a function, it is mainly because a state of being *visibly* other intensifies the outsider's demarcation (*NWO*, 290–1). Understanding this reveals some of the concerns of Phillips's own writing, not in race as the essential sign and substance of the outsider's identity, nor a flattening out of all outsiders in some

---

[17] See *NWO*, 266–8, 288; George Orwell, 'England Your England', in *A Collection of Essays* (New York: Harcourt Brace Jovanovich, 1981), 254.

[18] Anita Desai, Caryl Phillips, and Ilan Stavans, 'The Other Voice', *Transition*, 64 (1994): 82–3. Clingman, 'Other Voices': 135–6.

[19] In this regard, also see Caryl Phillips, ed., *Extravagant Strangers* (New York: Vintage, 1999), an anthology of writing by these figures among others.

formulaic manner, but an interest in all those asymmetrically marginal-ized and excluded people of whatever origins whose routes cross in ways that shift from the complex and complementary to the jagged, tangen-tial and disjunctive—in itself an underlying formal patterning in his work.

But on this question Phillips gets even closer to definition, for in his account there is a connection between certain structures of feeling and certain structures of fiction. As he sets out the pattern in his essay, the key feeling at issue is *ambivalence*—ambivalence towards (in this case) Britain, the 'host' country, the place to which the immigrant belongs as an outsider. Its results are not uniform or predictable: the jingoism of a Kipling, the social commitment of an Orwell, the political extremism of a Wyndham Lewis, may be prompted or accentuated by feelings of ambivalence (*NWO*, 290). But Phillips also takes a point that has been raised by Terry Eagleton among others, and gives it a particular slant.[20] In certain writers the reality of ambivalence, of doubleness and disjuncture, translates into a formal principle in their work, registered for Phillips primarily in relation to time. Indeed, some of the greatest formal innovators in the English language have been its outsiders who, precisely because of their alienation, 'experiment with discontinuities of time, and revel in the disruption of conventional narrative order'. Such writers are, as Phillips puts it, 'disrupters of national continuity' (*NWO*, 292). It is intriguing here that Phillips points to *chronology*, whether within the frame of the work or beyond, rather than say spatial disruption. Of course, time and space are connected, but if Phillips fixes on the temporal, this may be because, as distinct from other disjunctions we can imagine, there is something quite profound in the notion of a disruption of time. Here the route of time itself is broken, punctuated, made other to itself. The time of the nation is not only non-simultaneous, but its very assumption of flow is a fiction these fictions will disassemble—even as they assemble other kinds of correspondence and transmission through their versions of disjunction.

There are at least two consequences for Phillips's own writing. One is a set of elective affinities which in and of themselves adopt a cross-cutting modality. On the one hand Phillips has spoken of his veneration

---

[20] See Terry Eagleton, *Exiles and Émigrés: Studies in Modern Literature* (London: Chatto & Windus, 1970).

for Richard Wright and James Baldwin, black writers who, in different
ways, grappled with questions of identity, made their own transnational
journeys, and inspired him in his early decision to become a writer.[21]
On the other hand, there is a figure of inspiration who might on the
face of it be unexpected—none other than Joseph Conrad. Yet the
connection makes perfect sense, for Conrad, too, was one of those
'disrupters of national continuity' whose formal experimentations and
associative dynamics emerged directly from his experience as an outsider, his own oceanic wanderings. As Phillips puts it, Conrad was 'a
man of the water. . . . He's a man of travel, and he's a man who reinvented
himself. He changed his name; he had three languages at his disposal;
he understood, within himself, the fragility of identity.'[22] This is partly
what underlies Phillips's disagreement with Chinua Achebe regarding
Conrad; it is not Conrad on the question of race but Conrad as expo-
nent of the *route* that Phillips finds so evocative.[23] Overall, the pattern
is emblematic and characteristic. Phillips *frees up* his sense of affiliation,
creates new constellations. He is inheritor to Wright and Baldwin but
also to Conrad: a transnational literary mapping across quite marked
distances and spaces.

The second consequence is there in Phillips's work, for it is disrupted,
gapped, synaptic, in all the ways we might now anticipate. Indeed, in
a fitting paradox his writing raises disruption to a highly structured
principle. We see it, for example, in a non-fiction masterpiece such as
*The Atlantic Sound*, comprised of discontinuous but linked essays across
time, water, and land: a retracing of the first journey Phillips's parents
(and he himself) made across the Atlantic to England; two accounts
of persistence and heroism in former Atlantic slaving ports (an African
travelling to Liverpool in the 1800s, a white judge in Charleston in the
1950s); a description of a farcical 'Panafest' in Ghana, where the subject
is 'roots' rather than 'routes'; a meditation on a settlement of American

---

[21] For Phillips's discovery of Wright, see *ET*, 7–8.

[22] Clingman, 'Other Voices', 122–3.

[23] In Phillips's account of a conversation with Chinua Achebe on Conrad, he also
comes to understand that his own perspective is European rather than African—
i.e., beyond any straightforwardly racial version of affiliation. See 'Out of Africa',
*Guardian*, 22 February 2003; <http://books.guardian.co.uk/departments/classics/
story/0„900335,00.html> (accessed 10 January 2004). And see Phillips's sympathetic
Introduction to Joseph Conrad, *Heart of Darkness and Selections from The Congo Diary*
(New York: Random House, 1999).

'Black Israelites' in the desert town of Dimona in Israel, looking for their own version of the Promised Land. This kind of disruption is also marked in Phillips's fiction. *Higher Ground* tells three stories (discrete, but not wholly unconnected) regarding three characters: an African complicit in the workings of the slave trade; Rudy, a Black Power figure in jail in the United States at the end of the 1960s; and Irina, a Holocaust survivor from Poland living in England.[24] In *Crossing the River*, three siblings sold by their father into slavery turn up in such different settings as Liberia in the early nineteenth century, the American 'Wild West' of the late nineteenth century, and a Yorkshire village during the Second World War. In *Cambridge* Phillips takes on the voice of an early nineteenth-century slave as well as that of a young Englishwoman sent out to her father's estate in the West Indies. The stories in these works are not only set apart in space and time, but Phillips also presents them variously through first-person voicing, letters, and journals as well as third-person modes mixed with free indirect discourse—a stylistic gapping and rotation further complicating perspective, location, and approach.

It is worth emphasizing that these shifts implicate readers as much as writer, for it is readers who must navigate these passages and crossings, assess parallax, transmission, and distance, hear echo and resonance, comprehend connection, faultline, correlation. If Phillips's writings develop the kind of 'discrete combinatorial system' that expresses the generative aspect of syntax, then we can also understand them as profoundly syntactic. Across landscape and ocean Phillips measures himself in relation to histories, locations, and routes, and we too are put in transnational space—a transnational world of writing, of navigation.

## *THE NATURE OF BLOOD*: EVA STERN

All this—and more—is embedded in Caryl Phillips's sixth novel, *The Nature of Blood*, a novel worth considering in some detail both to see how these patterns emerge and to gain a sense of their larger resonance.

[24] Publication details for Caryl Phillips's works mentioned here: *The Atlantic Sound* (London: Faber, 2000); *Higher Ground* (Viking: New York, 1989); *Crossing the River* (London: Bloomsbury, 1993); *Cambridge* (New York: Knopf, 1992).

The novel has four major narratives. The most prominent, related mainly in the first person, concerns Eva Stern, a Holocaust survivor. A second, written mainly in the third person, is set in the town of Portobuffole, near Venice, in the fifteenth century, telling of the blood-libel execution of members of its Jewish community. The third is set in Venice in the sixteenth century, chiefly a first-person account of the story of Othello. Enclosing these, beginning and end, is the novel's fourth major narrative, concerning Eva Stern's Uncle Stephan, who left Europe for Palestine in the 1930s and who, in the Israel of the 1990s, encounters a young Jewish woman from the Ethiopian immigrant community.

The characteristic Phillips 'shape' is apparent, therefore, dispersed across time and space, and various narrative voicings. Yet the novel also heightens the model in a number of ways. Where, say, in *Crossing the River* or *Higher Ground* the different narratives are kept distinct and told in sequence, here—though each story may take centre-focus for a while—they are *interlaced*, told in a series of variably gapped paragraphs liable to shift from one to the other without preface or transition.[25] There are also other narratives and interventions: the notes of a psychiatrist who examines Eva in England; a series of encyclopedia-like entries on ghettos and other topics; excerpts from Eva's sister Margot's story, as well as that of an English soldier who befriends and then apparently betrays Eva; the inner monologue of the young Ethiopian woman, Malka; a stray voice contumaciously addressing Othello. There are no clues other than the intrinsic dynamics of these threads and voices on how to put them all together. Indeed, how to put them together becomes one of the productive problems of reading the novel. Yet before considering the stories in combination, it is worth thinking of each individually, just to gain a sense of Phillips's remarkable method. Here his approach to the 'route' becomes itself a varied narrative *route*.

We can see each of the stories as heightening a particular topic. In the case of Eva Stern it concerns Phillips's meticulous yet deeply compassionate imagining of a profoundly abandoned woman for whom navigation is both imperative and impossible. As a young Jewish girl

---

[25] Caryl Phillips, *The Nature of Blood* (London: Faber, 1997); henceforth referenced as *NOB*. There appear to be three kinds of gaps in the novel: normal paragraphing; small gaps between segments, marking 'episodic' moments within a story; and larger gaps, usually but not always across different stories.

growing up in Nazi Germany, and then as a concentration camp inmate, her experience has been all but unutterable. The invasion of the inner, a form of 'substitution' through image, stereotype, symbolic replacement, was part of the logic of the Holocaust—an evisceration of the self long before the literal exterminations applied. After Eva's liberation, there is equally no 'fix' between her inner and outer worlds—the distance between the two simply unnavigable. When children throw stones at her, her response is, 'They mock what I look like, not who I am' (*NOB*, 26)—a pattern of which someone such as Phillips would have been well aware. When a documentary crew comes to film the freed inmates, in a dark gesture of resistance Eva gives more than they want, undressing for them—indicating at one and the same time her vulnerability and the logic of their 'narrative'. The documentary 'film' in this sense is emblematic, both a massive intrusion as well as a 'covering'. This is part of the reason Phillips's novel adopts other forms of narration altogether.

In these circumstances, the most devastating aspect of Eva's life is that any version of inward syntax has been almost entirely broken. In her 'liberated' camp, her mother seems to live again, coming to stay with her, only to 'abandon' her once more. The projection of the mother in Eva's mind marks a form of psychic dissociation, the disrupted internal navigation which is perhaps one measure of the reiterations of trauma— where trauma *is* trauma because navigation is broken. Where Eva feels abandoned by her mother, she also feels guilt: in a dream she is the parent who leads the Nazis to her child-mother, and the sequence ends with the feel of bullets in the flesh. The dream manifests the most painful aspect of Eva's grief—her failure to be this mother, to protect others even as she needs protection; in short, the breakdown of the biological grammar of a life. Later, when she is in hospital in England, a different dream-like sequence is the very embodiment of dissociation. Eva appears to be remembering a scene in which she and her sister Margot discussed how many babies each would like to have, but the 'memory' ends with a man in the park taking children to a ditch where they are thrown into a fire, and he returns for the babies whom he smashes against a wall. Dream or reality: the question makes something else clear, that there are *levels* of Eva's subconscious to which she ascends or descends at various moments. But this dream has also come from external reality, broken syntax creating broken syntax.

Eva's entire narration in the novel is an inward one, itself a mark of her solitude and dissociation. Her voice moves through multiple times, both forwards and backwards: the relived present of the concentration camps; the past of what seems so distant as to be the prehistory of that experience; a different level of the present in the post-Holocaust aftermath she inhabits like some residue of all these pasts. Yet because her enunciation is always in the present, this movement is also akin to shifts in levels of consciousness, and it is difficult to know what time or space she inhabits. In this regard the gapped paragraphs, lending an episodic feel to the narrative, in which events are inspected, reconsidered, taken up tangentially, enact a principle of recursion—and indeed, time is recursive not only in Eva's narrative but in the novel as a whole. There are times within times, inward dimensions of time that suddenly open up without warning. This is not so much the mark of navigation but an indication of just how vast and complicated a problem navigation *is* in the conditions of trauma the novel approaches. It is nothing less than the very *medium* of the problem, as well as the task and obligation of those who address it.

In this regard it is fitting that certain aspects of Eva's experience remain obscure to us. Did her soldier friend Gerry actually invite her to marry him, or did she forge a letter from him in order to make her way to England? There, both before and after the impossibility of marriage to Gerry, Eva feels she has been followed by a girl with a red mouth: the girl is herself, other levels of herself, her alter ego, the person she might have been, the girl Rosa who committed suicide in the house where Eva was hiding to escape transportation. Eventually Eva too commits suicide—or she appears to, since we do not know for certain. Either way, having survived the Holocaust, she cannot survive the world it leaves behind. By definition Eva cannot narrate her suicide, and after that, only 'external' versions are left. No testimony through her narrative is wholly reliable, or it is reliable in terms we barely understand. A displaced person, Eva has a displaced narrative, without knowable purchase in the usual world. This is the *rupta via* in a most heartrending form.

It is worth reflecting on the nature of the boundary in such a narration. For in Eva's story two—apparently contradictory—principles are true at the same time: both that there is no 'outside' to her narration, and that there is *only* an outside, because of the things we cannot know, the space we cannot fully inhabit. In every meaningful sense, then, the boundary becomes a place of *approach*, the actual space of navigation, where transmission is both the objective and the problem to be encountered. Here Phillips's narrative—the narrative *of* Eva's narrative—models a form of navigation as well as the protocols of transmission. For Phillips will not tell us everything; will not enquire too much; will respect the boundary of incommunicable experience.[26] Here, in the transnational setting, in the space of the transnational imaginary, Levinas's difference in 'height' makes a difference, even between 'author' and 'character'. Here the unvoiced is as important as the voicing, but precisely because of that, something resonates in the boundary after all. It is a different kind of navigation—of respect, deferral, and tact: both a touching and not-touching. It offers a different kind of meaning. Approaching Eva's story, we approach the resonating boundary of silence, itself a form of transmission.

## SERVADIO, OTHELLO, MALKA

If the Portobuffole sections of the novel highlight anything—beyond yet another landscape of atrocity—it is the question of narrative as the form of the route. From one point of view the story is simple if horrendously familiar from the Middle Ages.[27] A Jewish community in a small town near Venice in the 1480s faces accusations that a Christian boy has been murdered for his blood during the Passover season. After due investigation the authorities oversee torture and the extraction of confessions, until ultimately three men named Servadio, Moses, and Giaccobe are burned at the stake in St Mark's. The spectacle of execution is elaborate enough to satisfy the analytical imaginings of a Foucault; discipline and punishment are inseparable from display. Here, as Servadio formulates his own inward resistance—fasting, refusing to drink, reciting the *shema* and calling out 'One, One!' as he dies—it is evident, as elsewhere in this study, that sacrifice takes on a vertical direction (the smoke, the

---

[26] For helping to clarify this discussion, I am grateful to a paper by Stef Craps, 'Linking Legacies of Loss: Traumatic Histories and Cross-Cultural Empathy in Caryl Phillips's *Higher Ground* and *The Nature of Blood*', Conference on Caryl Phillips, Twenty-Five Years of Writing, University of Liège, 1–2 December 2006.

[27] In *The Nature of Blood*, Phillips gives two of his major sources as R. Po-Chia Hsia, *Trent 1475*, and Salomone G. Radzik, *Portobuffole*.

fire, the surrender upwards) so that a community of crime may seal its
horizontal bonds.[28] Conversely, for the sacrificial victims, unity ('One,
One') can only be vertical where horizontal links are impossible or have
been obliterated.

Once again, however, part of Phillips's purpose is to complicate
things, not least in the story's narrative dimensions. For instance, on
one level the account is presented as objective, third-person chronicle. It
begins, 'In March of 1480, the people of the small town of Portobuffole,
near Venice, were preparing their houses for the much anticipated arrival
of relatives' (*NOB*, 48), and carries on in that vein. But soon it becomes
clear that this account is very much 'voiced'. So, when Andrea Dolfin,
the Doge's representative in Portobuffole, submits his report to Venice
on the first trial of the Jews, his account speaks with an untroubled
authority: 'Everything began on a day in September during the previous
year, when the Jews were celebrating a holiday known as the Feast of the
Tabernacles' (*NOB*, 100). But Dolfin's recitation is soon inextricably
mixed with certain 'supplements', as to how the sacrifice bled, how the
onlookers hissed blasphemies at the Saviour and his mother, how some
stuck out their tongues and 'exposed their private parts' in an attempt to
further humiliate the innocent young Christian victim (*NOB*, 102)—all
presented as 'fact'.

Moments such as this suggest that the neutrality of any chronicle is
only a performance of neutrality, especially in a setting of asymmetrical
and uneven boundaries. *Because* it refuses to acknowledge the problem
of transmission, chronicle—a different kind of history from the histories of this novel—can at best be only an inauthentic form. But lest
things become too straightforward, Phillips goes even further, for, as in
Eva's story, there is no 'alternative' narrative against which to measure
the problematic version. Dolfin's account, for instance, is not quoted
within the text but is inseparable from it, delivered without comment
in the voice of the larger narrative whose 'chronicled' voice it both
mimics and replicates. Voicing, perspective, angle—all become hugely
and deliberately troubled in such overlays, and not only for Dolfin's
account but the narrative that contains it. Sometimes, as in Conrad,
this is registered as a matter of tone. After the execution we hear that 'the

[28] For relations between the horizontal and vertical, see in particular ch. 4. The *shema*
is a daily prayer also recited by Jewish martyrs in many different settings: 'Hear O Israel,
the Lord is our God, the Lord is one.'

spectators . . . were deeply moved by the power of the Christian faith and its official Venetian guardians' (*NOB*, 155). The point here is that this statement might not be ironic but laconically true. It is enigma raised almost to a philosophical principle, because we have no firm ground on which to stand. In this guise, enigma becomes nothing less than the territory of navigation across the transnational space and time of the novel—and, among other things, it is readers who are both invited and challenged to navigate it.

The novel's version of the Othello story brings other perspectives to bear on these matters, among them the question of *language*. This is an issue which has been somewhat misunderstood by commentators. J. M. Coetzee regards Phillips's Othello as 'lifelessly prosaic'; Hilary Mantel remarks that if readers try to think where they have heard his voice before, 'you may be put in mind of the butler in *The Remains of the Day*.'[29] And it is true that in his reflections Othello is apt to refer to 'my person being ever vigilant'—exactly the kind of construction Stevens uses in Ishiguro's novel. Yet where does such language come from? It must at least cross our radar screens to ask what Othello might be beyond a kind of African butler to Europe—someone to cater to its grandness, admitted to the halls of power but only in service to the state—the 'black European success' of *The European Tribe*. In this respect Othello's language, like his adoption of Venetian clothing, is a kind of dress he puts on, the inevitably artificial sign of the dignity he feels should rightly be his.[30] In this sense, and not only because of the original Shakespearean platform, 'staged' is the appropriate term for the outsider's presence. The question of language has of course been a fraught one for Africans, both colonized and in the diaspora: whose language one adopts, and in what form.[31] In Othello's case, it literally speaks to a form of self-alienation. At 'the very centre of the empire' (*NOB*, 108) he is a 'mimic man', struggling to balance his sense of self with the weightless non-recognition afforded him by Venice.

[29] J. M. Coetzee, 'What We Like to Forget', *New York Review of Books*, 6 November 1997, 40; Hilary Mantel, 'Black is not Jewish', *Literary Review*, February 1997, 39.
[30] On the connection between clothing and language, see Phillips, *ET*, 46.
[31] For lineaments of the dispute between Chinua Achebe and Ngũgĩ wa Thiong'o on the use of English in African writing see Chinua Achebe, 'The African Writer and the English Language', in *Morning Yet on Creation Day* (Garden City: Anchor Press, 1975) and Ngũgĩ wa Thiong'o, 'Return to the Roots', in *Writers in Politics* (London: Heinemann, 1981).

It also has a bearing on his relationship with Desdemona. Beyond language they are able to meet with their eyes. But when language enters in, they are in a world of more complex negotiations. We see this on one occasion when Othello visits the Jewish ghetto in Venice: he has received a letter from Desdemona and needs help in deciphering her handwriting. There a scribe reads the letter and writes a dictated reply. How are we to regard this? As a form of triangulation, in which the Jewish scribe mediates between the oppressive European power and the African figure?[32] Or as a circulating 'route' in which the scribe, Othello, and Desdemona struggle to find different kinds of connection, a different metonymic model? Again, what is at stake is the nature of the boundary, the possibilities of the transitive. Ultimately, Phillips neglects to tell the end of the Othello story, and this is fitting in a way. In a sense there is of course no need to: its end is contained in its beginning, in the Shakespearean paradigm. Or, as in the case of Eva, this may be Phillips's token of respect, a refusal to intrude in Othello and Desdemona's ultimate anguish. Beyond that, however, is perhaps another dimension: that we do not yet have the narrative, or the language, to tell the end of Othello's story in any full way—a story which exists—resonating like Eva's silence—in still unending space.

In the novel's last major narrative, of Eva's Uncle Stephan's encounter with the Ethiopian woman Malka, we can find other echoes both within and beyond the novel. Where Eva was transported by train to the camps, Malka has been transported by aeroplane, and not to doom but to supposed liberation. Yet, like Eva, she finds 'liberation' to be a distinctly ambiguous concept. Though Malka is Jewish, and in Israel, her African identity means that she and her family are, in relative terms, segregated, kept in a ghetto of sorts; the nature of 'blood' still applies. Where time stopped in the camps, Malka's African family finds itself subjected within a different kind of time-regime—of clocks and watches, a kind of reverse chronometric surveillance. As for Stephan, though he is related by blood and experience to Eva, in relation to Malka he is more like the Englishman Gerry; he is Malka's 'interrogator', wanting to intrude into her private space to find her 'truth'. Not spoken to Stephan, but in a silent interior monologue Malka asks, '*What are you trying to prove?*'

---

[32] For the archetypal definition of inauthentic triangulation, which has nothing like even the limited promise visible here, see Jean-Paul Sartre, *Anti-Semite and Jew*, trans. George J. Becker (New York: Schocken, 1995).

(*NOB*, 209). The celebrated rescue of the Ethiopian Jews is at risk of being a probationary exercise in exactly the sense Malka discerns, also a form of display with its equivalent dispositions of power as well as violations of the truth and of inwardness.

'She had lived. She was living,' (*NOB*, 212) is Stephan's thought in relation to Malka, and this at least differentiates her from Eva and the others who have suffered before her. Eventually, after Stephan's night with Malka—both a connection and much less than that—he is put in mind of his two nieces, Eva and Margot, and the moment in their European garden when he decided finally to leave for Palestine. Sitting on a bench in the morning in Tel Aviv, it is as if he is sitting on the bench in their garden at that moment in the 1930s, as his memory reaches out to them across the years. They did not hear him then, they cannot hear him now; he does not know if they are alive or dead. Connections are fragile and tenuous, as one time speaks to another without a reply but soundings of a kind. Given these echoes, it is almost as if time works in two directions in the novel, the living remembering the dead, the dead remembering the living. We are in transitive, transitional space, navigating relations between one part and another, the part and the whole.

## CONSTELLATION

Mirrorings, refractions, reflections: there are any number of them in *The Nature of Blood*. Eva's father's name, Ernst Stern, is an anagrammatic self-reflection, or a syntactic palindrome of an asymmetrical kind (which has more than a little resonance for the novel's form). Stephan Stern, who appears to have fought in the underground Haganah in Palestine against the British, might call to mind the name of the Stern Gang, but it is probably a mistake to identify him with Avraham Stern, its leader, as Marina Warner suggests we are 'only allowed to suspect' in the novel.[33] Eva's sister Margot has the same name as Anne Frank's sister;

[33] Marina Warner, 'Its Own Dark Styx', *London Review of Books*, 20 March 1997, 23. Such an identification would be a mistake, not least because the underground Haganah, with which Stephan Stern appears to be (fictionally) associated, was fiercely opposed in both ideological and political terms to the right-wing Irgun and its breakaway, the Stern group.

but she is not that sister, nor is Eva the same as Anne Frank, though, as always, there are ripples of association. There are also outright intrusions of a different kind. Across the years a voice suddenly reaches out to accuse Othello: 'And so you shadow her every move, attend to her every whim, like the black Uncle Tom that you are. Fighting the white man's war for him/ Wide receiver in the Venetian army/ The republic's grinning Satchmo hoisting his sword like a trumpet' (*NOB*, 181). We might be tempted to identify this voice as Caryl Phillips's, at last giving his true opinion of Othello—but that would be a mistake too.[34] Rather, this Black Power presence (almost as if Rudy from *Higher Ground* had stepped across textual space) is yet another voice in the novel, to be added to the multitude we have to put in relation to one another.

Beyond resonance and echo, what are we to make of this pattern? In approaching *The Nature of Blood*, critics have offered various concepts, whether of 'palimpsest', 'labyrinth', or the Levinasian idea of 'facing'.[35] Phillips himself has spoken of how he has been inspired by the idea of musical form, which lends credence to Warner's suggestion of a musical architecture in the novel.[36] Certainly one aspect of this pattern is a recasting of our standard models of time, and in this respect Malka's experience is emblematic. For in Malka's 'route' from Ethiopia to Israel, as she herself says, she has crossed centuries as well as space (*NOB*, 209). Malka, in other words, is a *time-migrant*, in that two times are suddenly layered in her life, a kind of temporal crossing that she, like many migrants, must navigate. In a larger sense the novel has generalized this principle, setting different times and spaces as well as

---

[34] In this regard Warner is surely correct in saying that Phillips's 'sentences mimic the histories he's excavating'—handed over tightlipped to the reader who has to work hard to interpret them: 'Its Own Dark Styx', 23.

[35] See, respectively, the following: Andrew Armstrong, 'BLOODY HISTORY! Exploring a Capacity for Revision. Restaging History in Wilson Harris's *Jonestown* and Caryl Phillips', *The Nature of Blood*', *Jouvert*, 6/3 (2002); <http://social.chass.ncsu.edu/jouvert/v613/armstr.htm> (accessed 24 September 2004); Bénédicte Ledent, 'A Fictional and Cultural Labyrinth: Caryl Phillips's "The Nature of Blood"', *Ariel* 32/1 (2001): 185–95; Wendy Zierler, ' "My Holocaust Is Not Your Holocaust": "Facing" Black and Jewish Experience in *The Pawnbroker*, *Higher Ground*, and *The Nature of Blood*', *Holocaust and Genocide Studies* 18/1 (2004): 46–67. Armstrong adopts the idea of 'palimpsest' from Ashraf Rushdy, and Zierler takes 'facing' from Adam Zachary Newton.

[36] See Clingman, 'Other Voices', 130; and Warner, 'Its Own Dark Styx', 23.

narratives together—the matter of its own migrant and transitive explorations. It is these multiple times and spaces that define—in Bakhtin's term—the novel's *chronotope*: the combination of its periods and locations, which comprise a kind of hyper-landscape and temporality of its own.[37]

To say the least, this also describes the novel's transnational dimension, but we have to consider more deeply how it works, assessing not only the effects but the risks. What does it mean, for instance, for a black British writer to inhabit the voice and mind of a female Jewish victim of the Holocaust? What does it mean to set that account in relation to the story of Othello? In this regard, Hilary Mantel has bridled strongly at what she takes to be an implicit parallel between different experiences. Concerning the idea—which Phillips had drawn on via Fanon—that when someone talks about the Jews he is also talking about blacks, she comments that it is

the devil's sentimentality: it is demented cosiness, that denies the differences between people, denies how easily the interests of human beings become divided. It is indecent to lay claim to other people's suffering: it is a colonial impulse, dressed up as altruism. The heart may be pure, but more than heart is needed; good motives sometimes paralyse thought. We are not all Jews. That is a simple fact. It is why the Holocaust happened.[38]

Yet, as Peter Singer has remarked in a different context, '[A] comparison is not necessarily an equation.'[39] And indeed, it may be the *problem* of resonance—both its reach and its limits—that Phillips's fiction is designed to explore. As Wendy Zierler has suggested, these stories are about 'contiguity, not sameness',[40] and in that light it may be what happens at the *boundary between* them that matters: the essential question of transmission. The grammar of identity across these stories is,

[37] For the chronotope, see M. M. Bakhtin, 'Forms of Time and of the Chronotope in the Novel', in *The Dialogic Imagination*, ed. Michael Holquist (Austin: University of Texas Press, 1981), 84–5.

[38] Hilary Mantel, 'Black is not Jewish', *Literary Review*, February 1997, 40. In making this accusation, Mantel attributes the remarks of Fanon's philosophy professor to James Baldwin.

[39] Peter Singer, 'Reflection', in J. M. Coetzee, *The Lives of Animals*, ed. Amy Gutmann (Princeton: Princeton University Press, 1999), 86. Laura Wright mentions this statement in *Writing 'Out of All the Camps': J. M. Coetzee's Narratives of Displacement* (New York: Routledge, 2006), 111.

[40] Zierler, ' "My Holocaust" ', 58.

paradoxically, *non-identical*. Rather it is a grammar of the transitive—
with all the difficulties that entails, whether philosophical, ethical, or
navigational.

Particular moments in the novel indicate the subtleties of this
approach. So, as Phillips's narrative recounts the history of Jewish migration to Portobuffole from Cologne—the violent origins of which, we
learn, went back to the fourteenth century until the final expulsion
in the 1420s—suddenly the thought intrudes: 'Such is the way of the
Germans with their Jews' (*NOB*, 51). We might ask whose voice this
is: a Venetian perspective on Germans, or some latter-day view that
shades into Eva Stern's story? Or is it a view that enters Eva's life only to
reflect back on Venice—oscillating back and forth across that boundary?
Either way, the intrusion becomes a kind of *route*: contiguous but not
continuous, connected but not identical. Similarly, in the Portobuffole
story, when (in Dolfin's account) Moses takes the (allegedly) murdered
boy's body and clothing to burn in his 'huge oven', this may be a reverse
projection of the ovens Eva will face in the concentration camps, but it
exists primarily as a kind of haunting, an uncanny presence across the
novel's chronotope. When Servadio's servant, Donato, wins his freedom
by converting to Christianity and taking the name of the (alleged)
victim, Sebastian, this is a syndrome that might be recognized in the
novel's Othello: attempting to gain legitimacy by adopting the guise
of an oppressive culture which creates its innocence through the racial
guilt of others. But by this definition it is not the same story—more
a metonymic link which allows transition as well as the transitive. In
other words, these narratives *travel* into one another, but that does not
mean they are equated. If anything in such moments, it is the nature of
the narrative boundary that comes into focus as a space for readers to
navigate.

Let us consider one other powerful example which introduces a
crucial idea for the shape and implications of Phillips's novel. At the end
of the Portobuffole story, when the Jewish victims have been burned, we
are told how an executioner approached the pyre with a long-handled
shovel, put it between the smoking coals and pulled it out full of white
ash which the air dispersed (*NOB*, 155–6). In the very next—gapped—
paragraph we are back in Eva Stern's story: she is in a boxcar being
transported to the concentration camps. In such a moment there is

something like a narrative flash of horror and recognition. We are put in mind of Walter Benjamin's definition:

image is that wherein what has been comes together in a flash with the now to form a constellation. In other words: image is dialectics at a standstill.[41]

It is this idea of constellation that is crucial, and, as Benjamin suggested elsewhere, it takes us not into but *out* of 'homogeneous, empty time' as one moment stands in relation to another.[42] This version of constellation does not involve superimposition or equation but distance and difference: without that, there could be no flash of meaning in the first place. As it happens, Phillips's novel multiplies the sense of constellation, because in *The Nature of Blood* we have the multiple times and locations of its chronotope. In such a model, the constellation becomes like its 'original', the kind we see in the night sky, whose pattern depends on vast differences in time and space. The pattern depends too on the viewer—who, knowingly or unknowingly—is part of the constellation. In such a way, we as readers become part of the constellation of *The Nature of Blood*, seeing its patterns, reconstructing them, negotiating difference and distance, part of its transnational and transtemporal navigation.

In such a way, the individual routes of the novel, taken together, become its constellation, opening up in the four dimensions of time and space. It is quite remarkable that *The Nature of Blood* invents a grammar of identity to go along with this design which approaches it from the other direction. So, in the constelled narratives of the novel, we proceed from a German/Jew (Eva) to Jewish/Venetians (in Portobuffole) to a Venetian/African (Othello) to an African/Jew (Malka). Note how each pairing hands on to the next—Jew to Jew, Venetian to Venetian, African to African, and then back to Jew—but also how the progression *shifts*, as Jew becomes Venetian, then African, and then Jewish once

---

[41] Walter Benjamin, *The Arcades Project*, trans. Howard Eiland and Kevin McLaughlin (Cambridge, MA: Belknap Press, 1999), 463.

[42] For the classic definitions of '*Jetztzeit*' and 'constellation', see Walter Benjamin, 'Theses on the Philosophy of History', in *Illuminations*, ed. Hannah Arendt (Glasgow: Fontana, 1973), 263, 265. It may be a matter of familiarity, but I prefer the translation in this version to that in the *Selected Writings*, vol. 4: *1938–40*, ed. Howard Eiland and Michael W. Jennings (Cambridge, MA and London: Belknap Press, 2003), even though both translations are apparently by Harry Zohn.

again. This is an astonishing transition, showing just how far Phillips has managed to go along this series. It might be tempting to see it as a chain of substitution, in which specific details may change but the outcome—the tragic nature of blood—is the same. This would justify Hilary Mantel's complaint, that different experiences in the novel are being equated. But far more meaningful is to see it as a metonymic chain, a chain of combination, in which Jew can become Venetian, Venetian become African, African become Jew again. This is identity as syntactic, transitional, transitive, a navigation of an extraordinary kind, not to mention a radically different account of what we are accustomed to think of as 'self'. Perhaps most important of all, out of the constellations of the novel, *identity itself has become a route*—punctuated, transitional, altering, in the way that our identity as a species out of Africa has undertaken exactly such a set of transitions.

Route, constellation, navigation: no wonder that in ancient times they were linked as people found their way by the stars. Here constellation and the route are the very form and sign of navigation in the transnational imaginary of Caryl Phillips's fiction.


## SPINOZA'S LENS

Across time, across space, there are other forms of correspondence which invite their own contemplations.

In November 1665 Baruch Spinoza, then living in Voorburg, just outside The Hague, wrote to Henry Oldenburg in London. Oldenburg was secretary of the Royal Society and had asked Spinoza to explain to himself and the scientist Robert Boyle a central part of his philosophy: 'how we know the way in which each part of Nature agrees with the whole, and the manner of its coherence with the other parts.'[43] Spinoza replied by means of a physiological analogy:

---

[43] Baruch Spinoza, *The Ethics; Treatise on the Emendation of the Intellect; Selected Letters*, trans. Samuel Shirley, ed. Seymour Feldman (Indianapolis: Hackett, 1992), 280. For a wealth of reliable information on Spinoza during this period, see Steven Nadler, *Spinoza: A Life* (Cambridge: Cambridge University Press, 1999), esp. ch. 9, 'The Jew of Voorburg'.

Now let us imagine, if you please, a tiny worm living in the blood, capable of distinguishing by sight the particles of the blood—lymph, etc—and of intelligently observing how each particle, on colliding with another, either rebounds or communicates some degree of its motion, and so forth. That worm would be living in the blood as we are living in our part of the universe, and it would regard each individual particle as a whole, not a part, and it would have no idea as to how all the parts are modified by the overall nature of the blood...[44]

The nature of blood, *natura sanguinis*: the echo may be accidental, but how fascinating that it is the same phrase as in Phillips's novel. Let us add accident to accident, for there are other echoes. Spinoza was born in the Netherlands of Portuguese Ladino extraction, later to be excommunicated by the Jewish community because of his transpersonal and transnational view of God. He grew up in the heart of Europe, in Amsterdam, the later city of Anne Frank, who meant so much to Phillips, born in the Caribbean. In the midst of the plague, Spinoza's brother, Gabriel, who ran the family shipping and trading business after Baruch's excommunication, left Holland for the West Indies—Barbados and Jamaica—where he ultimately became a British citizen. A few years after Spinoza died in 1677, his sister (or half-sister) Rebecca relocated to Curaçao, in the New World, with her sons.[45] Globally as well as personally, Spinoza may have had reason to consider how 'each part of Nature agrees with the whole, and the manner of its coherence with the other parts'.

He kept on extending his vision, extension after extension. To Oldenburg, he pointed out that even if we think the 'blood' is the whole which contains its constituent parts, it too is subject to larger causes which modify it and are reciprocally modified. And there is the vastness of that central image: 'That worm would be living in the blood as we are living in our part of the universe.' Note, our *part* of the universe; note, our part of the *universe*. For Spinoza, lens polisher, clarifying our view, just as there is no final boundary to identity, so there is none to location, or, in the largest sense, our space of habitation. There are only extensions and modalities of being, a grand cosmic syntax flowing in every direction. To the worm living in the blood, watching each particle

---

[44] Spinoza, *Ethics, Emendation, and Letters*, 281.
[45] Nadler, *Spinoza*, 45, 86–7. Nadler says Rebecca moved some time between 1679 and 1685.

collide with another, the relation between animate and inanimate might be obscure: the particles unliving, yet comprising a living whole. So too, perhaps, in the cosmos, Spinoza's Nature, *natura naturans*, the inflectional shift in the word become a syntactic phrase, become process and movement. Across the distances of space, constellations make up greater and ever greater combinations, all flowing and turning endlessly. 'So much, then,' as Spinoza remarked to Oldenburg, 'for the question of whole and part.' For Spinoza the *trans* was trans-everything, the truly sublime grammar of identity. But for a writer such as Phillips, as for the others in this study, that grammar is still the project of a journey, a journey we scarcely know how to make.

## FAULTLINE

To route, constellation, navigation, we must also add faultline—another constituent element of Phillips's fiction. One way to see this is through the contrast between *The Nature of Blood* and Phillips's following novel, *A Distant Shore*. For the two novels are mirror images of one another, their relative structures reversed. Where, across the faultlines of varied national settings, *The Nature of Blood* creates a transnational setting, *A Distant Shore* shows transnational faultlines within national space. Where separate routes have created the constellation, what ought to be the constellation resolves tragically into a set of routes—broken, disparate, finally unconnected. Respectively, the two novels map the national in the transnational, the transnational in the national. But if *A Distant Shore* explores the latter, it comes up mainly in negative form.

The two main characters of the novel are in this regard emblematic. Both are exiles, though of different kinds. Dorothy, born English, is a woman living in a state of internal exile in the new housing development of Stoneleigh in the north of England; Solomon, formerly known as Gabriel, is a refugee from war and disaster in Africa, who becomes Stoneleigh's caretaker-cum-watchman and Dorothy's neighbour.[46] The two meet, and have an instinctive understanding—because

---

[46] Publication details for the novel: Caryl Phillips, *A Distant Shore* (New York: Knopf, 2003). Henceforth referenced as *ADS*.

of their respective experiences, because of their alienation, because of their solitude. But also because of those experiences, each of them inhabits a different world; they connect but cannot connect with each other.

For both characters, as we might now expect in a work by Phillips, there is a sense of broken navigation, broken routes. The novel opens with the thought 'England has changed', and Dorothy becomes one example of what that means. She is divorced, in crisis, in apparent mental breakdown; as a former school and piano teacher, her music does not 'fit' or flow. She is the first-person narrator of her story, but like Eva in *The Nature of Blood*, hers is an account filled with disruptive internal recursions, where events come out of sequence, where *after* Solomon has died—brutally murdered by local white youths and dumped in the local canal—he comes to Dorothy's door: her version of their first meeting. Such moments might seem to be flashback, but rather than reflecting any deliberate re-ordering, Dorothy's narrative reveals primarily that sequence is beyond her. Dorothy is wholly caught up in her narrative, she is its *expression* more than its 'author'. Like Eva's, her story is less narration than recitation—the world as it comes to her at different moments or strata in her mind; the gaps are her experience, not her technique. Yet if *faultline* is the motif of her condition, that is not only personal but national. It is partly because 'England has changed' that Dorothy feels so alien, so alone, so disconnected; but equally, her disconnection is one sign of an inner national condition.

For Solomon/Gabriel, experience itself is a faultline, a broken archaeology, reflected in the split in his name. In Africa he was soldier, victim, perpetrator, who finally left his country by boat for France, and then by hazardous passage to England. We meet him in prison, where he is watching a fellow detainee die of abuse and neglect. Gabriel is there because he has been falsely accused of rape, and when his lawyers ask for an explanation of what occurred, to them he offers only silence: the hidden realm of the fugitive. But internally, the question prompts the deepest accounts of his memories: everything he knows and has experienced but cannot possibly explain. Within this past there are also the intrusions of dreams—of his mother, who died in his place when government soldiers came looking for him: layer within layer of interior time, strata of conscious and unconscious memory. Travelling from France, Gabriel perched on the thin ledge of a boat with his friend

Bright and a Chinese man who probably fell off in the waves. But it is as Gabriel jumps into the waters approaching England, as his leg snaps with the impact, that his narrative also snaps back, now into a first-person narrative of his life in Africa as a member of a minority tribe, and his experiences as a rebel soldier. There are dimensions within dimensions of time and interiority in his mind.

None of this is accidental in a Phillips novel. The passage across water—as in the original Black Atlantic passage—is a place of transition but also rupture and temporal fracture: an experience that paradoxically will live on for ever. (It is no coincidence that the pub Dorothy frequents is called the Waterman's Arms, or that Gabriel dies in a sordidly domestic canal.) In Gabriel/Solomon's passage across water, time forward produces time back—the succession of receding pasts that underlie the present of his story. As in his other fiction, Phillips complicates the modalities of these accounts even further. The third-person narrative of Solomon's past as Gabriel is told in the present tense: it is a stratum of time that still resonates. But when his story is told in the first person, it goes into the past tense: more like a conventional memory. Overall, it is as if time and narration were being pulled inside out, or rotating in different directions: not only are there times within times in the novel, but they are aligned with shifting versions of narration. All this is layered, ever-present in Gabriel's body and mind: it is the fractured nature, in vast and disparate form, of the migrant experience. As in the case of Malka, but more overt now, we see the multiple times the migrant brings with him.

In such an account we are light years away from Benedict Anderson's notion of national temporality—everyone experiencing everything at the same time. Rather, separately and together, Dorothy and Gabriel's lives suggest parallel universes within the nation, operating within different fields of time and space. Here we see the cavernous and disjunctive simultaneity of the national—times within times, narratives within narratives—precisely because of migrant and exilic experience, whether (in Dorothy's case) domestic or (in Gabriel's) across formal borders. Especially in relation to Gabriel, the experience of the migrant reveals a different kind of simultaneity—all the faultlines and crossings of his experience, all to be negotiated in the same moment, a vast world of disjunction invisible and unspoken in national time. Indeed, one of the crucial revelations of Gabriel's story is its *non-revelation* in any public form. Gabriel's pasts, all the layerings of his present, are the forgotten and hidden of the national everyday. These *are* the faultlines of the transnational within the national, the underside of what we mean by the transnational itself.

That too is the significance of the fact that Gabriel and Dorothy never really discover one another's stories, despite their empathy for each another. The novel's sequence ends with the beginning of their encounter: told now through Gabriel's eyes, he approaches Dorothy's house to knock on her door. He of course is long dead, and the feeling is uncanny, as if the dead were walking again. But it is part of the force of Phillips's novel that they are: that people such as Gabriel/Solomon are always among us, not only as the dead but as the living whose existence has no foothold in public space and time. Solomon approaches Dorothy primarily in order to tell his story—his Gabriel story, the whole account of who he is and where he has come from—but it is a story he will never tell, not to her, not to his killers, and maybe not to us; just as she will never tell her story fully to him. It is as if the tectonic plates of the novel's major narratives slide over and under one another with very few points of contact or purchase—these hidden stories of migrant and exilic time and space. As we shall see elsewhere in this study, in that light the transnational—in Gabriel's world, in Dorothy's—is the uncanny of the national: its shadow, its hidden home, its suppressed grammar, its broken possibility. And where the national represses the transnational, we experience it only as the uncanny—a shadow, a loss, an evocation.

'If I do not share my story, then I have only this one year to my life. I am a one-year-old man who walks with heavy steps': thus Gabriel, approaching Dorothy's door (*ADS*, 266). He is also, inevitably, Othello, confronting the youths who will eventually kill him: 'They do not know who I am. I am the son of an elder, a man who decided disputes and punished crimes. . . . I am a man who has survived, and I would rather die like a free man than suffer my blood to be drawn like a slave's' (*ADS*, 251). Like Othello, Gabriel's problem is also one of speech—the words he is forgetting, the new ones he has to negotiate: 'My language was drying up in my mouth, and sometimes, when nobody was around, I would place my language on my tongue and speak some words so that I could be sure that I was still in possession of it' (*ADS*, 253). In Gabriel's mouth language is the route as *rupta via*, a transnational syntax that cannot be properly expressed.

## NOTHING LIKE OTHELLO

These, then, are some of the patterns of the transnational in Caryl Phillips's life and his fiction. Through migration and travel, his own constellations comprise many points of connection, transition, and reference. His personal routes and combinatory sense of identity—West Indian, black, British, Jewish—have come into his novels to be played out as matters of form and theme. He has explored the nature of the boundary: its distances, its differences, its transitivities, the full force of the broken route. He has shown us various conundrums. The world may be intransitive, but navigation always occurs. Where the boundary becomes absolute, it still links those who suffer from its intransitivities—across space, time, the narratives we are able to comprehend. We have to think not only in the images we see but in negative space—beyond the visible, not least the visible of the nation, what edges into the transnational. But of course this too can only be incomplete. For now we live in the space of transition; it is the space of our navigation.

'These days,' remarks Caryl Phillips in *A New World Order*, 'we are all unmoored' (*NWO*, 6). The pun may or may not be intentional. Othello 'unmoored': he is in transition, no longer the Moor, perhaps voyaging, not to Cyprus—where he fought the Turk, where Stephan at the beginning of *The Nature of Blood* awaits his own promised land—but across space that is now configured quite differently.

'That's he that was Othello. Here I am,' is Shakespeare's version. Who is Othello? We do not know and cannot answer. 'I saw only one other black man in Venice. He looked nothing like Othello.' We only know the 'nothing like' him, though he may arrive in a different form, by a different route, in a transnational world.

# 3

# Combination, Divination

*Salman Rushdie*

Roughly speaking, to say of two things that they are identical is nonsense, and to say of one thing that it is identical with itself is to say nothing at all.

> Ludwig Wittgenstein, *Tractatus Logico-Philosophicus*

In all creation
Nothing endures, all is in endless flux,
Each wandering shape a pilgrim passing by . . .

> Ovid, *Metamorphoses*, Book 15

In short, there is no end of it . . .

> Laurence Sterne, *The Life and Opinions of Tristram Shandy, Gentleman*

'How does newness come into the world?' This is Salman Rushdie's text, and his two great novels, *Midnight's Children* and *The Satanic Verses*, tackle its themes in different ways. The one takes place in an (apparently) national setting, its presiding mood comic, tinged with darkness. The other is overtly transnational, its mood dark, yet with its own comedies and illuminations. Together they compose the national–transnational in a paradigm we might as well call, as if it were a kind of language, *Rushdie*. Endlessly generative—where *generation* becomes the motive principle in every way—the novels are linked by at least one aspect: the force of overflow or excess, where identity cannot be contained, where nothing is what it seems. *Midnight's Children* overflows boundaries of self, location, and the national, so that the national cannot simply be its frame. In *The Satanic Verses* the overflow is between countries, times, spaces, as well as modes of reality. In both novels we see transitivity, morphology, transition; or, when these forces are held at bay, pathology, whether within the self or beyond.

And so the novels are not simply opposites but modulations of one another, different phases of the national–transnational, even as they explore different phases of the self. It is as if, applying the vision of *Midnight's Children* more globally in *The Satanic Verses*, Rushdie found the hazards as well as promise of a transnational world. Beyond the national, apprising the transnational, we see morphology and meta-morphosis in all. Primarily, in both novels these patterns are embodied not only as content but *form*—form which becomes a kind of content, from the most sweeping of structures to the smallest of mirrorings and oscillations.

Emboldened by the irrepressible geometries of those forms—in ways that affect the form of this chapter—what follows here is a series of contemplations of Rushdie's navigations. The first task is to show that in its grammar of identity, *Midnight's Children*, on one level the most 'national' of novels, is also a transnational fiction.[1]

## *MIDNIGHT'S CHILDREN*: COMBINATION

1. 'There will be two heads—but you shall see only one—there will be knees and a nose, a nose and knees.'[2] Nose and knees, knees and nose: palindrome of a phrase, reversible, mirrored. Morphology of the word, phonology of the sound: the n—s goes through a shift, adds or drops

---

[1] There has of course been debate on *Midnight's Children* in relation to nationalism. Timothy Brennan, in *Salman Rushdie and the Third World: Myths of the Nation* (New York: St Martin, 1989), remarks that the novel belongs to a larger tradition of the ' "nationalism of mourning" found everywhere in Third-World fiction' (100). Aamir Mufti, in 'Reading the Rushdie Affair: An Essay on Islam and Politics', *Social Text*, 29 (1991), critiques Fredric Jameson's reading of third-world literature as intrinsically linked to 'national allegory' in that it falls short of understanding novels such as *Shame* and *Midnight's Children* and cannot measure up to the 'self-consciously supra-national concerns' of *The Satanic Verses* (96). Josna E. Rege, in *Colonial Karma: Self, Action, and Nation in the Indian English Novel* (New York: Palgrave Macmillan, 2004), writes that *Midnight's Children* 'declared that there were as many valid versions of Indian identity as there were Indians' (108), yet also that the novel is 'emotionally committed to the narrative of nation' (126).

[2] Salman Rushdie, *Midnight's Children* (Harmondsworth: Penguin, 2000), 96. All further page references in this section and the first paragraph of the next are to this edition. *Midnight's Children* was first published in 1981.

a silent 'k', trades an outside 'e' for an inside 'o', and from that makes a pair, a pattern, a half-rhyme and rhythm, the same but different, a transition, opposed. The word works along a continuum of sound to find quite different meanings, except that both are joined to the idea of a body, except that these are two bodies, Shiva's and Saleem's. The internal syntax of the word's morphology suggests alternate possibilities of the body's (two bodies') syntax. A nose sniffs the world, while two knees attack it; the former protrudes, the latter proceed. Knees criss-cross, make an 'X', knees and nose are a criss-crossing, the body above and the body below. Criss-cross, 'X', χ, chiasmus: chiastic metonymy, the sign of *Midnight's Children*. From this one can make an identity and a nation where both are never simply themselves. Or one could turn it (chiastically) into a question. Can one make an identity and a nation from this? Yes, but only in the form of reversal, change, overflow. This is not where identity is '*x*'—an algebra of tautology—but the 'χ' of crossing, excess.

2. In the person of Saleem, central character and narrator born at the moment of India's independence on the stroke of midnight on 15 August 1947, a great allegory evolves. Birth for birth, move for move, somehow the history of the country is implanted in the individual and vice versa. And yet, what kind of an allegory is it? Saleem tests the idea that the individual can represent the nation by quoting Mrs Gandhi's election slogan, '*India is Indira and Indira is India*' (483). Once again the construction is palindromic, mirroring as well as tongue-twisting. But Saleem cites the slogan mainly to consider whether Mrs Gandhi took the idea from his own grandiose assumptions regarding 'the equation between the State and myself'. If so, the dangers of messianic substitution are evident. But note that Saleem also wonders whether the idea 'leaked' from his thoughts into Mrs Gandhi's—a different form of correspondence. And in his own case Saleem offers a different version of what the national connection means. India, he remarks, 'was not only my twin-in-birth but also joined to me (so to speak) at the hip, so that what happened to either of us, happened to us both' (444). Twins joined: the same-but-not-same linked by contiguity, across the 'X' of the hip. They cannot substitute for one another, and yet they cannot be separated. This is a form of syntax rather than simple representation, and much can happen backwards and forwards across the conjunction—opposition as well as connection. Same and not-same,

chiasmus: *Midnight's Children* will play on this throughout the novel, so that even where Saleem 'represents' the nation he does so by embodying a principle of non-identity: linkage rather than substitution.

3. Salman Rushdie is *the* writer of the late twentieth and early twenty-first centuries whose life and fiction seem to be joined at the hip, so that what happens to him seems to come from one of his novels even as his novels take their shape from his imagination. From his fiction comes a character simultaneously omnivorous and gargantuan—even as the 'cracks' threaten to make him fall apart. From one of his novels the singular brand of religion he addresses will rise up in such a way that it takes on human form and threatens to kill him. Some twenty years after he wrote *Midnight's Children*, he will marry someone who bears the same first name as the woman who listens to his narrator in the novel. Does life 'leak' into fiction, or is it the other way round? And what exactly is the nature of 'leaking', the 'seepages', blends and combinations of cooking, so central to the novel? Mysteries to be tasted and tested. In the meantime, a thousand and one nights, one of Rushdie's deepest inspirations: the recursive possibilities of stories looping one out of the other, within one another, endlessly flowing and, in a sense, saving a life. 1001: a palindromic number whose internal syntax can go backwards as well as forwards.

4. As Saleem says at the end of the novel, 'perhaps the story you finish is not the one you begin' (491). All narrative relations are chiastic in this account: the end is not the one you expected at the start, if you knew the end you might not have known where to begin. Time, the very ground of syntax, involves morphology and navigation, not least in this business of beginnings and ends. And yet, underlying the shifts are certain patterns that may be the motor and design of change. Saleem is 'handcuffed to history' (3)—chained by links or linked by chains that make his history a part of the non-self, and vice versa. He is an ingester who must, impossibly, be ingested: 'I have been a swallower of lives; and to know me, just the one of me, you'll have to swallow the lot as well' (4). This proves to be self-probationary in the novel, as Saleem's life is inseparable from all the lives that have produced him and to which he is attached. But if swallowing is a metaphor for a certain kind of knowledge, then the knowledge it proposes is essentially recursive and transitive: to understand *this* person you have to understand *that* one, and the *next*—one within the other, one next to the other, each linked in

an endless chain. Saleem says, 'To understand just one life, you have to swallow the world', and he adds (as if it were Rushdie's own signature), 'I told you that' (121). But this is not because the self represents the world or can swallow it whole. Instead, it is *like* a world because *like* the world it is connected through an infinitude of linkages. This presence of the metonymic: the mark of syntax and transition within the metaphor.

5. Let us look more closely at the idea. Rushdie's metaphors are a marvel, because he makes them so *literal*, often features of the body. Metaphor—the most ethereal of forms—is chiastically linked with its opposite, the physical, so that if Ahmed Sinai's 'assets are frozen', then so are his testicles. Apart from anything else, Rushdie *rejoins* metaphor to the hidden metonymies within it, if not an actual chain of linkages then a sense of physical connection along what might be a chain. Metaphors, in other words, project real connections in the world, and they have actual effects. As we saw in the Introduction, Rushdie returns to etymology to pursue the idea. Both 'translation' and 'metaphor' derive from the meaning 'to carry across', in Latin and Greek respectively, and he connects both of them to the idea of migration: 'I formed the idea that the act of migration was to turn people somehow into things, into people who had been translated, who had, so to speak, entered the condition of metaphor'.[3] Metaphor, carrying across, translation: there is a notion of physical contiguity in the shift from one place or meaning to another, but as in any such move, something may get lost—or as Rushdie puts it elsewhere—gained in the translation.[4] In this respect metaphor is itself not a sign of substitution but of transition and metamorphosis: the thing no longer identical with itself. That, as we also saw earlier, is the radical idea embedded in Kafka's famous story on the subject: an insect has not been substituted for Gregor Samsa, nor he for an insect. Rather, he has been *combined* with an insect—his own consciousness wedded to the strangely alien body. If the combination itself becomes a metaphor, it is only to suggest the dread possibilities of human combination.

---

[3] Salman Rushdie and Günter Grass, 'Fictions are Lies that Tell the Truth: Salman Rushdie and Günter Grass in Conversation', in *Conversations with Salman Rushdie*, ed. Michael Reder (Jackson: University Press of Mississippi, 2000), 77.
[4] Salman Rushdie, *Imaginary Homelands* (London: Granta, 1991), 17.

6. Saleem's nose, gargantuan, dripping, sniffing, is metonym rather than metaphor. It is his main *attachment*, protruding from him, leading to him, and in that sense it represents him, becomes his sign. It is also the sign of his attachment to India, for Saleem has a 'map-face': as his geography teacher Emile Zagallo asks his class, 'In the face of thees ugly ape you don't see the whole map of *India?*' (265) (with, as Fat Perce Fishwala adds, the drip from its end the island of Ceylon). The nose, then, is a kind of *node* (the way that Saleem might even pronounce it on his more adenoidal days) connecting the human geography of Saleem with the geology of his continent. Yet in this literalness, of shape, of physicality, it offers a specific form of understanding. Tai, the ancient and malodorous boatman, who saw Isa ('that Christ') pass through Kashmir, taps his left nostril and tells Saleem, 'You know what this is, nakkoo? It's the place where the outside world meets the world inside you' (13). The phrasing is relentlessly chiastic (outside world, world inside), and it marks the most fundamental navigation of all, where inside intersects with outside as the mysterious boundary of nothing less than life. If the nose is metaphor in this regard, even if it is a literal metaphor, it represents metonymy and chiasmus as intrinsic to our very existence. Or, as we might put it, no transubstantiation (air, breathing, food, eating) without combination. And no combination without alteration, no nation without alternation.

7. To this we might add holes and wholes. Saleem's nose is a part representing the whole, something we know as synecdoche. Yet to this Rushdie adds other ideas: each 'whole' contains a 'hole', and each 'hole' is a way of envisioning wholes (the very words embody the idea). At the beginning of the novel, in addition to knees and nose we have rubies and diamonds, and a grandfather, Aadam Aziz, oblique echo to E. M. Forster's Aziz and God's Adam. But if Allah fashioned man from clots of blood, Aadam's blood on the prayer mat ends his simple worship of God. Aadam is 'knocked forever into that middle place, unable to worship a God in whose existence he could not wholly disbelieve. Permanent alteration: a hole' (6). There is the hole inside Aadam, and outside himself Aadam the doctor sees by means of a hole, as he discovers the body of his wife-to-be Naseem through the perforated sheet held aloft by the muscular female wrestlers. These are two spaces of absence, a negative linkage, though absence also allows vision. In Aadam's case, it is the hole that allows him to see the parts of his wife and

surmise her body: the combination of her elements which he navigates as he comes to know the whole. No syntax without absence or synapse: the gap that must be crossed like the sea from one continent to another with its own versions of translation. But when the sheet with the hole is finally dropped and the whole of Naseem is suddenly there, vision is reversed, crossing recrossed. It is the seer who is seen, and she the one to exclaim about the part for the whole, 'But Doctor, my God, what a *nose!*' (24)

8. Saleem's birth, like other mythic versions where heaven and earth meet, begins with an annunciation. His mother Amina, Muslim saviour of a Hindu whose peep-show (viewing through a hole) promises to reveal the whole world, makes her way to the seer, Ramram Seth. Presiding in the throng of the impoverished in the alleys of Delhi's Red Fort is a white *hijra, transvestite*—a haunting figure of crossing. The narrative too is crossed, doubled: as Amina makes her way to the Red Fort, her husband Ahmed is approaching the Old Fort, to pay off the Ravana gang threatening to burn his godown. There Ahmed is frustrated by a monkey—human-not-human, whom Saleem calls Hanuman, after the monkey-god who helped Prince Rama defeat the original Ravana in the *Ramayana*. Rama is avatar of Vishnu; 'Ram' as mantra may contain the universe, and provide the source of all language.[5] Annunciation, *Ramayana*, the courage of the Muslim woman who saves the peep-show wallah: major religious and cultural traditions criss-cross, and connect too with the prophecies of fairy tale. Hindu man leads Muslim woman to Hindu prophet, and that is where Amina learns the formula of the child: 'There will be two heads—but you shall see only one—there will be knees and a nose, a nose and knees.' And hence the logic of the birth where one is more than one, founded on crossings of all kinds. Why is all this important? Because it shows the *many* and the *one* in a new form. In *Midnight's Children* 'one' is never identical with itself, let alone with any other, but at the same time it is never disconnected. Instead, pairings or multiple connections, whether of similitude, doubling, or reversal, mean that nothing comes singly, in and of itself. There is no simple substitution or representation: rather there is the elaboration of

[5] John Bowker, ed., *The Concise Oxford Dictionary of World Religions* (Oxford: Oxford University Press, 2000), *s.v.* 'Rama'; *Oxford Reference Online*, Oxford University Press. University of Massachusetts, Amherst, <http://www.oxfordreference.com > (accessed 21 December 2004).

identity through contiguity, often through crossing. 'My annunciation saved a life' (84), remarks Saleem, and this is the myth of the glorious child. Except, as we find out later, it was not really 'his' annunciation; or he was only its twinned and crossed registration.

9. Saleem describes his intrauterine growth: 'What had been (at the beginning) no bigger than a full stop had expanded into a comma, a word, a sentence, a paragraph, a chapter; now it was bursting into more complex developments, becoming, one might say, a book—perhaps an encyclopedia—even a whole language...' (111). This is a grand Rushdiean conceit, invoking distantly Joyce's 'Oxen of the Sun' chapter in *Ulysses*, but the point is no less resonant for that. A life is like a language, full of expansive generative possibilities, an internal universe opening out in every phase into multiple dimensions. It is not only a navigation *using* language, but life *is* the language to be navigated. As Saleem's birth approaches, he—the narrator who has not yet been born (a different kind of 'crossing')—recites everything that has gone before, in fast-forward replay from Aadam Aziz to Ramram Seth and onwards, a work of recapitulation, recombination. When it comes to the question of his parents, Saleem's view is a particular one: he has, as he remarks, '[t]he power of giving birth to fathers and mothers' (120). In this regard the arrow of cause and effect is reversed, and biology is crossed by narrative. Here are Saleem's fathers: Ahmed Sinai, Wee Willie Winkie, Methwold, Joseph D'Costa, Uncle Hanif, Schaapsteker the snake-man, General Zulfikar, and Picture Singh (the Most Charming Man In The World). And mothers: Amina Sinai, Vanita, Alice Pereira, Mary Pereira, Pia-Aunty, Parvati-the-Witch, the Widow (as dark mother), and Bharat-Mata, mother India herself. Moreover, Saleem is not using the terms 'mother' and 'father' metaphorically. It is not as if all these people are *like* parents to him. Since biology counts for almost nothing in the book, these really are his mothers and fathers—each part of a metonymic chain leading from one to another by contiguity and linkage, not substitution or allegory. His father is *simultaneously* Ahmed–Wee Willie Winkie–Methwold–Joseph, and so on, and his mother Amina–Vanita–Alice–Mary... in a continuing series. Of course, Mary and Joseph step straight out of these pages and link with that other miraculous birth—a nice joke. As always in this novel, high and low forms come together, another form of insistent crossing and shift. Chiasmus may sometimes lead

to tragedy, but it is also the sign of the eternal joke—of resilience, of life.

10. So lineage, which we think of as vertical, a form of 'reproduction', turns out to have horizontal (or metonymic) aspects. Insofar as the vertical is involved, it takes the form, as we might predict, of the 'X'. This is because, primarily, of the switch, the central joke of the novel, but also its most serious suggestion. At the moment of double-birth, or triple-birth, as India, Saleem, and Shiva are born, Mary Pereira switches the two babies. The child of the middle-class Muslim Sinais is given to the impoverished Hindu Wee Willie Winkie, whose wife Vanita has just died in childbirth. And the switch goes further back than that, because WWW is not the real father. Methwold, he of the charismatic hairpiece with its magnetic centre-parting (a line of division and crossing), had seduced Vanita. And so the switched-Saleem's father is an Englishman, one who quite successfully hands on his colonial traditions and culture to the Indian community he leaves behind in Bombay. Here is allegory in some guise: India's lineage is unutterably mixed, whether through Mughal Emperors or British Empire. And the logic of the switch, if both Saleem and Shiva 'map' onto India, indicates that the new country is no singularity, perhaps not even a 'blend'. Because of the 'X', both Shiva and Saleem are twinned with India, and their brotherly equation, in the true tradition of Cain and Abel, Jacob and Esau, is one of opposition as much as identity. Not least Saleem's false birthright—his *possession* of place, recognition, reward—is Shiva's *dispossession*: a crossing of privilege and poverty, inclusion and exclusion, in the prophetic moment of independence. Later, as Saleem's fortunes fall, Shiva (as Major Shiva) rises in the world; there is always a crossing between them. But of course, even the 'X' is doubled. For Shiva's son with Parvati (the iconic holy pairing) is adopted by Saleem, whose own powers of reproduction have been neutralized. It is in fact a double-crossing, and it produces a lineage of a kind, for Saleem's non-son will be the true grandson of his grandparents. Reproduction is not strictly or only biological, and what we take for the validations of biology can be thoroughly misleading. As Saleem indicates in his own case, a distinctive nose can come from more than one direction; it is one of life's little jokes. Amina remarks to her husband, 'Look, janum, the poor fellow, he's got his grandfather's nose' (131).

11. It is worth mapping the pattern. Across the generations, this is the shape that lineage takes:

X
X

Or, we can expand the image, so:

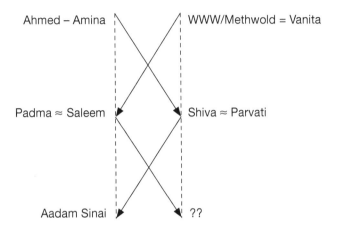

The map is asymmetrical: three parents in the top-right corner, no child in the bottom right. Or at least, no child if we insist on the biological as the basis of lineage. Yet biologically it is clear that vertical lines of reproduction are putative; only the oblique is real. The image itself may be a metaphor—a form of representation. Yet it represents the reality of crossing and linkage as the very *principle* of reproduction, even in the most 'linear' forms. For what birth, after all, is not the product of a 'crossing'? Any birth, any identity, sustains this principle in its deepest grammar. And so it is no vast leap of the imagination to add a curve or two to the double-X above, to see it as the double-helix, the sign of DNA, the building block of life.[6] The code of DNA is itself a kind of syntax (AGCT), repeated in intricate chains of combination

[6] For an inventive exploration of meiosis as a more promising concept than hybridity in postcolonial as well as other settings, see Nicole Matos, 'Meiotic Fictions: Hybridity and the Reproduction of the New', *Rhizomes*, 9 (2004); <http://www.rhizomes.net/issue9/matos.htm> (accessed 12 January 2008). Matos considers Rushdie (*The Satanic Verses*), along with Robert Antoni and Italo Calvino.

and recombination, which allows gene to combine with gene and the being as a whole to enter into combination with the world outside it.[7] Accident-no-accident, it is no surprise to find this pattern at the heart of *Midnight's Children.*

12. This is Padma's accusation when she first hears of the switched babies from Saleem: 'You are an Anglo-Indian? Your name is not your own?' (131). To which Saleem replies, 'I am Saleem Sinai...Snotnose, Stainface, Sniffer, Baldy, Piece-of-the-Moon. Whatever do you mean—not my own?' The relation of name to object cannot, in some significant sense, be 'identical'; this is suggested by Wittgenstein's paradox on the identical, and has a bearing on Derrida's notion of 'différance' as well. But Saleem's response is equally significant: even at this level, he has a *chain* of names rather than a single one. So Saleem is a combination, and he is correct: what could it possibly mean that his name is not his own, since a word will never fully name us, nor is there any single name to 'own'? This is naming as spectrum rather than reference, and Saleem may find himself anywhere along that chain. But does that make the chain in any serious regard unreal? Ask his mother, who might be a perfect witness on the topic. Amina, who has become adept at loving 'in bits' (except for the one piece of her husband she cannot love), tells Saleem that love is a thing 'that every mother learns; it is not born with a baby, but made' (328). And later even his father says 'Come, son; come here and let me love you' (329). It is as Saleem tells Padma: 'when we eventually discovered the crime of Mary Pereira, we all found that it *made no difference!* I was still their son: they remained my parents' (139). Metonymy, in other words, trumps biology. Acceptance of linkage and metamorphosis is at the heart of being and becoming human; a lineage all of its own.[8]

---

[7] 'But it is in appreciating the dual nature of DNA—that it is not just inherited but is also environmentally responsive—that we will understand better how genes influence behavior.' Gene Robinson, 'The Behavior of Genes', *New York Times,* 13 December 2004, A27. For Steven Pinker on the similarities between language and DNA as 'discrete combinatorial systems', see the Introduction to this book.

[8] On this question, and for a reading of Rushdie that is very sympathetic to my own, see M. Keith Booker, 'Beauty and the Beast: Dualism as Despotism in the Fiction of Salman Rushdie', in *Reading Rushdie: Perspectives on the Fiction of Salman Rushdie,* ed. M. D. Fletcher (Amsterdam and Atlanta: Rodopi, 1994). Booker argues that Rushdie raises dualisms of all kinds only to deconstruct them, not least around questions of identity, good/evil, etc. As Booker remarks, the 'intolerance of otherness amounts to

13. If, biologically, only the diagonal lines are real and even the vertical are metonymic, does that mean we should give up on, or overthrow, 'reproduction' as direct lineage? Yes and no; or only insofar as we revise it. The point is obvious enough to be almost embarrassing. Reproduction is not cloning; it is not substitution. It is not 'I produce you, and you are therefore a form of me.' In reproduction, you are also a form of not-me. In other words, reproduction is a vector of the vertical (the same, substitution) and the horizontal (contiguous but not the same). Therefore it appears as a diagonal, and *Midnight's Children* is deeply invested in that form of attachment-shifting-displacement. But should we not equally be suspicious of such geometric scheming, such clear patterning? Isn't it too 'structural', mapping one-to-one on the vertical and horizontal axes of the graph? What about some irregular or broken lines for a change? Well, the non-biological lineage (Aadam Sinai in relation to Saleem and his grandparents) is a form of broken line. And there is the whole topic of excess in the novel—something still to be discussed.

14. The question of names applies not only to Saleem, for many names change in the novel. So, Saleem's mother, Mumtaz, becomes Amina, and the Brass Monkey becomes Jamila Singer. Saleem's grand-mother Naseem at some point becomes the Reverend Mother, and with that seems to undergo a whole personality shift—as does the Brass Monkey when she moves to Pakistan and becomes Jamila. Conversely, where names stay the same, they can mean very different things, travel through a whole morphology of meaning. So, the MCC is the Metro Cub Club, the Marylebone Cricket Club (England's overseas touring team from that era), the Midnight Children's Conference, and later the Midnite Confidential Club, where Picture Singh takes on his challenger for the title of Most Charming Man In The World. What can this mean but that identity over time may be a version of metonymy? One person can have many names, one name can mean many things, and the self continuous in space is in transition through time—one version of itself always morphing into another possibility. Duration of identity through time is one of the oldest philosophical and existential puzzles, but it

a dual opposition between self and other of the type that Rushdie relentlessly challenges in his fiction' (249).

may be slightly less puzzling if we accept it as a kind of navigation, an unfolding syntax.

15. When Saleem is born, Nehru writes to him: 'You are the newest bearer of that ancient face of India which is also eternally young. We shall be watching over your life with the closest attention; it will be, in a sense, the mirror of our own' (139). If Saleem is the 'newest bearer' of the face of India then there is a form of substitution at work, but only in terms of his association with previous 'bearers'. In other words, it is a face that changes according to its representatives; it is the chain of bearers that makes a face never identical with itself, as if the map's outlines were always shifting and blurring.[9] And if Saleem is a 'mirror' to India, then we have a familiar pattern: for mirrors preserve vertical symmetry, but their left-right symmetries are reversed.

16. Let us list some of the novel's insistent chiastic patterns, remembering that chiasmus involves both contiguity and reversal. There is Nadir Khan's friend, the painter, who had tried to get the whole of life into his art, beginning as a miniaturist and ending with elephantiasis (49). Nadir is saved in the cornfield by Rashid the rickshaw boy who has just been to see a film called *Gai-Wallah* (loosely, 'cow-man'), 'an eastern Western' (50). There is Saleem's celebrated comparison of reality with movies: if you are nose up to the screen it makes no sense, but with distance comes the illusion of shape (189). Where does optimism lie, asks Saleem, in fate or in chaos? (86) (He adds that his mother's pregnancy was fated, but his birth owed much to accident; unless, we might wonder, the accident was fated.) Saleem falls in love with the game of Snakes and Ladders, and uses it as a central chiastic image of rise and fall—except, as he points out, that the game lacks ambiguity 'because...it is also possible to slither down a ladder and climb to triumph on the venom of a snake' (161). When Saleem falls ill, snake venom in the hands of Schaapsteker heals (169). A washing chest is the site of revelations: not Mount Hira or Mount Sinai, but Mrs

---

[9] Partha Chatterjee cites Nehru explaining to Indian peasants that they themselves constituted India: 'You are parts of this *Bharat Mata*, I told them, you are in a manner yourselves *Bharat Mata*, and as this idea slowly soaked into their brains, their eyes would light up as if they had made a great discovery.' *Nationalist Thought and the Colonial World: A Derivative Discourse* (Minneapolis: University of Minnesota Press, 1986), 146. Chatterjee tends to translate this as manipulative nationalist ideology, but Rushdie's version, as argued here, appears to be different.

Sinai's 'mount' (the 'black mango') and the inhalation of a pyjama cord
that produces Saleem's 'radio' (182–6). When Saleem contemplates the
affair of Homi Catrack and Lila Sabarmati, he lists the avatars: 'Radha
and Krishna, and Rama and Sita, and Laila and Majnu; also (because
we are not unaffected by the West), Romeo and Juliet, and Spencer
Tracy and Katherine Hepburn' (297). The Widow's hair-parting (black
on one side, white on the other) is paired with Methwold's, which
began the whole fantastic business, fertility crossed with sterility. High
and low forms, soiled underwear and heaven. Saleem's combination of
megalomania and paranoia ('it's all about me') is also a vastly enter-
taining and self-aware joke, a chiastic doubling at the heart of its
invention.

   17.  As if he were writing purely for Benedict Anderson's inspiration,
Saleem defines the birth of India:

a nation which had never previously existed was about to win its freedom,
catapulting us into a world which, although it had five thousand years of history,
although it had invented the game of chess and traded with Middle Kingdom
Egypt, was nevertheless quite imaginary; into a mythical land, a country which
would never exist except by the efforts of a phenomenal collective will—except
in a dream we all agreed to dream . . . (124)

   The nature of this 'imagined homeland' has been commented on
enough, but there are aspects of it that remain absorbing. For one thing
it is intriguing that Saleem becomes 'a sort of radio', 'All-India Radio'
receiving and broadcasting on the invisible airwaves of this dream. But
if the radio is an instrument of national consolidation (Saleem tells
us that the bribe for sterilization under Rajiv Gandhi's scheme was a
transistor), it is also (as Ian Baucom suggests in another context) a form
of national dispersal.[10] Saleem hears all the voices in his head: 'From far
to the North, "I". And the South East West: "I." "I." "And I"' (192).
'I' is the shifter: same name, many voices; they all compete in Saleem's
head, while he is nothing less than a compilation of all of those 'I-I-I's—
of course together with his own 'I', presiding in this assembly. Saleem's
birth is heralded by newspaper—the *Times of India* (Bombay edition)—
another key instrument of Andersonian national consciousness—but

---

[10]  See Ian Baucom, 'Frantz Fanon's Radio: Solidarity, Diaspora, and the Tactics of
Listening', *Contemporary Literature*, 42/1 (2001): 15–49.

Rushdie allows just a hint of doubleness here too. Reverend Mother, who hates photographs, comments on the image of Amina and child that celebrated the birth: 'Photos take away pieces of you. My God, whatsitsname, when I saw your picture, you had become so transparent I could see the writing from the other side coming right through your face!' (157). For Rushdie the national photograph is doubled, 'ghosted', uncanny; there is a story from the other side always coming through. (In reverse.)

18. But then it is amazing that the geographical boundaries are so fixed for Saleem. This may be because for Rushdie there is nothing so scandalous and lamentable as Partition—both the idea and the historical fact of it in India/Pakistan. What should be a node or nexus, a place of transition, becomes a limit, a fixity, an emptiness. This explains the fact that when Saleem goes to Pakistan, he finds the airwaves of his radio blocked by the border: there has been and can be no exchange between the two countries. Moreover, Pakistan has become a place of metaphor, a place of representation: it is an Islamic republic, the 'Land of the Pure'. Where purity admits no mixture or metonymy, this form of singular representation *always* constructs an absolute boundary. Saleem enters Pakistan via the Rann of Kutch, and he leaves via the Sundarbans—the waterways of the Indus and the Ganges respectively, where land and sea mingle in amphibious confusion, with the Indo-Gangetic plain of India subtended between. But the intransitive boundary contradicts water, flow, the river, the mythic origins of India (water flowing down from Shiva's hair into the Ganges), the continuities of land. The land is divided by a space that cannot be crossed because it is not synaptic, syntactic. Pakistan is a place of persistent mourning for Saleem, principally because its linkages are all vertical, towards God, not horizontal: we might say it is a country not of CombiNation but DiviNation.

19. But not only Pakistan. To divide, from the Latin *divido*, itself from the root *vidh-*, to part, to split. Thus, the Sanskrit *vidhava*, equivalent to the Latin *vidua*, a widow.[11] Sanskrit and Latin, East, West. In *Midnight's Children* the Widow returns with a vengeance, to separate

[11] Charlton T. Lewis and Charles D. Short, *A Latin Dictionary* (Oxford: Clarendon, 1879), *s.v.* 'Divido, visi, visum'; <http://www.perseus.tufts.edu> (accessed 14 January 2008).

and divide, to cut out fertility and hope. It is, etymologically, a form of divi-nation.

20. What then of time? Time too is a marvel in the book, not least because there are so many kinds, from Tai-time to national time, myth time and Methwold's sundowner time. It too is subject—though not entirely—to the warpings of national history. With Partition the clocks in Pakistan run half an hour ahead of their Indian counterparts (86). Saleem, confessing the chronological errors of his narration (which he cannot or will not fix), remarks, 'in my India, Gandhi will continue to die at the wrong time' (190). But this is not merely an acknowledgement of the intrinsic unreliabilities of Rushdie's own memories of India, as he has averred.[12] More than that, we might ask when would be the *right* time for Gandhi to die, in *any* narration? But if synchronicity is the mark of national time, then Rushdie shows that it can, so to speak, take on other dimensions: multiple times resonating at once, not least at the moment of national birth. 'Think of this,' says Saleem, 'history in my version entered a new phase on August 15th, 1947' (223). But he points out that in another version the date is nothing more than a fleeting instant in the age of darkness, Kali-Yuga, which began in 3102 BC and will last 'a mere 432,000 years!' And the Age of Darkness is only the fourth phase of the current Maha-Yuga cycle, which is in total ten times as long; 'and when you consider that it takes a thousand Maha-Yugas to make just one day of Brahma, you'll see what I mean about proportion' (223). Time within and surrounding time: in this light, time itself is capable of vast recursions based on alternate frames of measurement—a syntax of cavernous recessions and enclosures. So much for national time; this is not-the-national within the national.[13]

---

[12] Rushdie, *Imaginary Homelands*, 10–11.

[13] It is not clear that Saleem's appeal to an older version of time is what Benedict Anderson calls 'simultaneity-along-time' a past moment or representation that has a living presence in the 'now'. Nor is it an appeal to the legitimations of the past, which often underwrite nationalism. Rather, it is a doubled *frame* of time that in some ways undermines the 'national' model. For an account of time that sounds almost exactly like Saleem's, taken from Mrityunjay Vidyalankar's *Rājābali* (1808), see Chatterjee, *The Nation and its Fragments*, 78. Chatterjee argues that this formulation is pre-national— and if so, it is one more way of complicating the 'national' temporality of *Midnight's Children*.

21. Saleem's musings on time open up a circle in the novel. For Padma, listening to his whirlings, is embarrassed. But Padma of the hairy forearms, she who Possesses Dung, the receptacle if not of Saleem's bodily then of his narrative emissions, also has mythic proportions. We are told that Padma is one of the Guardians of Life, along with the sacred treasures of the earth, the sacred rivers, and the tree goddesses, 'beguiling and comforting mortal men while they pass through the dream web of Maya . . . Padma, the Lotus calyx, which grew out of Vishnu's navel, and from which Brahma himself was born; Padma the Source, the mother of Time!' (223) Here is chiasmus with a cosmic vengeance: Padma, the 'end' of the story is also its foundation and beginning, for there is no story without time, its essential medium. And this means, too, another reversal, of narrative hierarchy: for the audience of the story, purportedly its passive receptacle, is actually its 'end' in another guise: its purpose, and the origin of its deepest needs.

22. Questions of form. Saleem is the narrator whose presence—like Tristram Shandy's in the work which provided some inspiration for *Midnight's Children*—precedes his existence for a serious proportion of the length of the novel. 'At this rate,' complains Padma, 'you'll be two hundred years old before you manage to tell about your birth' (37). The narrative inversion is accompanied, often, by a sense of dissociation between Saleem-character and Saleem-narrator: 'He and I, I and he . . . I no longer have his gift; he never had mine' (190). Chiastic syntax tells a tale of crossing even within the continuities of identity, and this crossing is also the difference between he who tells and he who is told. In the midst of this Saleem in his two guises has two quests: the quest for meaning, and the quest for purpose. Saleem as character perpetually puts the question to his fellow Midnight's Children Conferencers: ' "We must think," I said, "what we are for" ' (261). And at the outset of the novel, Saleem as narrator announces that he must work faster than Scheherazade 'if I am to end up meaning—yes, meaning—something. I admit it: above all things, I fear absurdity' (4). But meaning and purpose are connected: if Saleem-N can find meaning, then Saleem-C will have found a purpose. The pursuit of significance: this may be what the novel calls the 'national longing for form' (344). But the question might still remain: is this the same as a form of *national* longing? Can meaning be found only in the nation? Or is the national

displaced by the forms that Saleem discovers as character/narrator? He-not-I.

23. Saleem expands on his definition this way: 'As a people, we are obsessed with correspondences. Similarities between this and that, between apparently unconnected things, make us clap our hands delightedly when we find them out. It is a sort of national longing for form—or perhaps simply an expression of our deep belief that forms lie hidden within reality; that meaning reveals itself only in flashes' (343–4). It is so easy, within this formulation, to focus on the quotable kernel of nation and form, but look at Saleem's terms on either side of it: 'people' as much as 'nation', 'unconnected' as well as 'similarity', meaning that reveals itself 'only in flashes'. At the heart of it is the notion of 'correspondence', but, as Saleem indicates, correspondence is not the same as identity—if it were it would not be correspondence. Elsewhere, Saleem explores what it means in his case, and intriguingly he tackles it in grammatical terms: 'I was linked to history both literally and metaphorically, both actively and passively, in what (our admirably modern) scientists might term "modes of connection" composed of "dualistically-combined configurations" of the two pairs of opposed adverbs given above. This is why hyphens are necessary: actively-literally, passively-metaphorically, actively-metaphorically and passively-literally, I was inextricably entwined with my world' (272–3). Whether this analysis is correct may be doubted—that is, whether the options are only active or passive, literal or metaphoric—for we have seen much richer patterns of crossing in the novel. Instead we should note the deeper structure of Saleem's formulation: the chiastic switchings of the 'opposed' pairs; the organizing concept of 'modes of connection'; the fact that 'hyphens are necessary'. There we get closer to Rushdie's grammar. It is a *generative* grammar rather than pedagogical, the motive principle of navigation in language as well as identity.

24. Alpha and Omega. The mid-point of the book introduces the idea of beginning and end, not only as a question of narrative and plot, but as a matter of alphabet (Greek), and also Saleem's blood type, which will reveal his chiastic, biological-metonymic identity, his overflow beyond the boundaries of his family. Not only A and O, and zygosity and Kell bodies, but also, as Saleem says, 'that most mysterious

of sanguinary attributes known as rhesus, which is also a type of monkey' (259). As he adds, 'Everything has shape, if you look for it. There is no escape from form.' But the form of Saleem's identity is explosive: what A and O reveal when his finger is amputated in the door incident with Masha Miovic and his schoolfriends is the incontinent grammar of his genetic code. To reveal this in a family, whether domestic or national, is to invite disaster and exile: exactly what occurs. Saleem summarizes:

O eternal opposition of inside and outside! Because a human being, inside himself, is anything but a whole, anything but homogeneous; all kinds of everywhichthing are jumbled up inside him, and he is one person one minute and another the next. The body, on the other hand, is as homogeneous as anything. Indivisible, a one-piece suit, a sacred temple, if you will. . . . Uncork the body, and God knows what you permit to come tumbling out. Suddenly you are forever other than you were; and the world becomes such that parents can cease to be parents, and love can turn to hate. (270–1)

The indivisible at odds with the irrepressible; the One containing the Many; the self that is other to itself. Whether national or familial, Saleem tells of the A that is connected with O, beginning with middle with end, and the whole ceaseless alphabet soup in between that inevitably overflows any containment. This is identity as excess, which in spilling over becomes a kind of *trans*-identity: both the boundary *and* its beyond.

25. In the chapter entitled 'Revelations', when Musa the servant returns, leprosy-ridden, to be mistaken by Aadam Aziz for God, and to prompt Mary Pereira (haunted by images of her once-loved Joseph D'Costa) to tell the truth regarding the baby-switch, Saleem comments: 'Someone was called God who was not God; someone else was taken for a ghost, and was not a ghost; and a third person discovered that although his name was Saleem Sinai, he was not his parents' son' (321). We have not-God, the not-ghost, and not-the-son. A sort of unholy trinity, chiastic and fallen version of that other combination.

26. Versions of metonymy, syntax, recursion everywhere. When Saleem's Uncle Hanif reinvents a form of eroticism for the censored world of Indian cinema, he does it through what comes to be known as the indirect kiss: the actress (his aunty Pia) plants a sensuous kiss

on one side of an apple, then passes it to an actor who does the same
on its opposite face. This is the apple as metonymic transition of the
kiss, and when Saleem spies on his mother at the Pioneer Café, he
sees her imitate the gesture exactly (with a glass of *lassi*) in her illicit
meeting with Nadir Khan. Later, when Saleem tries to act on his mother
and Nadir at a distance, by sabotaging the affair of Lila Sabarmati
and Homi Catrack, he employs eminently recursive means. Taking to
the newspapers, he cuts out words and letters to send an anonymous
message to Commander Sabarmati, who then kills both his wife and
Homi. The method is one of recombination: one syntax available within
another, a possibility always permitted by the alphabet string, offered up
in this case by the 'national' newspapers—generative capacities available
even there to contradict their apparent intentions. As Saleem says, he is
also '[c]utting up history' (297)—the substance of the newspaper stories
he dissects like a surgeon and recombines. And later still, in Pakistan,
when Saleem is brained by the family spittoon ('hit the spittoon': in
colliding with Saleem's skull the Indian national pastime is reversed),
the object becomes the only index of the memory he has lost. He
carries the spittoon everywhere—the attachment that tells him who
he is, the metonym of his identity. When Saleem is there-and-not-
there, being transported back to India in Parvati's magic basket, it is
likewise the spittoon that saves him, 'a reminder of the outside' (439).
Donated to the family by the Rani of Cooch Naheen (translation: the
Rani of Nothing), the metonym almost outlasts those to whom it is
attached.

27.  In Pakistan, the Land of the Pure, Jamila Singer becomes a singer
of patriotic songs, 'Pakistan's Angel', 'The Voice of the Nation', the
'Bulbul-e-Din', or nightingale of the faith—a series of substitutions in
which she represents both country and Islam. To preserve her modesty,
Jamila sings behind a perforated sheet; in the street she wears a gold
and white *burqa* at all times—in her case a refusal of the metonymies
of contact, the contract between artist and audience. Saleem, however,
becomes an artist of a different kind; using his nasal skills he becomes
a virtuoso of smell, that most metonymic of sensory navigations. Moreover, where Jamila opts for country and heaven ('The President's will is
the voice of my heart' [360]), Saleem, like Stephen Dedalus in Joyce's *A
Portrait of the Artist as a Young Man*, opts instead for 'the pungency of

the gutter' (364). This is his discovery when he attempts to develop a science of nasal ethics regarding the difference between the sacred and profane—that the profane is far more attractive. But it produces an ethics of a different kind. When Saleem visits Tai Bibi, the 512-year-old whore, he discovers his secret lust for Jamila (Tai imitates her scent). He has it all worked out, and pleads with Jamila: they are not brother and sister after all, they are divided and not united by their blood. But even as he speaks his words sound hollow to himself, and Jamila is revolted. Saleem realizes that 'although what he was saying was the literal truth, there were other truths which had become more important because they had been sanctified by time' (372). What he has discovered, though he does not put it in these terms, is that once again biology is outdone by metonymy. And perhaps even more important: that metonymy does not mean the abandonment of ethics. Indeed, it may produce a higher form of ethics, because it is an ethics that goes beyond blood relation.

28. 'Begin all over again,' Padma exhorts Saleem after he tells of the death of his parents and his braining by the spittoon (399). It is an imprecation that has to do with Saleem's life as well as his narrative, for, slate wiped clean, both himself and not himself, he starts another existence as the Buddha. Even here, his links are insistently doubled: 'Buddha', depending on how one pronounces it, means both 'old man' (in Urdu) and 'he-who-achieved-enlightenment-under-the-bodhi-tree' (402); and Saleem, now in the top-secret CUTIA section of the Pakistan army, becomes the composite 'dog-man', the tracker, with nothing more than his nose to guide him as he follows the metonymies of scent for his movement. But, as befits a Buddha, there is separation from self and time. Saleem is severed from both his previous life and his present one: 'not I. He,' he insists to Padma, describing the Buddha (414). And to Ayooba Shaheed Farooq, his comrades solicitous about his past and family, his response is clear: 'I am who I am, that's all there is' (403). But if the self is now perfect, contemplative, singular, existing only in the present, there are downsides. As Saleem remarks, 'emptied of history, the Buddha learned the arts of submission, and did only what was required of him. To sum up: I became a citizen of Pakistan' (403).

29. Saleem's trackings in the war against Bangla Desh lead him and Ayooba Shaheed Farooq into the Sundarbans, a mythographic

descent into the underworld and the unconscious, where time and space become hallucinatory planes. This is the Qur'an's Jahannam, a version of hell; it is also reminiscent of Book 6 of the *Aeneid*, where Aeneas visits Hades, and beyond that Book 11 in the *Odyssey*, where Odysseus does the same. But if there are parallels, the differences are also significant. Aeneas visits the underworld in a reverential quest to find his father, and hear directly from him the future lineage of the new Imperium he will found in Rome.[14] Virgil was the Imperial poet, and this is his national epic. But Saleem—no Aeneas he—returns from the Sundarbans disillusioned and horrified by national wars. Instead, Rushdie appears to take a different classical model: Ovid, who was exiled and not honoured by Augustus; whose conventional paeans to Julius Caesar and Augustus are set off by considerations of how Empires rise only to fall; whose full name, most fittingly in relation to this novel, was Publius Ovidius Naso—'The Nose'. Ovid's lineages are based not on patrimony but on the subtle exchanges of *metamorphosis*—between the human and the natural, between humans and the gods, between humans and one another or within themselves, what Calvino called a vision of 'universal contiguity'.[15] And so it is only 'natural' that when Saleem finally recovers 'consciousness' after the Sundarbans, it is because he has been bitten by a snake—just as in the *Metamorphoses* the god of healing, Aesculapius, takes the form of a snake. 'For two days,' Saleem says of himself, 'he became as rigid as a tree, and his eyes crossed, so that

---

[14] Virgil's lineages are uncomplicated and unambiguous—'Here is Caesar, and all the line of Iulus/ . . . Caesar Augustus, son of the deified'—and Anchises' instructions to his son equally clear:

> Roman, remember by your strength [*imperio*] to rule
> Earth's peoples—for your arts are to be these:
> To pacify, to impose the rule of law,
> To spare the conquered, battle down the proud.

See Virgil, *The Aeneid*, trans. Robert Fitzgerald (New York: Vintage, 1990), Bk 6, 1060–8, 1151–4 (in the original, lines 789–95, 851–3).

[15] See Italo Calvino, 'Ovid and Universal Contiguity', in *The Literature Machine* (London: Secker and Warburg, 1987). Calvino shows how Ovid was himself a great combiner, taking not only some of his stories but also his techniques from the East, including embedded or recursive structures. He points out that according to L. P. Wilkinson, Ovid took the story of Pyramus and Thisbe 'from some ancestor of the *Thousand and One Nights*' (153). Also see Booker, 'Beauty and the Beast', 240, for Bakhtin on metamorphosis.

he saw the world in mirror-image, with the right side on the left' (419). Saleem comes back to life through reversal, through nature, and through the chiastic crossings of the mirror. And rather than found a lineage and Empire as an expression of *virtus* or manhood, Empire undoes both him and his lineage. Saleem is unmanned by sterilization programmes and sperectomy.

30. Back-to-Bom: Saleem cannot contain his excitement returning to Bombay, home of all the world's multiplicities, and in some respects the excitement is Rushdie's. On the train with Picture Singh, following the line of the railway (always metonymic) across the landscape of India, to Saleem the wheels seem to sing 'abracadabra abracadabra' (519). This is Aadam Sinai's first word too, when, silent from birth, he finally speaks: 'Abba...' (Saleem thinks he is saying 'father') '... cadabba' (528). In young Aadam's version the word is *almost* palindromic—just 'c' and 'd', adjacent letters after all, counterposed. In Bombay, after another descent into Jahannam (each saga requires at least one, remarks Saleem) at the Midnite Confidential Club, he makes his way to the Braganza Pickle Factory, where he finds Padma and Mary (now Mrs) Pereira, who in an ecstasy of recognition cannot restrain herself: 'look how thin you've got, come, come, let me kiss you, let me give you cake!' (526). As Saleem points out, she is the only mother he has left, and Padma will be the one to listen to his narrative. As in all good sagas, the end of the journey is the beginning of the story. A and O; chiasmus.

31. In telling of his emergence from the Sundarbans, Saleem muses on identity: 'What you were is forever who you are' (423). This seems to contradict the principle of morphology. But later, recounting his emergence from the non-being of Parvati's magic basket, he muses again:

I no longer want to be anything except what who I am. Who what am I? My answer: I am the sum total of everything that went before me, of all I have been seen done, of everything done-to-me. I am everyone everything whose being-in-the-world affected was affected by mine. I am anything that happens after I've gone which would not have happened if I had not come. Nor am I particularly exceptional in this matter; each 'I', every one of the now six-hundred-million-plus of us, contains a similar multitude. I repeat for the last time: to understand me, you'll have to swallow a world. (440–1)

Is inner being a one-piece suit, like the body? It may be, as a matter of intrinsic spirit or attitude. Perhaps each of us has our own metaphoric 'imprint' or representation which we enact throughout our lives. But Saleem's imprint—the very signature that defines him—is one attuned to endless linkage: the contiguities and morphologies of being that always exist and will continue for ever. Even the syntax of his sentences doubles and works in two directions: 'I am everyone everything whose being-in-the-world affected was affected by mine.'

32. And so we come to the question of chutneyfication. All through the novel we have had 'leakages' and 'seepages', the way that not only food but even clothing will seep into an identity. And in the most innovative conceit in the novel Saleem reveals that each chapter is like a pickle jar, with its own 'special blends' (442). Thirty of them for the novel, and one left over for the future. This, as Saleem famously remarks, is 'the chutneyfication of history' (529). But what is the nature of a 'blend'? Saleem asks what is required for chutneyfication, and lists his ingredients: fruit, vegetables, fish, vinegar, spices; but also eyes blue as ice, and a nose; and the more unusual blends of memories, dreams, and ideas. In some ways, as Saleem admits, chutneyfication introduces 'the inevitable distortions of the pickling process', but this is what produces immortality: 'The art is to change the flavour in degree, but not in kind; and above all ... to give it shape and form—that is to say, meaning' (531). Changing the flavour in degree but not in kind: these are the metamorphoses of metonymy and not substitution. And consider the blend, its strange ambiguities. As Steven Pinker has pointed out, in a blend individual properties are lost, while in a combinatorial system those properties remain distinct.[16] But one might ask: at what level? Before a blend is a blend it is a combination of elements, and may remain so, even down to the molecular level. Or, we might say: a blend is a combination that endures through time, but its underlying grammar remains that of the combination, of its ingredients. And if the grammar of form gives meaning, then in Rushdie's model the grammar of excess (A and O that overflows, one jar left over) will always be an intrinsic part of that form.

---

[16] See the Introduction, p. 18.

33. Thirty-one jars for Saleem; a few more paragraphs than that here. After sperectomy, after the Widow's hand, Saleem feels the cracks creeping up on him. Joyce's peroration to *Ulysses* is all about Molly Bloom's 'yes', but Rushdie is not so unequivocal. His penultimate paragraph begins, 'No, that won't do', and the last begins 'Yes,' but only to say 'Yes, they will trample me underfoot' (532–3). This is Rushdie's no-yes, the ultimate chiastic pairing when it comes to matters of the future, of hope. Rushdie responded to allegations of despair in the concluding vision of *Midnight's Children* by saying that Saleem's impending disintegration is counterbalanced by the endlessly regenerative capacities of the novel.[17] And that is surely correct. Yes, they will trample Saleem underfoot, but this is the 'crowd without boundaries, growing until it fills the world' (532). This is not just the cycle of regeneration contained in unceasing patterns of life and death, it is also the national become transnational, the grammar of the multitude, a recursive principle working within and beyond the boundary until it overflows—as Saleem says—into a space that becomes global, the world. 'I have been so-many too-many persons,' remarks Saleem, 'life unlike syntax allows one more than three' (533). But in this novel life and syntax have become mutually informing in endlessly generative combinations. Combi- and divi-nations: there is no such thing as the singular nation or the singular self, only principles of division, doubling, mirroring, reversal, overflow—both the *less* and *more*, both the cracks and the crowd, both the lack and—always—the excess. This is navigation not so much for a new country but for a new and transformed way of conceiving it.

\* \* \*

## *THE SATANIC VERSES*: DIVINATION

1. In *Midnight's Children*, when Saleem first hears his voices, his mind is drawn to others who have had similar experiences—Moses on Mount Sinai, the prophet Muhammad on Mount Hira. In suggesting the comparisons, Saleem is aware of the potential susceptibilities of his audience: 'Muhammad (on whose name be peace, let me add; I don't

---

[17] Rushdie, *Imaginary Homelands*, 16.

want to offend anyone) heard a voice saying "Recite!" and thought he
was going mad' (185). Yet elsewhere Saleem is less concerned about
affront. Family history, he remarks, has its own dietary laws, and one is
supposed to tell only the halal portions of it, 'drained of their redness,
their blood. Unfortunately, this makes the stories less juicy; so I am
about to become the only member of my family to flout the laws of
halal' (62). It is a statement of artistic independence, and it provides
the impetus to push beyond questions of offence. Two novels later,
in *The Satanic Verses*, Rushdie returned to the story of Muhammad—
or someone very much like him who, within the dream sections of
the novel, is called Mahound, the offensive medieval Christian term;
and what followed after that was fury, *fatwa*, and persecution. Yet if
Rushdie came up against the boundaries of religious sensitivity only to
traverse them, this was in keeping with the form of a novel profoundly
transnational in its conception and cast. For here boundaries exist in
nothing but transformation, while the self is intrinsically multiple and
metamorphic. Time–space–dream: the connective modes of *The Satanic
Verses*, a novel which provides us with vast and unsettling dimensions of
the transnational, and a book the world will take a while to get the
measure of.

2. The transnational is built into the very premises of *The Satanic
Verses*. It is a novel of places, migrations, transmigrations, which begins
with two of its characters falling out of the sky, victims of a national
fiction that demands—as such fictions often do—'sacrifice'. Tavleen,
the woman who uses that word and blows up the plane carrying
Saladin Chamcha and Gibreel Farishta from India to England, is a
Sikh nationalist, and in the form of some mythic creature has grenades
strapped to her body like fatal breasts. Saladin and Gibreel cartwheel
through the sky, clasping each other head to tail—knees and nose—
like a whirling 'X' in rotation. Much of the story is theirs, and much
of it takes on chiastic form.[18] They land miraculously on the beach,
and find themselves metamorphosed. Gibreel takes on the halo of the
angel, Saladin the horns of the goat and the devil. But in the rise
and fall of this book, who is angel and who devil alternate like two

---

[18]  For a particularly perceptive understanding of Gibreel and Chamcha's fall from the
sky, see Gillian Gane, 'Migrancy, the Cosmopolitan Intellectual, and the Global City in
*The Satanic Verses*', *Modern Fiction Studies*, 48/1 (2002): 23–5.

intersecting sine-curves. When Saladin takes on goat-form, it is partly a function of his construction in the eyes of a hostile host country, partly a function of his acceptance of that construction. Conversely, when he takes on 'normal' form, he is not above behaving like the devil, prompting Gibreel with his own kind of 'satanic verses' to rampant destructive jealousy. And Gibreel's 'angelic' nature cannot be separated from a kind of schizophrenia. The sign does not represent the thing; or it represents it only as a form of oscillation, every now and then coinciding with its object. But if there are discontinuities in the metonymies of the sign ('horns' do not necessarily connect to 'devil'), nothing can remove the sense that Saladin–Gibreel are connected, two parts of the same being. 'For are they not conjoined opposites, these two,' the narrator of the novel remarks, 'each man the other's shadow?'[19] Saladin and Gibreel cross each other on lines that stretch from earth to heaven, and from one country to another. All this is part of Rushdie's explicit concern in the novel: 'How does newness come into the world?' (8).

3. But the 'Xs' are muted, mutant, or mutilated: *Mutilasians*—the characters on 'Dr Who' Chamcha watches on TV when he has lost his job in the voiceover market. Rushdie adds asymmetry to chiasmus: Chamcha's chromosomes—his genetic 'Xs'—are non-standard: 'two sticks too long, or too short, he couldn't remember' (51); and when he is trying to bed Zeeny Vakil, his disjunctions produce unsustainable crossings in his vision, 'as if his right eye saw the world moving to the left while his left eye saw it sliding to the right' (52). Chamcha has tried to invent an internal discontinuity in taking on a dedicated version of Anglo identity, but this is transformation without transition—a dangerous undertaking in a novel interested in the difference. Chamcha is 'The Man of a Thousand Voices', the voiceover artist on radio and television whose own bodily or visual identity is repressed. Or, in his desperate wish to be 'properly' English, he is the mimic man whose self has been substituted. If, as Rushdie has said, migration is a form of translation ('entering the condition of metaphor'), Chamcha's radical disruptions produce particularly violent results—the horned goat accepted neither by his host country nor himself, the Kafkan 'insect'

---

[19] Salman Rushdie, *The Satanic Verses* (New York: Picador, 1988), 441. All further page references in the text and notes are to this edition.

on the floor of the police van. In this way, his experience begins to define a pattern: the horizontal break in metonymic continuity in the self converts into a vertical split or repression in the psyche—his anger, his desire, his loss. And so we can understand Rushdie's formulation in a new way: where transition, continuity, navigation is lost, one enters the condition of a different kind of metaphor. Metaphor not *as* but *versus* metamorphosis.

4. How does this happen? Metaphor involves oscillation, shift, movement. But settled into finality it can lose a sense of transition. It becomes comparison, representation, fixed order, the 'having crossed', stasis. But metamorphosis accepts no finality: one can grow horns and lose them again, the halo is deceptive, compared objects will drift out of focus, the boundary change its shape, the metaphor itself undergo transition. The crossing is all, the only true illusion the intransitive.

5. What continues through metamorphosis: the novel is necessarily drawn to this issue. For Otto Cone, Alleluia's father, Holocaust survivor who contracted his name from 'Cohen', the most dangerous lie of all is 'the idea of the continuum'. As he puts it, 'The world is incompatible, just never forget it: gaga. Ghosts, Nazis, saints, all alive at the same time; in one spot, blissful happiness, while down the road, the inferno' (305). By contrast, Muhammad Sufyan, owner of the Shandaar Café, tries to encourage Chamcha by proclaiming his preference for Ovid rather than Lucretius. For Lucretius, whatever goes 'beyond its boundaries' through change brings immediate death to its former self, while for Ovid the more compelling analogy is 'yielding wax':

As yielding wax is stamped with new designs
And changes shape and seems not still the same,
Yet is indeed the same, even so our souls
Are still the same for ever, but adopt
In their migrations ever-varying forms.[20]

---

[20] *Satanic Verses* (285); Ovid, *Metamorphoses*, trans. A. D. Melville (Oxford and New York: Oxford University Press, 1998), 357. Interestingly, this is the exact translation Rushdie uses, and the Introduction to the Ovid (first published in this version in 1986, just as Rushdie would have been writing *The Satanic Verses*) raises exactly the same contrast between Lucretius and Ovid (xv–xvi); it was almost certainly Rushdie's source. Note Pythagoras' line, 'The goat that gnawed the vine was sacrificed/ On vengeful Bacchus' altars' (*Metamorphoses*, 355), which lends a certain resonance both to a theme of sacrifice and Chamcha's goatish experience.

The source is 'The Doctrines of Pythagoras' in Book 15 of the *Metamorphoses*, and the context concerns the underlying continuity between humans and animals—quite apt for the goat-man. In the Ovidian view, the nature of the boundary is intrinsically mutable, and linked to migration; for Lucretius, it is absolute and linked to death. Migration, the transitive, demands mutability: it is the only way to survive. And if navigation is an intrinsic part of human grammar, then mutability is part of it too.

6. Yet that does not mean metamorphosis is easy or simple, the nature of the boundary easy to navigate. At times Lucretius seems to meet Ovid, as in the Hot Wax Club (the name not accidental), where mannequins of Mrs Thatcher and her entourage undergo total meltdown, to the delight of the immigrant patrons. Elsewhere the reference is to Blake, the poet of visions, for whom there is no progression without contraries. As Gibreel reads to Allie Cone from *The Marriage of Heaven and Hell*, 'The lust of the goat is the bounty of God' (315). Blake's paradoxical images—linking contraries across immense conceptual and metaphysical space—are particularly evocative for Gibreel, pursued as he is by ghosts and visions, not least of his own apotheosis. For him this is evidence that 'the world of dreams was leaking into that of the waking hours, that the seals dividing the two were breaking, and that at any moment the two firmaments could be joined' (314–15). Metamorphosis between dream and reality: another kind of syntax in the novel, another kind of crossing, another kind of grammar, involving both continuity and discontinuity.

7. Gibreel's dreams are uncanny in a form beyond the usual because each one takes up where the former left off; it is a kind of continuing narrative. In his guise as the Archangel Gabriel, he enters alternate worlds: the world of the Imam in London; of 'Mahound' in Jahilia; of Ayesha's pilgrimage from Titlipur to Mecca. At the heart of this process there is a strange doubling. From one perspective, Gibreel is the Archangel—the bringer of visions to his characters, who move at the behest of his imagining. Yet in some respects he is no more than a witness to dreams that control him, and his characters draw things from him he does not know are there. To him Mahound is a kind of listener, while he is 'inside the Prophet' who elicits his revelations: 'I am bound to him, navel to navel. . . . We flow in both directions

along the umbilical cord' (112). This is palindromic dreaming, where
distinctions of dreamer and dreamed fall away. Gibreel is both inside
and outside the frame of the dream: if he brings visions they are
only within visions to which he is subject. Beyond conundrums of
the creative imagination, the 'frame' problem extends further. When
Mahound tests out the false or 'Satanic' verses of his recitation by
'wrestling' with Gibreel and—because Gibreel defeats him—proving
the authenticity of the text which replaces them, it is Gibreel who
points out the difficulty, that he is the 'source' of both versions: 'a
bit of a problem here, namely that *it was me both times, baba, me
first and second also me*' (126). In other words, there is no outside or
context to these versions, just as there is no outside to the dream, just
as Gibreel is both Gibreels. Not for the first (or last) time in this study,
the transnational is linked with the problem of the frame. There is no
outside from which to gain perspective, no fixed horizons, no vanishing
points. We navigate within the frame as if in a dream, sometimes
with its dizzying and frightening logic, sometimes with its intuitive
and prophetic mappings. If we try to 'fix' the mappings, we will lose
them.

8. January 1961 is when Chamcha—the 'spoon', the toady—first
arrives in Ellowen Deeowen, metamorphic version of (the letters of)
London. It is a year that, inverted, is palindromic. Time in general
is neither so simple nor elegant in the novel, and that means space
is not either. When Gibreel 'dreams' the Imam (an imam who in a
different version would become only too real in Rushdie's life), the
latter is prophet of the end of time, the Untime of a purified and
singular world without history. This is truly homogeneous time, the
bad version of the transnational; but it is not the time of the book.
Instead, both in the splits of the novel's dream-times and their intersection with its 'real' times, the novel's temporality is more asymmetrical,
criss-crossed. Though Gibreel's dreams will at moments dart into one
another—he will call to Mishal Sufyan in London, and the narrative
enters the world of Mishal Akhtar in Titlipur—this is not simultaneity
but connection (and diversion) across a gap. By the same token, the
novel's various dreamscapes—Jahilia, Titlipur, London—do not occur
in simultaneous space or time, nor is 'Mahound's' dreamtime an exact
replica of the real time of Muhammad. From one point of view these

timescapes (as in Phillips's work) are constellated—invoking distance, difference, transitions of a kind, even if the flash between them is as jagged and fast as lightning. But there is also a shadowed quality, an afterimage, as if one left its trace on the other. From this perspective these dream- and timescapes are plateaus of the uncanny, each a foreshadowing, each with a shadow world just beneath the surface. The home—whichever home—becomes doubled, tripled, the *unheimlich*, the 'unhomely': Freud's term is 'uncannily' appropriate.[21] This is the transnational as the uncanny of the national, but it is not easy space in which to live. 'Airstrip One, Mahagonny, Alphaville...Babel...'The gate of God." Babylondon' (474). In exploring the transnational, *The Satanic Verses* does not underestimate its unanchored and even alarming dimensions.

9. Doublings, triplings, everywhere. One character who is present only as a trace (Muhammad) is 'doubled' in the person (or at least the shadow-name) of 'Mahound', while the latter's followers, Khalid, Bilal, and 'some sort of bum from Persia by the outlandish name of Salman' (103), appear to overlap with the historical originals, and reappear fictionally in the Imam section.[22] A number of other characters also have the same names as one another: Chamcha's mother and stepmother are both Nasreen (I and II, respectively); Mishal is the daughter of Muhammad Sufyan in the London story, and wife of the Zamindar, Mirza Saeed Akhtar, in the Titlipur story. Ayesha is quadrupled: she is the Empress in the Imam story; the girl–visionary in the Titlipur story; the youngest wife of Mahound; and the youngest whore behind the Curtain in Jahilia. This last aspect constitutes one of the most daring doublings in the book—that the twelve whores in

---

[21] See the discussion of the uncanny in ch. 5.

[22] Bilal was the former slave who became Islam's first *muezzin*. According to tradition, Salman Al-Farsi (or Al-Farisi, 'the Persian') was the scribe to whom Muhammad dictated the Qur'an: Brennan, *Salman Rushdie*, 152. Also, John L. Esposito, ed., *Oxford Dictionary of Islam* (Oxford: Oxford University Press, 2003), *s.v.* 'Salman the Persian'; *Oxford Reference Online*, Oxford University Press, University of Massachusetts, Amherst, <http://www.oxfordreference.com> (accessed 9 February 2005). Khalid ibn Said was, according to several traditions, one of the early Companions of Muhammad; Khalid ibn al-Walid was a commander who first fought against Muhammad, but was later converted and led various campaigns (Muhammad called him 'the Sword of Allah', which suits his epithet in the novel as 'the General'). See H. A. R. Gibb *et al.*, eds, *The Encyclopaedia of Islam*, vol. 4 (Leiden: Brill, 1978), 927–8.

post-conversion Jahilia take on the names of Mahound's wives (who
have the same names as Muhammad's wives),[23] while the refugee poet
Baal takes Mahound's name himself. But if the Curtain represents the
ultimate chiastic inversion in the novel—night to day, vice to virtue—it
also slides away from simple opposition, as the multiplication of names
in the book suggests. For within the dreamscapes of the novel these are
copies which are not identical either to any original nor to one another,
yet where there are transitive, metamorphic continuities. Perhaps it is no
surprise that in a hostile world fiction leaked back into history as these
questions collapsed into more single-minded allegations of blasphemy
and travesty, a binary imagining of truth and falsity—a substitution for
the book itself.

10. As commentators have suggested, if *The Satanic Verses* is 'blasphemous' it is so only in the way that something that takes religion
seriously can be blasphemous.[24] Yet in effect its approach is much more
transitional than that. What are the claims of religion the novel explores?
Primarily the premises of the One and the Frame, which the novel takes
acutely enough to question. But it is a novel that by no means offers
itself as an alternate measure of truth. When the narrator allows himself
to enter Gibreel's dreamworld—appearing as a bespectacled, balding,
dandruff-ridden 'Supreme Being' on his bed, there is some question: is
he 'Ooparvala' (the fellow upstairs) or 'Neechayvala' (the one below)
(329)? And with the many hints as to his (possibly) Satanic self, a
different frame-problem arises: if not the liar's paradox, then what may
be termed the 'devil's paradox'. That is, how are we to take a story told

---

[23] There appears to be some variation in the number of Muhammad's wives (I have
seen lists of eleven, twelve, and thirteen); in *The Satanic Verses* by the time of the 'Return
to Jahilia' there are twelve wives of Mahound, while his first wife, Khadija, has long since
died. With some variation in spelling, all the wives listed on pp. 394–5 in the novel
are the same as Muhammad's wives. I am grateful to Mazen Naous for some of this
background.
[24] Sara Suleri remarks that *The Satanic Verses* is 'a deeply Islamic book' and comments
on the possibility that it shows 'the profound cultural fidelity represented by specific
acts of religious betrayal'. See Suleri, 'Contraband Histories: Salman Rushdie and the
Embodiment of Blasphemy', in *Reading Rushdie*, ed. Fletcher, 222. Brennan points out
that '[t]o betray a religion one has first to be a real part of it' (*Salman Rushdie*, 145).
Aamir Mufti argues that the novel is a Derridean 'supplement' to the totalizing narratives
of contemporary Islam: 'It is an act of "substitution" that undermines all essentialisms'
('Reading the Rushdie Affair', 112). But substitution may produce essentialisms of
another kind.

to us by the 'devil'? Or is that form of singularity, even at the level of narrative identity, simply not applicable?[25] In that regard the novel explores versions of continuity and connection across the various binary logics of our imaginings. Fairly early in the Mahound story the narrator asks the question, 'What is the opposite of faith?' The answer comes that it is 'Not disbelief. Too final, certain, closed. Itself a kind of belief,' but 'Doubt' (94). Doubt, exists on a metonymic continuum between belief and disbelief. It participates in both, a point of intersection that allows the two to communicate, just as Satan remains the angel who fell. This combination of belief/doubt also provides the novel with its traditional formula for storytelling: believe-don't-believe; 'It was so, it was not'; '*Kan ma kan/Fi qadim azzaman*' (147). And so Salman the scribe, the 'immigrant bum from Persia', will alter the recitation of Mahound to test doubt, just as another migrant Salman alters the original story of Muhammad to inhabit the territory of translation, transformation, and search. In that regard the narrator—the voice of narration—is neither the devil's nor the angel's but the voice of the writer in all its metonymies, displacements, and navigations. It is a different form of divination.

11. The book is generous towards belief. Ayesha, Mahound's wife, has the last word on his death, affirming that if her husband has died, God still lives; and the pilgrims of Titlipur walk through the Arabian sea on their way to Mecca.[26] For Rushdie, a fabulous writer in every sense, fable is the mode which enables that mix of doubt–belief, and the fables of this book are one of its most powerful elements. In the image of the pilgrims walking through the sea we understand metamorphosis as the very mode of fable—Ovid's mode, a way of writing, seeing, storytelling that links the real to the non-real, the ordinary to the mutable to the transcendent. Yet such fables can also tell the story of illusion. Ayesha leads the pilgrims through the waters of purification towards Mecca— and they drown, or do not drown. In allowing this doubleness, the fable belies the unitary quest of the pure. It participates in their purity— those magnificent images of the butterfly girl—but encompasses them

---

[25] Booker points out that in the novel 'God and Satan are indistinguishable, irrevocably intertwined, and the narrator himself does nothing to clear up the confusion' ('Beauty and the Beast', 247).

[26] For the 'original' of this event (the 'Hawkes Bay case' of 1983), see Suleri, 'Contraband Histories', 232.

in a different kind of morphology. The Imam drinks water for purity, Ayesha and the pilgrims march through it, but for the novel water is the language of the dream.

12. This may have a bearing on Gibreel and his fate. For Gibreel there is no resolution, at least not one which allows for transition in his life. Unable to separate himself from the Archangel (the one substituted for the other), he ends in madness and suicide. This is a high price to pay in a novel which can make anything happen, and may seem unjust. Yet there is a logic here. For Gibreel is (finally) Lucretian, Chamcha (finally) Ovidian. Gibreel, consigned to substitution, the fixity of identity, proves the Lucretian point: whatever goes beyond its boundaries dies. Chamcha is initially Lucretian, attempting to discard his former self. He goes through hell, becomes demonic, but *accepting* the self in metamorphosis can recover, find peace, reconnect with his former life. Lucretian identity will bring disaster, the Ovidian allows malleability and boundaries that can be navigated through life—a version of identity for a world beyond fixed mappings.

13. Yet from another point of view—the narrative that can make anything happen—Gibreel's fate shows something else. Finally, Gibreel is left out of the frame, unconsoled, unresolved, irremediable. Again we have the novel's shift towards asymmetry. Not all 'Xs' are crossed, not all journeys successfully revisited, there can be serious ruptures in the grammar of the self, as well as the sense of belonging. Rushdie pays tribute to the principle of excess in a different way: what overflows or is left out of our stories—also part of a transnational picture.

14. How does newness come into the world? The novel has answered its question, but only through a dizzying array of possibilities, morphologies, and disjunctions. *The Satanic Verses* has recognized the fuller import of the more buoyant visions of *Midnight's Children*. Yet the intrinsic thrust of the two novels towards alternation, combination, overflow, has remained consistent and deepened—a vision for a transitive and transnational world. Underlying it all is an eternal tale of transition. Towards the end of *The Satanic Verses* Chamcha visits his dying father, Changez, an episode apparently written after the death of Rushdie's own father.[27] It is a moment at peace with

---

[27] See Ian Hamilton, 'The First Life of Salman Rushdie', *New Yorker*, 25 December 1995 and 1 January 1996, 108–09.

itself and strangely radiant, and it prefaces Chamcha's acceptance of his own mutabilities. 'Changez': the Indian name morphs its reality into English. A world of 'Changes' is a world of mortality, but that too has its secret. Accepting death, we try not to hold on to ourselves, our territory, our belonging, and that means others may have space for their own.

# 4

# Vertical and Horizontal

*Charlotte Brontë, Jean Rhys, and Anne Michaels*

I longed only for what suited me—for the Antipodes of the Creole:
and I longed vainly.

> Rochester, in Charlotte Brontë, *Jane Eyre*

Je regrette l'Europe aux anciens parapets!

> Arthur Rimbaud, 'Le Bateau Ivre'

It stands to reason that resemblance does not necessarily appear
where there is kinship.

> Walter Benjamin, 'The Task of the Translator'

So far we have seen the transnational in a variety of aspects. We have
explored it along waterways that both connect and divide an earth without fixed horizon: patterns of navigation that always apply, no matter
how our frameworks might change. We have seen it as a constellation of
broken routes across multiple timescapes both within and beyond the
visible of the national. We have followed it as a version of identity that
cannot be contained, whether in personal or national terms—a vision
both exhilarating and daunting. In all these forms the transnational is
still a space of exploration, a world both within and beyond our reach,
a place of intimation, possibility.

Now we need to consider it from yet another angle—one that initially invokes the impossible rather than the possible. For the question
must arise, what happens when many of the themes discussed so far—
metonymy, contiguity, transition, navigation—become bordered and
blocked? How does this happen and why, and what effects does it
have both in personal and wider terms? What is the nature of the

boundary in such conditions, and what are its larger consequences? And because we are interested not only in pathologies, can we draw more hopeful conclusions, not only despite but *because* of the implications of these dynamics? Sometimes, as in other investigations, one comes to understand the positive and functional by examining the fractured and broken.

These are some of the issues this chapter sets out to explore by considering three novels. Two of them are directly related: Charlotte Brontë's *Jane Eyre* and Jean Rhys's *Wide Sargasso Sea*. The third— *Fugitive Pieces*, by Anne Michaels—is not related at all, except implicitly by way of these themes. For, beyond questions of topic, all three novels are linked through deep imaginative structures concerned with a matrix first mentioned in the Introduction to this book: the horizontal, and vertical. Part of its significance was also suggested there, and can be given in a kind of shorthand here. Both within the psyche and beyond, vertical and horizontal are interrelated, indeed dynamically so. The horizontal involves the possibility of navigation, while the vertical has a bearing on, and depends on, that possibility. Where horizontal connection is prevented, vertical alignments—of repression, substitution, sacrifice— result. Similarly, where repression, substitution, sacrifice exist, horizontal connection is either prevented or permitted only in pathological forms. But where trauma or damage has produced repression or sacrifice, opening up horizontal boundaries admits healing, navigation, connection.

These processes are complex, but remarkably insistent, and we see them at work in these novels—all of which involve transnational dimensions. In this way we enter into territory that is at one and the same time symbolic, psychological, and cultural, linked to broader imaginaries of self, time, and space. The idea is to proceed from pathology—the dysfunctional grammars of identity both explored and embedded in *Jane Eyre* and *Wide Sargasso Sea*—to the potential for recuperation heralded in *Fugitive Pieces*. Loosely, this corresponds to the transition from a damaged world of nationality towards transnational possibility. Along the way we discover something about the mechanisms of a grammar of identity—how it actually *works* in and towards a transnational world. Here patterns present but less overt in the other novels in this study become more explicit.

*Wide Sargasso Sea* is of course a celebrated response to *Jane Eyre*, and so these two novels exist along a spectrum of imagining, reimagining, and realignment. There was something Jean Rhys saw in Brontë's novel that she wanted to rewrite. The reasons probably had much to do with her own life, and so it is worth considering aspects of that too, under the rubric of the horizontal and the impossible.

## JEAN RHYS: NOT *BÉKÉ* LIKE YOU

One cannot tell the whole story, but let us consider the following patterns.

She was born Ella Gwendoline Rees Williams (a name she changed) on the island of Dominica, and from her early years came lasting imprints. Her mother was distant and intimidating, beating Ella, and telling her she would never 'learn to be like other people'.[1] On her mother's side, Rhys came from a long-standing slave-owning Dominican patrimony, something of which she was deeply ashamed. Yet no alternative version of identity was available. Rhys recorded how her Dominican nanny and surrogate mother, Meta (the original for Christophine in *Wide Sargasso Sea*), filled her with terror, telling her of zombies, souciants, loup-garoux, and fearful cockroaches whose bites would never heal.[2] In some ways, the young Ella longed to be black, and felt that blacks were 'more alive, more a part of the place than we were', but there could be no miraculous transformation. Once she and her sister were given dolls: her sister's was black, and hers white, but she wanted the black one, so she took hers outside and smashed it with a large stone—a strangely metonymic response of and towards the self.[3] Sometimes that sense of metonymy was expressed in other ways. When Rhys was young, and looking at a photograph of herself, she realized with some melancholy that the dress was still the same, but the person wearing it had changed.[4] In one of her short stories, 'A Solid

---

[1] Carol Angier, *Jean Rhys: Life and Work* (Boston: Little, Brown, 1990), 24. Much of my information on Rhys comes from Angier's biography.

[2] Jean Rhys, *Smile Please: An Unfinished Autobiography* (London: Andre Deutsch, 1979), 30.

[3] Rhys, *Smile Please*, 50, 39–40.    [4] Rhys, *Smile Please*, 19–20.

House', when the heroine wants to commit suicide, she feels 'I must wear my pretty dress for this'.[5] Here we see metonymy not so much as the means of attachment but more profoundly as a sign of the *need* for it.

For that is the developing theme, of the desire for connection, and the lack of it. When Rhys left Dominica for England at the age of sixteen, the syndrome was only reinforced. She suffered endless cold in the succession of boarding houses she slept in as a chorus girl. She plumbed the depths at a young age, living as a kept woman for a while, at times on the verge of prostitution—the life she wrote about in *Voyage in the Dark*. That was when she had an abortion—her 'illegal operation' as she called it—and as for being kept (primarily by the early love of her life, Lancelot Smith), she wrote that she got quite used 'to changing that cheque, because you can get used to anything'.[6] She moved once again, to the continent, and entered into the affair with Ford Madox Ford that also introduced her to a world of writers and writing, but her life remained chaotic. Her first husband, John (or Jean, or Johan) Lenglet, was jailed in the 1930s for reasons that probably involved theft or currency dealings. When Rhys gave birth, she and her husband had to leave their daughter in a clinic because they could not afford to take care of her.

Afterwards, back in England, the story became, if anything, even more dismal. From the late 1940s to early 1950s Rhys faced a steady succession of court appearances for aggressive and disorderly behaviour—throwing a brick through a neighbour's window, physically attacking her lodgers, railing outside the Beckenham police station that '[y]ou can't get justice. This country is run by rotten stinking Jews.'[7] Her third husband, Max Hamer, like Lenglet before him, was imprisoned on financial charges, and Rhys was remanded to the medical wing of Holloway Prison. By 1966 Rhys had been moving from one leaky shack to another, trying to complete *Wide Sargasso Sea*, still in virtually endless

---

[5] For some of these 'dress patterns', both fictional and non-fictional, see Angier, *Jean Rhys*, 417–18, 521. Later, finding the right cheap pretty dress in a window was Rhys's spur to finishing *Wide Sargasso Sea*, and in the novel Antoinette's dresses are used in a metonymic way.

[6] Rhys, *Smile Please*, 122.

[7] Angier, *Jean Rhys*, 453. This whole alarming segment of Rhys's life is dealt with in Part 3, ch. 2 of Angier's book.

conflict with her neighbours (on whom she depended). When Hamer—recently released from prison—was ill and dying, he would put up his umbrella in hospital when it rained because he expected to get wet.[8] At times Rhys confronted her failings and anguish. 'There is something as unstable as water about me,' she remarked. Or, reversing the image, she described herself as 'Le Bateau Ivre as well as the Volga boatman but always a boat for some reason and in stormy weather too.'[9] Of one suicidal moment she wrote, 'I would never belong anywhere, and I knew it, and all my life would be the same, trying to belong and failing. . . . I am a stranger and I always will be, and after all I didn't really care.'[10] But she ended that episode, as she recalled, in a fit of gleeful drunken defiance with a friend.

Suffering and making others suffer: there are monstrous aspects to Rhys's story, and if she recognized something in Brontë's Bertha—isolated, confined, demonized—perhaps this had a good deal to do with it. But beyond that was another dimension which one can describe as a breakdown in personal geography, without continuity, transition, connection. Decades later Caribbean writers such as Jean Bernabé, Patrick Chamoiseau, and Raphaël Confiant could develop a notion of *créolité* that was celebratory and triumphant in its combinatory possibilities. Like the archipelago of islands strung out across the Caribbean sea, identity for them was composite, drawing on the region's multifarious roots, routes, and histories.[11] But this was not the case for Jean Rhys. For her no combination or substitution would work. She had not felt at home in the Caribbean, she could not connect the Caribbean with England, England could not replace the world she had left behind. In *Wide Sargasso Sea*, Christophine describes Antoinette to her husband: 'She is not *béké* like you, but she is *béké*, and not like us either.'[12] *Béké* is white, foreign: Antoinette, like Rhys, is in the non-place of identity,

    [8] Angier, *Jean Rhys*, 524.

    [9] Respectively, Rhys, *Smile Please*, 123, and Rhys to Francis Wyndham [14 May 1964], in Jean Rhys, *Letters, 1931–1966*, ed. Francis Wyndham and Diana Melly (London: André Deutsch, 1984), 276.

    [10] Rhys, *Smile Please*, 124.

    [11] Jean Bernabé, Patrick Chamoiseau, and Raphaël Confiant, *Éloge de la Créolité*, trans. M. B. Taleb-Khyar (Paris: Gallimard, 1993).

    [12] Jean Rhys, *Wide Sargasso Sea*, Judith L. Raiskin ed., *Norton Critical Edition* (New York and London: Norton, 1999), 93. Henceforth referenced as *WSS*.

between but not connective, contiguous but not transitive. Rhys was the non-Creole in Dominica, the monstrous Creole in England.

Some of this was reinforced for Rhys on her sole return to Dominica in 1935, where she found mainly a sense of rupture and loss. She visited Geneva, the ancestral slave estate which had passed down to her family. In 1844 the house had been burned down by labourers, during a riot following rumours that slavery was to be reinstated. In the early 1930s it had burned down once again, and Rhys now confronted the ruins: '[T]here was nothing, nothing,' she wrote. 'Nothing to look at. Nothing to say.'[13] On that trip Rhys wanted to take her second husband, Leslie Tilden-Smith, across the island on the old Imperial Road, but the road had disappeared, and the trip was a calamitous one.[14] The moment appears emblematic: the Caribbean island had broken down the 'Imperial Road'; it was a road that could not even connect the island's two sides. On board ship to Dominica, Rhys had discovered another barrier as they entered the Sargasso Sea with its floating and ensnaring weeds. As her biographer Carol Angier puts it, 'the image was fixed in her mind of a bar: a place where sea and air conspired to stop you, to prevent passage from the West Indies to England, from England to the West Indies.'[15]

Rhys could not conjoin the different parts of her life; continuity and connection were barred. Yet where that occurred, a different kind of syntax could take over. From the historic fire at Geneva to the more recent one, to a famous fictional fire involving a Creole woman from the West Indies, Rhys's imagination sparked. She gave a number of reasons why she turned to the story of the 'first Mrs Rochester' in *Jane Eyre*, and part of it clearly was a wish to rethink everything it suppressed. 'I've never believed in Charlotte's lunatic,' she wrote to Diana Athill, 'that's why I wrote this book and really what a *devil* it's been.'[16] But beneath, beyond, and enclosing that were the possibilities and impossibilities of navigation to which she herself had been subject, and which she had to reveal and revise in Brontë's novel.

---

[13] Details on Geneva and Rhys's trip: Angier, *Jean Rhys*, 7, 357; also, Rhys, *Smile Please*, 37–8. Rhys appeared to be uncertain whether the house had been burned down two or three times.

[14] Angier, *Jean Rhys*, 356.    [15] Angier, *Jean Rhys*, 352.

[16] The quotations come, in reverse order, from Rhys to Athill, 15 February [1966] and 20 [February 1966], in Rhys, *Letters*, 296, 297.

## GHOST IN THE NATIONAL
## MACHINE: *JANE EYRE*

There is a transnational secret at the heart of *Jane Eyre*, and her name is Bertha Mason. That much is clear. What may be less clear, at least initially, is how far Bertha's presence and fate are connected with patterns of the horizontal and vertical—and how they are in turn connected with that secret. We can see this by seeking out some of the essentials in the novel.

For the matrix underlies so much in the story, as if Brontë could not do without it. Consider various moments. The novel opens with Jane in a small breakfast room *adjoining* the drawing room from which her aunt, Mrs Reed, has excluded her.[17] There is a horizontal contiguity, in other words, but also division; Jane is (as Homi Bhabha might put it) *'almost the same, but not quite'* in this family.[18] The Reeds live, as Sandra Gilbert and Susan Gubar are attuned to, at Gateshead;[19] in the breakfast room Jane sits on a window seat, where she looks through 'clear panes of glass, protecting, but not separating me from the drear November day'.[20] Gates and windows: Jane occupies threshold positions; the vertical gives a glimpse of, but contains, the horizontal. Later, Jane makes her way across the landscape of England to various places which offer refuge but also confinement. The school at Lowood offers little escape for young girls but death and (as in the case of Helen Burns) heaven—both down and up at the same time. When Jane flees Thornfield Hall she makes her way to Marsh End, where she finds the family she discovers to be, obliquely, her own: Diana, Mary, St John. But even this is not without its dangers, for St John wants to press

---

[17] Gayatri Chakravorty Spivak mentions this point in 'Three Women's Texts and a Critique of Imperialism', *Critical Inquiry*, 12/1 (1985): 246.

[18] Homi Bhabha, 'Of Mimicry and Man: The Ambivalence of Colonial Discourse', in *The Location of Culture* (London and New York: Routledge, 1994), 86. Helpfully, for my discussion in this chapter, Bhabha indicates that '[i]n mimicry, the reproduction of identity and meaning is rearticulated along the axis of metonymy' (90). Elsewhere, Bhabha writes of 'the metonymy of the substitutive chain of ethical and cultural discourse' (91), but in Jakobson's model metonymy and the substitutive are opposed.

[19] Sandra M. Gilbert and Susan Gubar, *The Madwoman in the Attic: The Woman Writer and the Nineteenth-Century Literary Imagination*, 2nd edn (New Haven and London: Yale University Press, 2000), 342.

[20] Charlotte Brontë, *Jane Eyre*, ed. Richard J. Dunn, 3rd edn, *Norton Critical Edition* (New York: Norton, 2001), 5–6. Henceforth referenced as *JE*.

her into marriage and missionary work—subjection to his will (down) and service to God (up). Nothing sets off this sense of horizontal and vertical more than the battlements of Thornfield Hall where Jane paces, musing on the fate of women and their desire for action. Here is the threshold again: the battlements rise above the manor, and Jane has glimpses of horizons, possibility. Yet vertical walls contain her, and they also contain a hidden secret—the madwoman whose laugh Jane hears, whose location is 'up' on the third floor, yet which has the feel of 'down', like a dungeon.

In all these ways, there is an impulse to the horizontal blocked by limits which are often vertical, or have vertical implications. The ultimate—broken—horizontal syntax in this regard concerns the suppressed links among the novel's characters: Jane, Grace Poole, the 'madwoman', Rochester. There are mirrorings and intimations everywhere. Jane, like Grace, is a plain, solitary, female servant. Grace is Bertha's prison-keeper, as is Rochester. Rochester cross-dresses in the 'gypsy' scene with Jane, becoming, like Bertha, the masculine-feminine and (in his case) morally monstrous. Of course the deepest and most hidden metonymic link is between Jane herself and Bertha—as Gilbert and Gubar put it, Jane's 'truest and darkest double'.[21] This is a connection that cannot be recognized, and is therefore suppressed within the larger system that is Thornfield Hall. But where suppression exists—pushing 'down' on the vertical axis—there is the constant threat of return: Grace's laugh, her spectral emanations, hints of the horizontal reflections in the mirror which could be Jane's own. The vertical can also return from a different direction, as we see after the evening in the orchard when Rochester finally asks Jane to marry him; that night a bolt of lightning strikes the horse-chestnut tree, splitting it in half. The lightning comes from heaven as if to say such a connection between Jane and Rochester is forbidden unless the wider links in their syntactic line are confronted and acknowledged. From this point of view there is what we might term a 'projection principle' in the novel, and it works in two ways. Any horizontal impetus, when blocked, converts into a vertical dynamic of repression, return, or some other manifestation. Similarly,

---

[21] See the discussion in Gilbert and Gubar, *Madwoman*, 359–62. Gilbert and Gubar are of course very good on many of these patterns, and I am in some respects following them, though pursuing their logic of 'doubling' in a different direction.

the vertical—whether acting from 'down' or 'up'—has significant horizontal implications.

The novel takes these matters even further in its geographies of the self, particularly in relation to the Caribbean. Here *Jane Eyre* both reveals certain syndromes *and* is subject to them, participating in patterns it otherwise decries. In general, the West Indies are figured in the novel as unstable, female, hot, and insane, all in contrast to Europe, and especially to England. Some of the implications of this, and some of its mechanisms, become apparent in one emblematic episode when Rochester recounts his past to Jane. Here Rochester remembers how he was woken one night by Bertha's mad yells. It was the kind of 'fiery West Indian night', he tells Jane, that frequently preceded 'the hurricanes of those climates'. He opened a window, only to let in the foul atmosphere, while inside all he could hear was Bertha's foul vocabulary, 'the thin partitions of the West India house opposing but slight obstruction to her wolfish cries' (*JE*, 262). The setting could not be clearer. The partition between Rochester and Bertha is 'thin'. He is separate from her, but too close. There is a contiguity Rochester cannot admit; he fears what Bhabha calls the menace of metonymy, enacted here in the colonial setting.[22] But relief is on the way. 'A wind fresh from Europe blew over the ocean and rushed through the open casement.' The Atlantic 'was thundering in glorious liberty'. 'I reasoned thus, Jane ... it was true Wisdom that consoled me in that hour. ... "Go," said Hope, "and live again in Europe" ' (*JE*, 263). This is then the pattern: where the direct horizontal connection is threatening, a more distant—racial and national one—will intervene to save, but only by suppressing the immediate link. It is as if a middle term on the spectrum drops away, allowing those on either side to close up, forming more congenial bonds, but it can only happen through violence. This is the logic whereby 'thin' partitions must become walls—thick and heavy—in order to maintain racial and national identity. Reason, hope, consolation: these are vastly superior to the other part of the self one may find behind the thin partition or across the tropical sea. The Antipodes of the Creole Rochester longs for are also the Antipodes of the self—at least any self he might discover in the Caribbean.

---

[22] See Bhabha, 'Of Mimicry and Man', 88, 91; for Bhabha, these manifestations are primarily discursive, and doubled, split.

What happens to Bertha, therefore, has substantial implications not only for the novel but in wider understandings of a grammar of identity. Here, par excellence, is the Freudian *délire du toucher*—both the neurosis and the taboo of touching which cannot bear contagion.[23] The taboo—product of the unconscious—sets up the boundary; the boundary reinforces the dynamic of the taboo. The ramifications in a transnational context are considerable, for here we see not only how intransitive boundaries are structured by the unconscious. Equally importantly, we see how this form of the unconscious is *structured by intransitive boundaries*. Wherever such boundaries are established, it is only on the basis of repression or some other form of elision, but this will always have consequences—of secrecy, volatility, return. Here we see how boundaries of this kind have both internal and external dimensions, operating both within the mind and in the external world. Just as internal boundaries are externalized, so external taboos become internal boundaries, in an unstable yet self-reinforcing system. In this perspective, and most profoundly, *Jane Eyre* intimates what *Wide Sargasso Sea* makes more overt: in a transnational world, cartography is also a mapping of the psyche, in all its complex dynamics of fear and rejection, the realities of suppression and return as well as possibilities of connection.

We can also see the pattern more technically, in terms of the grammar we have been using. For instance, *combination* between Rochester and Bertha is clearly impossible; this is a syntax Rochester will not permit. At the same time, beyond the boundary he constructs, Bertha represents an illicit *combination*. In particular, she is the male/female/black-white/animal (we remember her bloated features, her purple visage, her wolf-like cries; if nothing else, this is the Freudian contagion, which as we know works by a kind of negative metonymy). But Bertha—who she is, who she might be—also becomes a function of *substitution*: the forbidden compound, the $x-y-z$ that substitutes for her. Or, we might say even more precisely, *she becomes subject to a substitution effect*, as the illicit combination is invented and substituted for her in a particularly threatening form. No matter who Bertha is or might be, it is the space of this effect she must occupy in a wider system, and as for where that space is, Brontë has given it physical form. It is no more or less than

---

[23] See the discussion on *Totem and Taboo* in the Introduction to this book.

Bertha's walled-up quarters within Thornfield Hall—the unconscious of the regime that contains her. Here Freud's axes and Jakobson's come together, both the psychic and the syntactic: the logic of repression, the workings of substitution, the inherent instabilities of the result—all situated around questions of identity in a national and transnational setting. We can understand the Freudian dynamic as having navigational aspects, its own version of a generative grammar of identity, and vice versa.

If these are major revelations for a novel published in the 1840s—pre-Freud, pre-Jakobson, almost pre-everything—it has to be said they are expressed mainly symptomatically, because for the most part *Jane Eyre* subscribes to the syndromes it cannot fully confront. Because of the novel's predilections—Jane must marry Rochester, a certain version of identity result—it has to propose a specific geometry in seeking resolution. Here, as in the case of Rochester himself, the pattern entails suppression—specifically, of Bertha. In this regard, the realities are clear. Given the series of implicit metonymies between Jane, Bertha, and Rochester—each linked with the other in different ways—in this triad Bertha must be repressed for any alliance between Jane and Rochester to result. In this way, far from being the connective link between Jane and Rochester, Bertha instead becomes the *trace*—the hidden and then excluded term that permits Jane and Rochester's full association. The spectrum closes up, and even the usual consequence—Bertha becomes *spectral*—is overcome, because ultimately she is eradicated entirely. Bertha's substitution at the end becomes her complete evisceration, which allows the happy couple to unite, over her dead body, as it were. At that point the vertical for Bertha may be hell or heaven, but mostly it does not matter; the significant thing is that she is simply *not there*. She is the absence in a syntactic combination marked only by its removal, so that Jane can say successfully, 'Reader, I married him.' If this reminds us of anything, it is why combination *as such* is not always to be trusted, in matters of identity as elsewhere; we need to understand, too, its hidden and sacrificial traces, or the pathological repressions on which it may be founded.

Moreover, these resolutions in the novel evidently have national and transnational implications. By the end of the novel, Jane has come into her independent income, to place her on a par with Rochester. If she has always shown a 'masculine' mental autonomy, he is now 'feminized' in his weakened state. The vertical—the heavens—approve this parity and alliance: God has 'tempered justice with mercy' (*JE*, 385), and Jane and Rochester set up at Ferndean to live with good hope for the future. There are some strengths in this vision: Brontë has shown how pride will have its comeuppance; the thicker the walls of secrecy, the more certainly they will come down; the repressed will return with violence to meet the violence of its repression. And yet at another level the novel has simply repeated the pattern. If, in the words of the proverb, an Englishman's home is his castle, Brontë has brought the house down only to reconstitute it on more acceptable foundations. Ferndean is not Thornfield Hall; it is more modest, more moral, more equitable in gender terms. Yet it is *adjacent*, contiguous, near to Thornfield, 'almost the same, but not quite', a version not of menace but renewal. The novel has embodied a form of, if not renovation, then at least a project of *home improvement*, which in some ways makes the result even more properly national. It has established a metonymy that overcomes a dangerous and intrusive element through its suppression and then eradication. But this prevents an even more wide-ranging spectrum of recognition, simply inconceivable to the novel.

What that recognition might be is intimated by what is left out. *Jane Eyre* has shown a Caribbean presence at the heart of the national, which within a logic of public consciousness and recognition must be hidden, contained, and repressed. And yet the novel reproduces that repression. Bertha is the 'ghost' in the national machine, the secret that allows it to work in both psychic and symbolic terms—but only by remaining the hidden trace, the threatening and then elided term. Brontë might have been horrified to think of it this way, but in effect the novel has practised a form of immigration control, even a kind of ethnic cleansing, purifying the national body by sacrificing the alien.[24] If Jane, or Rochester, or Brontë herself had been able to understand their implicit connections with Bertha, this would have been a different novel, and Europe might have had a different history. But they did not, and this is the fiction as well as the history we have. Jane, as we understand her, can exist only in the absence of Bertha. She comes

[24] Spivak sees the Creole woman as the sacrificial figure for *Jane Eyre*'s 'feminist individualist' resolution; and, as she suggests, the imperial 'work of conscience' will continue in India through the missionary quest of St John. See 'Three Women's Texts', 248–51.

to replace Bertha's memory, except as a threat overcome, as a wound that is healed. She replaces her as well in the national imaginary, as the transnational is sacrificed to the national. In *Jane Eyre* we see with a tremendous clarity how the repression of the transnational is specifically what *allows* the national to be sustained.

## TRANSNATIONAL DREAMING: *WIDE SARGASSO SEA*

Perhaps it was because of the topic—which was not only topic, but topos, topography, topology—that when Jean Rhys turned to the story of *Jane Eyre*, it became a work of rewriting and revision but also repetition. This had to do not only with the details of the story but also its underlying matrices, which remained in place though its points of focus and implication shifted. *Wide Sargasso Sea* was in some respects a modernist undertaking with postcolonial and gendered inflections—rewriting the classic prior text, here not of the travelling male hero who returns home by sea, but of the creole female whose passage beyond or over the sea is only one of confinement. The novel was in its own way an act of translation, but if so, then in Walter Benjamin's enlightening sense, not a substitution or imitation, but fitting the fragments of a broken vessel together, making up a larger language, a larger narrative of which both texts are a part.[25] It was—and is—a form of textual navigation, even if it described impossible navigations.

'They say when trouble comes close ranks, and so the white people did. But we were not in their ranks.' This is how *Wide Sargasso Sea* opens, in the voice of Antoinette Cosway. As we might now expect, based on the precedents we have seen in *Jane Eyre*, it is a statement that invokes both adjacency (closing ranks) and exclusion ('we were not in their ranks'). In this regard Antoinette is already the trace that

---

[25] In this way both the original and the translation become 'recognizable as fragments of a greater language, just as fragments are part of a vessel'. Walter Benjamin, 'The Task of the Translator', in *Selected Writings*, vol. 1: *1913–1926*, ed. Marcus Bullock and Michael W. Jennings (Cambridge, MA and London: Belknap Press, 1996), 260. For Derek Walcott's gloss on Benjamin's image in his Nobel Prize Speech, as well as an exploration of Walcott's poetry in terms congenial to this chapter, see Nicole Matos, ' "Join, Interchangeable Phantoms": From Metaphor to Metonymy in Walcott's *Omeros*', *Small Axe*, 10/2 (2006): 40–60.

Bertha becomes, the suppressed term that both permits and establishes a horizontal alignment among those who are 'like' one another. But if Rhys repeats Brontë's law of the excluded middle in matters of identity, she also shifts it overtly in a direction only implicit in her model—the direction of race. For if those who close ranks are white people, then *ipso facto*, those who are excluded cannot properly be white. Already Antoinette is the 'almost the same, but not quite' in this context: hers is the metonymy of menace, as far as both the whites and blacks around her are concerned—the contagion, the reflection, the fear. Antoinette remarks that her family lives in the Garden of Eden, 'large and beautiful as that garden in the Bible—the tree of life grew there. But it had gone wild' (*WSS*, 10–11). The branches of the tree are rhizomatic, connective, syntactic, but also uncontrolled—precisely what those around the Cosways reject by way of contact.

Some of the complexities of this dynamic are apparent from the start. Antoinette, projected as menace by others, also feels them as threat. Consequently (and with some reason) her version of safety becomes the vertical: 'The barrier of the cliffs and the high mountains. And the barrier of the sea. I am safe. I am safe from strangers' (*WSS*, 16). Cliffs have height and the sea has depth as well as distance, but if Antoinette is safe from strangers, these barriers also make her the stranger who must be kept from others. In this regard the sea is conceived by the characters of this novel in much the same way as Rochester (and Brontë) did in *Jane Eyre*. It is *not* a space of transition, a connective, transitive boundary, but a boundary of division across which acts of normalization and suppression take place. So, Mr Mason's idea is to take Antoinette's retarded brother, Pierre, to England, where (in a repetition of Rhys's mother's fear regarding her daughter) he will be 'cured, made like other people' (*WSS*, 22). And of course Antoinette is taken to England if not to be cured, then to 'disappear'—which may amount to the same thing. The intransitive boundary, if crossed, is elided *as* transition: to be 'made like other people' is in effect to be made the *same*—to be substituted, suppressed, depersonalized. Or it is to remain forever the alien, another form of depersonalization. In these terms the intransitive boundary *creates* the intransitive identity, and it does so in ways that have national and transnational implications. Crossing without transition is a form of tautology or substitution—same for same, like for other.

Part of Rhys's achievement in the novel is to show how these dynamics are always intricately personal, where one syndrome may be overlaid on another. So, within her own family, Antoinette experiences all the patterns of connection and rejection that will later on be reinforced by Rochester.[26] She has no contact with her brother—the figure already 'disappeared', gone away. But her mother prefers this elided figure to the live flesh and blood of her daughter. She is the one who, when Antoinette says 'I am here', responds 'No'—a rejection both of her existence and her location: a location of contiguity, touch, linkage (*WSS*, 28–9). This occurs after the fire at Coulibri, when Antoinette visits her mother Annette at the house where she is cared for (shades of Bertha, and a prefiguring of Antoinette's future). But the mother rebuffs her daughter and flings her 'against the partition'. Rhys read Brontë carefully, and the image is not accidental: as in *Jane Eyre*, the West Indian partition signifies both the reality of proximity and the deep impulse to divide. There is a further dimension in this incident, for in Antoinette's description to Rochester, she tells how she saw her mother's black caregiver kiss Annette lasciviously—a moment when 'normal' boundaries seem to be completely overridden. This seems to be a rule in *Wide Sargasso Sea*: either contact is impossible, or it is deeply threatening and—as here—laden with racial and sexual overtones. In this regard, Rhys's novel, like *Jane Eyre* before it, is also subject to the patterns it analyses. In *Wide Sargasso Sea* the resolutions of the syntactic are both tantalizing and fearful, fascinating and repellent, invoked as well as rejected across boundaries either too open or impermeable.

In racial terms, these patterns configure a series of possible/impossible combinations. Given her own history, Rhys is of course fully alive to Antoinette's complex status as a white 'creole' (one of the provisional titles for the novel). Yet it seems for that very reason Antoinette's identity is one where any combinatory amalgam is unattainable. This is the significance of Christophine's remark to Rochester, that Antoinette is 'not *béké* like you, but she is *béké*, and not like us either'. Here the spectrum of possibilities inherent in the terms 'creole'—from white to black and anywhere in-between—and *béké* become versions of non-definition,

---

[26] I call the character 'Rochester' in the novel despite the fact that he is never named, because this is evidently the point of reference. To call him 'The Man' as some critics do seems to me to replicate the kind of substitutive logic I am arguing against in this book.

non-identity.[27] Antoinette is the doubly 'not-like', the 'almost the same, but not quite' in two directions, leaving her in a space of suspension, in between. This absence, this intransitive space, may be also why the novel stresses what we might call the 'contradictory category' when it comes to questions of identity—the 'white niggers' and 'black Englishmen' who seem to be rejected all round. Antoinette faces all this directly. When she explains the meaning of Amélie's 'white cockroach' song to Rochester, she says, 'That's what they call all of us who were here before their own people in Africa sold them to the slave traders. And I've heard English women call us white niggers. So between you I often wonder who I am and where is my country and where do I belong...' (*WSS*, 61). Here the very syntax of Antoinette's language—the 'between you I'— expresses it all: the proximity, the suspended and displaced term 'I', the element that should be connective subject instead to disappearance, division.

If Rhys works and reworks this territory in the novel, it must be because, drawing on her own experience, for her it was *the* central problem of identity without solution: the syntactic or horizontal impulse that can find no fulfilment, and which therefore appears in the novel only in insistent and partly symptomatic display. It is evident in some of the key moments of *Wide Sargasso Sea*, none more so than the climax in Antoinette's relationship with Tia, the young black girl who is sister, friend, and enemy because of these possible impossibilities. Indeed, the structure of their relationship is similar to that between Jane and Bertha in *Jane Eyre*, though shifted along the racial spectrum. In this novel, Tia steals Antoinette's dress—the metonymic attachment which now becomes an object of appropriation. After the fire at Coulibri, when Antoinette sees Tia and runs towards her, Tia throws the stone which hits Antoinette. The famous passage concludes: 'I looked at her and I saw her face crumple up as she began to cry. We stared at each other, blood on my face, tears on hers. It was as if I saw myself. Like in a looking-glass' (*WSS*, 27). The transactions here are reasonably complex. There are figurations of 'likeness', which might invoke possibilities of connection. But likeness is also reversal, because 'like' in a mirror is always reversed. There are 'blood' and 'tears', both bodily fluids but

---

[27] For one discussion of the 'inherently unstable category' of the creole, see H. Adlai Murdoch, 'Rhys's Pieces: Unhomeliness as Arbiter of Caribbean Creolization', *Callaloo*, 26/1 (2003): 253–4.

different; blood a sign of life as well as death; tears of guilt as well as pain. Most directly, there is the stone: *the* metonymic link between Tia and Antoinette in this moment, but also the most profound emblem of rejection. And this then crystallizes the pattern in *Wide Sargasso Sea*. Extending the model of *Jane Eyre*, in perverse cultural pathologies metonymy becomes the sign not of linkage but *partition*. The connective element divides, because connection is precisely what cannot be tolerated in a grammar of identity founded on demarcation and repression.

This may be why, where Antoinette can find no linkage in the world, she is subject to the irruption of dreams which are partly prophetic. The prophetic aspect—premonitions of her physically and emotionally violent relationship with Rochester—may simply be conventional: this is how dreams work in fiction. At another level, the pattern conforms to the projection principle we saw in Brontë: where horizontal connection is a matter of need or potential, but its realization is impossible, this is converted into a vertical dynamic within the psyche, of desire, fear, intimation, and return. As in Brontë, the model has Freudian aspects, but apparent here from yet a further angle. For Freud, dreams work by condensation and displacement, and it is conventional to say that where the element of displacement is metonymic, condensation—onto particular objects or symbols—is metaphoric.[28] There is a grammar *beyond* this of dreams, however. For the dream itself is syntactic in two ways, both in its filtered links with the external world of the everyday, and in the internal articulations of its 'language'—motifs, images, protocols of combination and so on. But to the extent the material of dreams *condenses* on certain symbols—that is, to the extent dreams in fact *become* symbolic—they are an index primarily of a *broken syntax*, of links that cannot otherwise be attained or acknowledged in waking life. This is the break that may produce the psychic operations of dreams in the first place. Broken navigations—impossible versions of horizontal syntax—produce the obscure navigations of dreams.

This dynamic is apparent in one of the most intriguing dream-moments in *Wide Sargasso Sea*, a moment which in reality is not a

---

[28] Terry Eagleton, *Literary Theory: An Introduction*, 2nd edn (Minneapolis: University of Minnesota Press, 1996), 137.

dream at all but has the overtones of a wakeful version. This is what we may call Antoinette's 'rat dream', and it is a narrative of thresholds. As Antoinette tells the story to Rochester, one night when she was visiting Granbois with her Aunt Cora she woke up to find 'two enormous rats', as big as cats, on the window-sill staring at her. Rochester, listening, expects to hear that she was frightened, but she was not: it was only when she fell asleep again and woke to find the rats *gone* that she became terrified, and went outside to sleep in the moonlight, which Christophine had warned her never to do. All the elements are here. There is Jane Eyre's window and window-sill—a portal to the outside, of sorts—as well as the moonlight, which in *Jane Eyre* marks the uncanny, intimating hidden secrets. Perhaps Antoinette prefers the rats she can see to the kind (Rochester) she cannot; perhaps the rats represent a certain untamed and natural wildness in herself that she herself needs to express. But most significant is the fact that, across the threshold of the window-sill, Antoinette finds the link between inside and outside strangely reassuring. For that reason, when she is able to see the rats, she does not conform to a symbolic logic: for her the rats do not represent any '*x*' that her unconscious might concoct. On the contrary, she quite calmly and resolutely *refuses* to give them any symbolic meaning. It is only when they *disappear*—when the syntactic link is no longer *there*— that the terror of the unconscious, the symbolic dimension, emerges. So Antoinette goes out into Jane Eyre's spectral moonlight. She has gone from spectrum to spectral; the possibility of the horizontal has become the ghosting and haunting of the vertical.

All considerations of dreams in *Wide Sargasso Sea* follow this pattern, including those discussions when Rochester and Antoinette refer respectively to the Caribbean or England as 'a dream' or 'dreamlike'. In terms of the novel's geography, as well as its geographies of the self, these disparate places are subject to an interplay not of linkage but inversion. Each place becomes the 'dream' of the other, subject to symbolic representation and the articulations of substitution, until finally Antoinette is walled up as the 'unconscious' of Thornfield Hall— its dream, as it were. As in *Jane Eyre*, the national is founded on the repression of the transnational; yet at the same time the dream figures an inevitable return, in a syntax that may be both desired and feared, and cannot (yet) fully be realized. It is part of the unusual strength of *Wide Sargasso Sea* that it makes this an overt and deliberate topic, one secreted only symptomatically in the earlier novel. Here, in effect, is a fairly profound mapping of the national and transnational in their interactions, mutual invocations, and projections, all rendered in ratios of the conscious and unconscious across problematic and (at best) only partially transitive boundaries. As in *Jane Eyre,* such a modelling allows us to understand the transnational not only as a political and cultural phenomenon, but at some deep level as a psychic cartography, with a symbolic economy and dynamic of its own.

Of course, much of this is enacted in *Wide Sargasso Sea* through the relationship of Antoinette and Rochester, not only at the level of character and action but quite as revealingly at the level of narrative. Here the paradox in the switches of narration between its two main figures (producing momentary confusion in a first-time reading) is not how different Rochester and Antoinette sound but how much they sound the *same.* Indeed, as Rhys was writing the book, she found herself confronted by an aesthetic problem, in that she did not know how to present Rochester's treachery without turning him into a one-dimensional villain—part of her long delay in completing the novel. Her solution was to give him his own narrative, an aspect which adds dimensions of perspective, control, and power (if not in wholly straightforward ways), but also some romance and vulnerability.[29] But for that very reason there is a horizontal fluency between Rochester and Antoinette which makes their voices sound extraordinarily similar, almost as if they were two sides of Rhys's own psyche, male and female, the English and the Caribbean.[30] And in so many respects the two characters are similar, connected. The real scandal in *Wide Sargasso Sea* is not how different Rochester and Antoinette are but how much they

---

[29] For Rhys's breakthrough on Rochester, see Angier, *Jean Rhys,* 514–15; also Jean Rhys to Francis Wyndham, 14 April [1964], including her poem 'Obeah Nights', in Rhys, *Letters,* 261–6. For an intriguing exploration of silence in the novel, showing how it counteracts any simple rule that 'speech is power', see Carine M. Mardorossian, 'Shutting up the Subaltern: Silences, Stereotypes, and Double-Entendre in Jean Rhys's *Wide Sargasso Sea*', *Callaloo,* 22/ 4 (1999): 1071–90.

[30] Angier, *Jean Rhys,* sees this as a matter of weakness in Rhys's writing, pointing to 'Jean's characteristic inability to inhabit any sympathetic point of view but her own' (553). But was this always the case? For a dialogue where Rhys put herself on trial, and where both voices—accusation and defence—were clearly her own, see Rhys, *Smile Please,* 161. Here the voices sound like those of Rochester and Antoinette, but both only intensify the sense of Rhys's solitude and culpability.

are *alike*. It is how—and why—likeness is converted into difference that presents *another* kind of scandal, something the novel observes in detail and depth.

What, then, does Rochester want? And what do we know about him, beyond the fact that he makes boys cry? We know that he is a second son, looked down on by father and older brother. He has been married off for money to secure his future; and he has been brought up to hide what he feels. In short, within a wider cultural framework, he has been feminized—part of his contiguity with Antoinette. He writes letters to his father that he does not post, and there are 'blanks' in his mind 'that cannot be filled up' (*WSS*, 45). In other words, Rochester is subject to exactly the same kinds of discontinuity that affect Antoinette, repressed by his father where she is rejected by her mother. Yet, where likeness and contiguity should create recognition and empathy, this is precisely the result Rochester cannot embrace. One of the most telling things we know about him is, as Christophine observes, that '[t]he man don't like scent' (*WSS*, 47). As in Rushdie, smell is the most metonymic of the senses, but Rochester has an absolute terror of metonymy. Where Antoinette is frequently associated with flowers, Rochester will lop off their heads or crush them underfoot. The metonymic link again becomes a marker of division, a way of reinforcing both hierarchy and the anxiety underlying it.

In this regard, one of the most suggestive moments in the novel comes when Rochester watches Antoinette throw stones into a pool. He meditates on the beauty of the place—its 'alien, disturbing, secret loveliness'—and by association his thoughts are also about Antoinette: 'I'd find myself thinking, "What I see is nothing—I want what it *hides*— that is not nothing"' (*WSS*, 52). The talk turns to snakes, as Rochester watches Antoinette with her chemise hitched up above her knees: 'She threw like a boy, with a sure graceful movement.' When he asks who taught her to aim so well, she replies that it was 'Sandi . . . a boy you never met.' Horizontal and vertical run rampant in this passage. A syntax of association connects an androgynous Antoinette, the island, and a particular boy, Sandi—Antoinette's 'coloured' relative, with whom she has her most meaningful emotional attachment. These are links that entail menace for Rochester, of sex, racial crossing, and the alien—but only because of the fact that in some respects they also involve desire. The talk of snakes is telling, as is Rochester's suggestive comment that he wants what is hidden, 'that is not nothing'. There is no need to lay too much stress on the Shakespearean 'nothing' to see the phallic element—the secret 'not nothing'. Rochester is drawn to Antoinette because of her girl–boyishness, just as he embodies a boy–girlishness—that kind of sexual syntax both within and between the two characters. Rochester's connection with Antoinette is his desire, but the recognition it involves is his fear—a fear of everything with which she is connected, a fear of his own repressions. It may not be accidental that boys fall in love with Rochester, or that he makes them cry. The crying boy is in some respects himself, but in the grammar of the identity he asserts, it is Antoinette who pays the price.

This, in its smaller and larger manifestations, is what then under-lies the pattern familiar from *Jane Eyre*: where metonymy entails the menace of attachment, it will be converted into the substitutions (or substitution effects) of representation. Here, if anything, the process occurs in an even more reductive, singular form. For where Bertha was at least complex if demonic as the male–female, black–white, human–animal, Antoinette becomes, in Rochester's version, simply 'insane'—even schematic versions of her chromatic texturings suppressed. Yet one difference between *Jane Eyre* and *Wide Sargasso Sea* is that where Brontë *shared* Rochester's vision of Bertha, here Rhys emerges from symptom more fully towards analysis, especially of Rochester. So, if Rochester and Antoinette are chiastic pairings as girl–boy, boy–girl, man–woman, European-Creole, 'crazy in truth' (in Christophine's phrase), it is clear that those are mirrorings ('like in a looking-glass') Rochester cannot bear, and so he must refuse them. He invokes repression both within himself and of Antoinette, until he turns her into what she becomes in *Jane Eyre*—the 'ghost' in Thornfield Hall, the hidden truth of its psychic economy. Moreover, this creates a substitute identity not only for Antoinette but also for Rochester. As he puts it, 'All the mad conflicting emotions had gone and left me wearied and empty. Sane' (*WSS*, 103). Part Two of the novel ends with a little boy crying for 'nothing'.

It is intriguing to see this dynamic operating at every level in the novel. So, in Rochester's relationship with the servant girl Amélie, she is the very emblem, if not of Homi Bhabha's 'sly civility', then a kind of 'sly servility'—seductively suggesting but also withholding the mastery

Rochester demands.[31] Daniel Cosway, who claims to be Antoinette's half-brother and poisons Rochester's mind with his Iago-like allegations, says of Amélie that '[*s*]*he belongs to this island*' (*WSS*, 59) and knows his story. This means Amélie is associated metonymically with the island and with Daniel, as well as the menace *he* embodies as a racial and familial danger to Rochester—very much a horizontal alignment and threat. In Rochester's mind there is also a kind of syntax between Amélie and Antoinette; in one of his many disputes with Antoinette he thinks the two women might be 'related' (*WSS*, 77). Consequently, when Rochester has sex with Amélie behind the thin partition in Antoinette's hearing, it is not just sex with Amélie he is having. It is sex with the whole damn *lot* of them—Antoinette, the island, Daniel, and the seductions and menace they all represent. Of course, in the servility (sly or otherwise) Amélie offers, and the compliant submission of the island with which she is connected, this is the sexuality of mastery, a 'vertical' manifestation beyond the more usual senses. Patriarchal grammars of sex and gender, geographies of the self, the severely boundaried nature of Rochester's resolutions—these become mutually and interactively defined. Substitution represses not only the 'other' (and the other within the self) but the whole contagious metonymic chain with which the other is associated. This again is Freud's syndrome of the *délire du toucher*—except that here touch is not avoided but enacted as mastery, the taboo object overcome.

It is worth reflecting on how these patterns in *Wide Sargasso Sea* reinforce and extend those we saw in *Jane Eyre*. Principally, the novel shows how navigation in a transnational world is not only disrupted and deflected but becomes translated into—and manifests—an inner dynamics of conscious and unconscious relations. The projection principle, converting the possibility of horizontal connection into vertical containment, enacts forms of substitution and repression. Versions of continuity along what Conrad called the waterways of the earth become a series of antinomies, where the transitive and transitional are interrupted by barriers, where those barriers also operate within the self. Connective elements divide, metonymy becomes menace, menace

---

[31] See Homi Bhabha, 'Sly Civility', in *The Location of Culture* (London and New York: Routledge, 1994), 93–101.

provokes suppression, suppression reinforces division. Locations enter the unconscious of other locations, where they are the objects of a primarily substitutive (therefore binary, therefore singular) form of containment. As in *Jane Eyre*, there is a transnational cartography of the psyche, and a psychological mapping of the transnational, with serious implications for grammars of identity and location in an alienated world. Here that world becomes a dreamworld, with navigations that can only be obscure, where barriers and broken syntax promote violence, where repression presents intimations of volatile return. These aspects are not separate from the transnational but built *into* it, profoundly complicating the nature of its boundaries. We are not free simply to supersede them, though ultimately—as in the case of Rochester— we may have to choose how far we reinforce transitive or intransitive versions.

This, then, is the setting in which we see Antoinette as the end of the novel, the zombie in the Englishman's castle, the female within the male, the Caribbean within England, the mad in the sane, the unconscious within the conscious. Like Bertha in *Jane Eyre*, she is not a separate part of those systems: she is what makes them *work,* and this is one definition of Empire, its power, its suppressions, its secrets. As for the sources of that power, '[g]old is the idol they worship', remarks Antoinette (*WSS*, 111). Rochester has come into the family money earlier denied him, because now both father and elder brother have died. There is allegory here after a sort: Empire is always impelled by a drive towards power and acquisition which has already been met. This is the secret contained in its repressions, and others suffer the consequences. Accordingly, any version of equality, connection, transitivity, becomes impossible, even between two figures otherwise so much alike as Rochester and Antoinette. If there is anyone in the novel who remains outside this system, it is perhaps only Christophine, the figure whom Benita Parry sees beyond its frame, as a kind of lasting echo and commentary on the distortions that otherwise dominate.[32] But nor, by that token, is any meaningful parity or connection achieved in a lasting

---

[32] Benita Parry, 'Problems in Current Theories of Colonial Discourse', *Oxford Literary Review*, 9/1–2 (1987): 27–58. There are of course debates on this matter: see Spivak, 'Three Women's Texts'. For a subtle discussion showing how Christophine's form of resistance is re-coded within Rochester's imperialist discourse, see Mardorossian, 'Shutting Up the Subaltern'.

sense between the two 'creole' figures, Christophine, from Martinique, and Antoinette, who is not *béké* like other whites. This was a syntax never achieved by Rhys in her own life, and with some honesty she could not put it into her book.

Yet some links are suggested in the final moments of *Wide Sargasso Sea*, indicating, if not the fact of connection, the drive of suppressed impulses emerging in the only form possible in the world of the novel. As might be expected, these come from a realm of the unconscious, as Antoinette awakes in Thornfield Hall as if from a dream within the dream of England, to enact what her dream has told her to do. All the motifs of *Jane Eyre* and *Wide Sargasso Sea* are there. At last there is the looking-glass (Jane's perpetual looking-glass) where Antoinette sees herself; or—just the slightest trace—it is Jane she sees by way of reflection. She has her red dress, metonymic sign of herself and also of fire, and the two together remind her of something she 'must do' (*WSS*, 111). The scent of the dress provides its own connections: it smells of frangipani, and cinnamon, and lime trees, and it provides a link, too, to Sandi, because Antoinette was wearing the dress the last time she saw him. The dream provides other 'passages': Antoinette is suddenly in Aunt Cora's room. She calls to Christophine to help, and finds she has been helped. She hears the sacrificial parrot, Coco, burned in the fire at Coulibri, and sees the pool there, and Tia, who dares her to jump—a jump that will resolve the link between her island and the battlements of Europe. For Antoinette, everything that has been repressed is revived in this moment, providing a syntax that allows her to navigate her way. In an inverse dynamic, the vertical becomes horizontal again—the emblem of a journey she can take to recognize herself and understand her location. The candle lights her along the passage, a pathway for her 'voyage in the dark'; she knows 'why I was brought here, and what I have to do' (*WSS*, 112).

A navigational grammar of metonymy resurrects and counteracts the obliterations of substitution. Yet it is a grammar still confined within the regime of Thornfield Hall, and that is why, perhaps, it ends in violence, in fire. If this has an eerie and premonitary resonance for our own era, then perhaps the implications are clear. The aim has to be to restore the transnational not as an unconscious but a conscious passage; neither through the violence of repression nor return, but through an open, transitive grammar capable of recognizing and navigating unevenness and difference. We have not yet been able to free the ghost in the machine, let her see what she can find by way of meaning or achieve.

## THE THIN MEMBRANE: *FUGITIVE PIECES*

*Fugitive Pieces* is, on the face of it, a novel unconnected with *Jane Eyre* and *Wide Sargasso Sea*, whether measured in terms of theme, character, or setting. And yet we should look not at the level of epiphenomenon, for at a deeper level there are correlations to be traced. Where both *Jane Eyre* and *Wide Sargasso Sea* have to do with the suppression of a syntactic grammar of identity (or its enablement only *through* repression), *Fugitive Pieces* concerns a syntax of reconnection: if not actually *raising* what has been buried, then allowing some form of linkage with it, and finding the healing power of horizontal and oblique links. In tackling one of the darkest areas of human history, it shows us what the resurrections of the syntactic might look like, across transnational space.

As if in intimation of these patterns, the novel begins with a child rising from the ground. Jakob Beer, concealed within a cupboard in the Polish town of Biskupin, has seen his parents and sister Bella murdered by the Nazis; or, not so much *seen,* because he was hidden away: this, like so much else in the novel, is an event defined by its imprint, its trace. Close as the moment was to Jakob, witnessing in this respect is not direct, but more a kind of vestige or echo. He was, as it were, in the next room, *adjacent* to the moment, but not quite of it, and for the rest of his life his problem is one of association: knowing what happened, not knowing if he is able to feel properly what it was or meant. Where his family was the closest thing to him, now there is a haunting that does not even invoke the uncanny because his home no longer exists and the unhomely is a place only of emptiness and absence. Jakob flees, burying himself by day and emerging at night, until he limps into the arms of the Greek geologist Athos Roussos, who sees a young boy thumping his fists on his chest and shouting the only words that come to mind, in German, Polish, and Yiddish, 'dirty Jew, dirty Jew, dirty Jew'.[33] This

---

[33] Anne Michaels, *Fugitive Pieces* (New York: Vintage, 1998), 13. Henceforth referenced as *FP.*

is Jakob's symbolic mirror-identity, his only sense of himself, and it is one of substitution and singularity, 'dirty' a synonym for 'Jew' and vice versa. Three languages but only one message: where translation should (in Benjamin's or any other version) involve variability, some difference in its continuities, this is a reduction of identity in every possible way.

But Athos shows Jakob another set of possibilities, and not only because he rescues him. To hide him from the Germans he wears the boy 'under his clothes'; Jakob feels they are a Russian doll, 'I inside Athos, Bella inside me' (*FP*, 13–14). In their composite formulation, they are a phrase within a phrase within a phrase, a recursive syntax of being and expression. And their links run very far: the Greek man encloses the Jewish boy, who encloses his sister, across the space of the living and the dead. The problem in such circumstances is how to make these boundaries properly transitive, so that Athos does not smother Jakob, so that Jakob does not smother his sister through excessive attachment to her memory nor, for the same reason, is smothered by her. This is what, over time, Athos provides, as a very model of navigation. He becomes *koumbaros* to the Jewish boy, his godfather who will connect him to a new existence;[34] yet he is always careful to provide space in Jakob's life for remembrance, always respecting the untouchable imprint of his experience. The novel is scrupulous in its ethic of touching therefore— not to violate what should be inviolable, nor replace what has disappeared, but to allow for the regeneration (in almost literal terms) that connection can provide. Athos does not substitute for Jakob's parents, nor does he even claim to stand *in loco parentis*. Rather, he is the 'almost the same, but not quite' in its positive form as a matter of responsibility and promise. If the vertical line of heredity has been lost, Athos provides a vector of the oblique—linking the past with a new horizontal. This is the alternative, non-biological family, and where in Rushdie it provided a model at once comic and cataclysmic, here it concerns trauma and the possibilities of healing.

Athos's place—the place he takes Jakob to—is the island of Zakynthos, off the coast of Greece: Mediterranean light to Europe's dark. There is no Sargasso Sea here, no barrier to protect, which to say the least in a world of global violence can be a problem. Again, the

[34] In Greece, the *koumbaros* is the best man at a wedding, traditionally the groom's godfather.

issue is not whether boundaries should exist, but what kinds of boundaries they should be—how and where, through transition, they should protect, how and where provide spaces for connection. Yet against the logic of impermeable barriers on the one hand and vulnerability to annexation on the other, even as the Nazis invade Jakob is exposed by Athos to a metonymic philosophy of the transitive. When he first sees Greek script it looks to him like Hebrew, not two languages and one meaning, but a form of resemblance and intertwining—almost a physical kind of 'translation'. Athos tells Jakob about his passions, principally for geology and its secrets, where strata hidden from the past can be revealed in the present, where faultlines reveal connection and disruption, where metamorphosis—of limestone transforming into marble, and fossils that *are* the past in the present—defines the very nature of being. For Athos the world is a 'terra mobilis' (*FP*, 21), a world in motion, and the opposite, perhaps, of a 'territorium', invoking possession, fixity, fear.[35] He also provides a *disciplinary* navigation, linking geology, palaeontology, and poetry. Not only are there residues, traces, preservations, and transformations in each, but their 'languages' are mutual 'translations' of one another—fragments of a larger vision and experience, so that poetry can be a kind of personal geology, geology provide its own record of transition and emergence. Later, Jakob's first volume of poetry will be entitled *Groundwork* because of its archaeology of self and time, in the intertwining that poetry becomes.

There are risks in gestures of this kind. Principally what Michaels risks is the aestheticization of terror and loss, the ecstasy of the luminous and visionary, the assumption of universal and mutual translatability. If there is a cautionary note here, it is that in understanding a transitive grammar of identity we should not subscribe too easily to an aestheticized model. As Brontë and Rhys remind us, boundaries are real, asymmetrical and abysmal; they operate intrinsically in our cartographies, deep within our conscious and unconscious minds, secreted within our cultures. Yet, if *Fugitive Pieces* romanticizes in some ways, on other levels it confronts the reality of gap and absence. It shows navigation as the

---

[35] Homi Bhabha points to the etymology of 'territory', which may incorporate both 'terra' (earth) and 'terrere' (to frighten): 'Sly Civility', 99–100.

complex space of crossing in an uneven and traumatized world; it shows the complexities and even mechanics of such crossings; and it shows how navigation *depends* on absence or gap—the nature of the boundary to be crossed, how navigation helps define and even create the nature of the boundary.

In this guise, as counterpart to the novel's voyages through space (Poland, Greece, Canada), there are serious contemplations of the fault-lines of time, and the paradoxes of their 'crossing'. Looking back, Jakob understands that simultaneity is far from being a unitary or unifying experience, so that even as Athos told him stories of Odessa, in that very city 'thirty thousand Jews were being doused with gasoline and burned alive' (*FP*, 26); or that, as French explorers uncovered the miraculous animal paintings in the caves of Lascaux in 1942, the ovens of Auschwitz were at work. This is the scandal of horizontal simultaneity—the obverse, in a transnational setting, of Anderson's version of the collective imaginary of the national. Here the horror of the global is the omnipresence of atrocity. Similarly, vertical time carries its own paradoxes. Jakob will be amazed at how the folds of time revealed in strata or fossils make it possible to go back millennia, while it is impossible for him to go back a year or two in his own life. 'Every moment is two moments,' observes Jakob (*FP*, 138); and he believes too in 'the gradual instant' (*FP*, 77)—history's build-up that suddenly releases change, just as the earth slowly prepares its cataclysms. Jakob's personal navigations become most intimate and complex in relation to his dead sister, with whom he can neither be at one nor leave behind. He will lie awake at night hearing her breathing or singing next to him in the dark, feeling 'half terrified that my ear was pressed against the thin wall between the living and the dead, that the vibrating membrane between them was so fragile' (*FP*, 31). Here time and space are complicated by memory, memory complicated by trauma, trauma a record of internal disruption imprinted by violence. Jakob's 'membrane' is a version of the 'thin partition' we saw in both Brontë and Rhys, and it is a hard distance not despite but *because* of its thinness. Proximity, crossing, navigation occur across a space close yet profound enough to measure the distance between life and death; the vibrating membrane is the very *image* of the terrifying, transitive, transformational boundary—a medium as thick with implication as it is 'thin'.

The major cataclysm the novel confronts is the Holocaust, and it deals with issues of identity, space, time, and memory not only in the face of it but also at the heart of it in the Nazi worldview, which we can take as a 'national' version in its most heightened form. In this form, as the novel suggests, spatial rapacity was accompanied by its temporal counterpart. This concerns Athos directly: he is writing a book called *Bearing False Witness* on how the Nazis abused archaeology to refashion the past. The town of Biskupin, known as the 'Polish Pompeii', was the product of an advanced non-Aryan culture, and so (according to the novel) Himmler ordered it should be obliterated.[36] Athos studied with a colleague who worked in the Ahnenerbe (the Bureau of Ancestral Inheritance), falsifying digs to prove that Greek civilization began in neolithic Germany. This, in a word, is the opposite of Walter Benjamin's constellation; it is the imposition of empty, homogeneous time without any sense of gap, distance, difference, gradation, or texture. What is now always was; what once was always will be. Similarly, the Ahnenerbe's version of identity was singular in the extreme, and its distaste for contamination total. This again was Freud's *délire du toucher*, in a manner that approached the asymptote of totality. No surprise, then, that the Nazis used metonymy in a particular form, the form of 'representation', so that the yellow star—literally attached to clothing— would represent the Jew, the Jew represent contagion on the other side of the impermeable boundary. At one stage Michaels writes that the Nazis destroyed metaphor, because they objectified human beings, reduced them to less than human. This suggests that when metaphor becomes absolutely reductive it loses its capacities in both morality and meaning. But equally important is to see what kind of metaphor this is. Whether by way of metaphor or metonym, as always what counts is how these figurations are used—towards the substitutions of singular representation, or the transitive oscillations of difference and connection.

Ultimately, it is displacement, connection, and combination that *Fugitive Pieces* pursues, a grammar of transition and transmission across time, space, and identity, both within the self and beyond. Jakob, the

[36] *FP*, 104. For an intriguing account of Biskupin and its archaeological history which does not tell exactly the same story as the novel, see Danuta Piotrowska, 'Biskupin 1933– 1996: Archaeology, Politics and Nationalism', *Archaeologia Polona*, 35–6 (1997–8): 255–85.

small boy who rose from the ground, becomes a poet. He also becomes a translator, working between and across languages, fitting their fragments together. With Athos he leaves Greece to live in Canada, then returns to Greece again, a transnational nomad whose search for meaning never stops. It is Jakob who gives us the idea of 'double exposure' (*FP*, 18), two images of the same object, superimposed and displaced. This is an evocative idea for the transnational: the shifted registration of self, location, perspective, outline—metonymy built into the imprint itself. Jakob remarks that he feels like a touch-typist 'who holds his hands above the keys slightly in the wrong place.... I thought of writing poems this way, in code, every letter askew, so that loss would wreck the language, become the language' (*FP*, 111). Echoing Rushdie's analogy, he compares both the poet and the translator to the immigrant, working across and between lines that are geographical, cultural, personal, and poetic. From that point of view, for him the mystery of metaphor is almost material in its transactions: 'It's no metaphor,' Jakob suggests, 'to feel the influence of the dead in the world, just as it's no metaphor to hear the radiocarbon chronometer, the Geiger counter amplifying the faint breathing of rock, fifty thousand years old' (*FP*, 53). If this is not simply 'metaphor', it is because here metaphor recovers the physics of its origins as metonym: the transmission of 'carrying across'. This *is* the grammar of navigation.

The novel's resolutions sustain this philosophy. Jakob is freed from submersion in Bella's afterlife through touch—through the love of his second wife, Michaela, who is both herself and a living connection to Bella. In this respect, he has found a way for the dead to remain in his life though absent, to be in contact with the past but not so that it substitutes for the present. His nomadic journeys, his poetry, his translations, are an incarnation of finding this way. But nor does he come to the end of the journey. Just as he completes Athos's unfinished *Bearing False Witness* after Athos dies, so too he has an afterlife in the novel—a membrane of crossing in and into the lives of others. This is provided by a third character, Ben, who meets Jakob in Toronto, and extends the patterns we have already seen. Ben is the child of Holocaust survivors who cannot escape the past; his name in Hebrew means 'son', but not son of anyone in particular. He becomes 'son' to Jakob, in the way that Jakob was son to Athos, but he does so only after Jakob dies; in these three men the law of the oblique is maintained, each making their horizontal way forward through resonance with the past, the metonymic family, as it were.

As in the shift of narration from Antoinette to Rochester in *Wide Sargasso Sea*, when Ben's voice takes over, unintroduced, from Jakob's, we are in a transition we have to work out, and the novel itself becomes a kind of syntax. Ben, whose marriage is troubled, travels to Greece to track down Jakob's notebooks, which are found almost by accident— another incarnation of the unforeseeable ways of connection. He ends up in the ancestral home of Athos, reaching back to a history before Athos's birth, and so these links have been constituted from Poland, to Greece, to Canada, and back to Greece again, in the geologic folds of time, space, memory, the contiguities and gaps of multiple lives and locations. Ben is the archaeologist of Jakob's life, just as the fragments he finds of Jakob's past help him to live his own, become 'translated' into his life—a version both of displacement and continuity. The novel has shown us that kinship does not always proceed by way of resemblance— Benjamin's striking idea from 'The Task of the Translator'.[37] It shows that kinship may in a sense be defined by *transmission*—who is willing to take it on, and what versions of connection they subscribe to. In a transnational world emerging from trauma—as the transnational world always is—such versions of transmission are both the risk and the very means of engagement.

Primarily, the novel has shown us identity *as a form of navigation* in a transnational setting. Confronting the horror of the Holocaust, it converts loss into the emblem of the journey, absence into the impulse of the syntactic, the syntactic into a redemptive version of self and location. This is the calculus it reveals in relations between the horizontal and vertical. Here repression—of the past, of memory, of the self—created by a history of trauma provides the impetus to resurrection through renewed forms of search. This is embedded in the novel almost as prophecy: the vertical—of history, of trauma, of loss—can become horizontal again, as part of a different definition of 'return'. It is an impetus that cannot ever fully be repressed; and it may, even in small measure, help heal the traumas of the past. Like *Jane Eyre* and *Wide Sargasso Sea* before it, *Fugitive Pieces* shows that repression is always more than personal, the

---

[37] Benjamin, 'Task of the Translator', 256.

possibility of regeneration never less than syntactic. Both have much to do with the future of a transnational world.

## NAVIGATIONS

Athos, Jakob, Ben: the syntax runs through the male line, almost a form of male parthenogenesis. Jane, Antoinette, Bertha: paradoxically, the females have no such pattern, and it is worth asking the question why. Or, we might ask why female syntax comes up in the forms we see in *Jane Eyre* and *Wide Sargasso Sea*.

It is a wider question for this study, for generally in these novels males have horizons, whereas females do not. (Julie Summers, in Nadine Gordimer's *The Pickup*, will present an intriguing mixture of these alternatives.) In a way, though, to ask the question is to provide the answer. It is no accident that questions of broken syntax will be explored by female writers and through female characters, given that topographies of enclosure, substitution, and vertical barriers have constituted their territory in various cultures for thousands of years. Conversely, when Anne Michaels explores horizons, she does it through the lives of her males. But this rule is by no means hard and fast. When a writer such as Caryl Phillips deals with these questions, certainly it is through the lives of women, and this may be one reason why they are prominent in his work; but he also writes of male characters, marginalized or obstructed because of the legacy of slavery, or as migrants in a fragmented and hugely oppressive world. W. G. Sebald, as we shall see in *Austerlitz*, is drawn to the motif of the fortress as the archetypal site of oppression and loss—Rimbaud's 'ancient parapets of Europe' in a particularly armoured form. And it is the possibilities of syntax in Austerlitz's life that they obliterate. The characteristic experience of men and women may be different, but precisely because of that there must be points of navigation between them as well.

This is why it is important to think about the reconstruction of a syntactic grammar of identity, of navigating a different way in the world, whether in female or male forms. Unlike Rochester or even Jane Eyre it means accepting the full implications of metonymy as transitive, refusing to acquiesce in the tempting ways of oppression, elision, or suppression. At the same time, it is not to ignore what barriers mean, the weight that structures their reality—the variable 'height' (or depth) in our respective experiences. Collectively, the contiguous 'fragments' of these novels extend one another's stories. Out of a world of horror, in which boundaries of power have reigned supreme, come hints of the journey as navigation, of navigation as a model of identity and belonging. Taking the journey means doing so not in ignorance of horror but *because* of it; the ghost that haunts either because it was the atrocity or because the atrocity is its continued suppression. This is the journey as syntactic, the syntactic as journey, accepting displacement from identities and locations that enclose us, and it can be taken without necessarily knowing the destination. Once upon a time the story was that of Odysseus, the canny man emerging from war who found his way home across the sea. Now, whether in the form of Bertha, Antoinette, Athos, Jakob, or Ben, the voyage is outwards, towards a definition of home as the navigation itself, through and beyond the barriers that enclose us.

It is an appropriate myth for our time. From Jamaica, Martinique, Dominica, to England, Poland, Germany, Europe, Canada, and Zakynthos—the Ionian island near Ithaca, Odysseus' home—it may be the only way to deal with the ghosts and hidden madness of our systems, voyage through the Sargasso Sea, allow the living and the dead to draw life from one another, send soundings across the partitions of our worlds, whether intimate membranes or—still—massive walls.

# 5

# Transfiction

## W. G. Sebald

A bridge—its two ends could not be embraced at a single glance
and its piers were resting on planets—led from one world to
another by a causeway of wonderfully smooth asphalt. The three-
hundred-and-thirty-three-thousandth pier rested on Saturn.

> *Grandville's Another World* (1844), quoted by
> Walter Benjamin, '*The Ring of Saturn*', c. 1928–9

'Everybody knows such things. Every place you go to, they always
knew.'

> Dan Jacobson, *Heshel's Kingdom*

In the fourth section of W. G. Sebald's *The Emigrants*, which revolves
around Max Ferber—a figure drawn from the life of the artist Frank
Auerbach—the narrator of the story (W. G. Sebald himself, or a figure
who both is and is not Sebald, and whom I shall therefore call S) visits
a cemetery in Bad Kissingen, north of Würzburg in Germany. It is a
pilgrimage of a kind. When Ferber finally filled in some of the silences
in his story, telling S of his flight out of Germany from Oberwiesenfeld
airport in Munich in 1939, and of the fate of his parents, who were
taken from Munich to Riga in 1941 and murdered, he also offered S
a brown paper package tied with string, containing photographs and
almost a hundred pages of memoirs handwritten by his mother between
1939 and 1941. What follows in the narrative is S's voicing of Luisa
Lanzberg's account of her life, but it is an account as significant for what
it leaves out as for what it remembers. Mostly it remembers childhood,
school, family, the enclosed, safe world of a domestic upbringing; what
it does not remember, except through incidental and ominous details, is

the 'outside' closing in, the narrowing Nazi horizon, the looming world of horror and terror. Ravelling and unravelling, covering and uncovering its subject like Ferber's own obsessional methods as an artist, it conceals as it reveals, the work of memory one of repression and postponement as much as it is of recapture. In the time of Luisa's account, voiced by S, there is a doubling of a different kind: the remembered past, rendered in the initial present tense of her narrative, we now know has become the absolute past, irredeemable. In Luisa's memoir, things that happen once happened always; and things that happened always . . . happened, once.

And so S finds himself in the cemetery in Bad Kissingen. He has been given the keys to unlock the gate (memory intimated but sealed in Germany), but the keys in both Freudian and post-Freudian ways do not fit. He must physically climb over the wall, across a barred boundary, to become a witness, and what he finds is a neglected wilderness of graves. A gravestone more recent than the others is inscribed for Lily and Lazarus Lanzberg, as well as for Fritz and Luisa Ferber, Max's grandparents and parents. Lazarus died in Theresienstadt in 1942, and the stone records the unknown fate of his parents. Only Lily Lanzberg is buried in the grave, and that primarily because she took her own life, in time to have a proper burial. In the cemetery, S finds other markers of note: a gravestone for one Maier Stern who died on Sebald's own birthday, and one with a quill on the headstone for a writer, Friederike Halbleib. Such echoes and hauntings mean a great deal to both S and Sebald. Though he does not comment on the name, we know that *Halb* means 'half', *bleib* means to 'remain', and *leib* means 'body'; the fate of a Jewish writer in Germany. S feels as if he himself had lost her, as if he is the one who cannot not get over the loss. It is then that he finds Lily Lanzberg's grave: 'I stood before it for some time, not knowing what I should think; but before I left I placed a stone on the grave, according to custom.'[1]

It is worth saying: this is according to Jewish custom. A German writer places a stone on a Jewish grave, and even if he does not know what to think, it is a mark of touching, of connection, earth to earth. In a sense chance has brought S there—the chance of finding Ferber,

---

[1] W. G. Sebald, *The Emigrants*, trans. Michael Hulse (New York: New Directions, 1997), 225. Henceforth referenced as *TE*.

of hearing his story, of being given Luisa's memoirs—and so this is a contingent moment, the culmination of a chain of chance events. But for Sebald such moments become both less and more than matters of chance. He is the kind of writer who continually migrates towards and into these stories as if some unknown fate or responsibility were leading him. He turns his life towards them, and in this respect a paradoxical reversal takes place. Instead of S being an extension of himself, Sebald's achievement has been to become an extension of S, an identity inseparable from its writing, its writing inseparable from a chain of connections. He presents himself as a kind of writing, writing as a form of being, being as a form of navigation. And so the idea of contingency takes on its original meaning: a place and mode of touching, being touched.[2] We see it here: the living and the dead touch through a mark of respect across the boundary of a massive and irredeemable horror. They touch for a moment through their metonymic link of memorial, a stone.

But what kind of boundary is it, what kind of crossing? This boundary is not the space of having crossed, of something completed. Rather it is a place almost of suspension, where crossing, connection, is the question in all its complexity to be encountered. That is the nature of this boundary, this navigation, and it brings up a definition significant for all of Sebald's work. Transmission: what is borne across at the limits of the self, where the self both must and cannot go; a particular kind of transition, of grammar.

## THE LIVING ROOM

W. G. Sebald was a writer who came to awareness—that is, who came into the form of his life—through this kind of migration and connection. He was born in May 1944 in the village of Wertach im Allgäu, a small and relatively remote village in Bavaria. It was a place the war did not get to, Sebald remarked, a silent place. 'Then you

---

[2] On this compare Homi Bhabha: 'the contingent is contiguity, metonymy, the touching of spatial boundaries at a tangent, and, at the same time, the contingent is the temporality of the indeterminate and the undecidable'. See 'The Postcolonial and the Postmodern: The Question of Agency', in *The Location of Culture* (London and New York: Routledge, 1994), 186.

find out it was the same month when Kafka's sister was deported to Auschwitz.' This is the horror of simultaneity Anne Michaels writes about in *Fugitive Pieces*, and for Sebald the implications were personal: 'It's the chronological contiguity that makes you think it is something to do with you.'[3] Sebald's father joined the army in 1929, in the despair of the depression, and finished the war as a captain. He was taken prisoner, returning home only in 1947, then found a job which kept him away much of the time, so that until Sebald was twelve he was brought up mostly by his grandfather. The postwar German 'economic miracle' allowed the Sebalds to enter the lower middle class, but the war itself remained clothed in silence. As Sebald recalled, it was only when he was sixteen or seventeen that his school was shown a film of the liberation of Belsen; afterwards there was a football match. Coming to understand the past took work and persistence, as well as a sense of involvement: 'If you know in the generation before you that your parents, your uncles and aunts were tacit accomplices, it's difficult to say you haven't anything to do with it. I've always felt I had to know what happened in detail, and to try to understand why it should have been so.'[4] This is the shadowed reality of complicity, a complicity which can be retroactive, affecting those not responsible for original crimes, yet for whom the crime would be in not taking on responsibility.[5] It becomes a haunting in which both present and future must become an inspection of the past, an obligation Sebald is drawn to as if by an irresistible compulsion.

For Sebald, origins were connected with destruction, rendered physically in the world he saw around him growing up. This was, as he put it, the 'rubble-world' (*die Trümmelwelten*) of immediate postwar Germany. Whenever he saw black and white photos of that period, he remarked, he would have the distinct feeling: 'That is it, where

---

[3] For information in this and following paragraphs see Maya Jaggi, 'Recovered Memories', *Guardian*, 22 September 2001; <http://books.guardian.co.uk/departments/politicsphilosophyandsociety/story/0,,555839,00.html> (accessed 10 September 2004); also Maya Jaggi, 'The Last Word', *Guardian*, 21 December 2001; <http://books.guardian.co.uk/departments/generalfiction/story/0,6000,624750,00.html> (accessed 1 July 2004).

[4] Jaggi, 'Recovered Memories'.

[5] For a thought-provoking exploration of the meaning of complicity as an almost universal responsibility, see Mark Sanders, *Complicities: The Intellectual and Apartheid* (Durham and London: Duke University Press, 2002).

you come from. There is your territory.'[6] It was partly because of this sense of territory that Sebald left his country. He studied first at the University of Freiburg where he felt stifled by a senior professoriate that had never left the mental universe of the 1930s.[7] While he was there the trial of Auschwitz functionaries began—people Sebald might have known as neighbours, while the small towns he did know had been emptied of their Jewish populations, and survivors had to come back from Sydney or Brooklyn to testify. In 1966 Sebald left to study in French-speaking Switzerland, then became a language assistant at the University of Manchester for two years. Following that, he became a schoolteacher in St Gallen in Switzerland, then returned to Manchester before taking up an appointment at the University of East Anglia in Norwich. At every step he observed the crossings of those who had gone before him: Ludwig Wittgenstein, who arrived in Manchester from Berlin in 1908 to pursue research in aeronautics (and who himself became a schoolteacher in a remote Austrian village in 1920); Elias Canetti, who, when he first came to Manchester from Bulgaria, lived in the same road as Sebald. This, according to Sebald, was Palatine Road; in *The Emigrants*, S places Max Ferber as living in that road, in the same house that was once occupied by Wittgenstein.[8]

Crossings, diffusions, retracings, other presences: Mark Anderson has commented on how Sebald spent some thirty years in a kind of extraterritorial limbo, writing from England in German about German and German-Jewish culture, slipping French and Italian into his spoken language rather than German, living in a more or less constant state of travel around Europe.[9] In *The Emigrants* the painter Frank Auerbach becomes Aurach in the original German version, then Ferber in the English—both the latter called 'Max', the name Sebald himself adopted as his own. The writing crosses into the life, the life into the writing, while migration and movement are built into everything, both the self and the world it explores. But in a world of connections, none of this can be by way of evasion. On the contrary, the movement *away* is also

[6] 'Ich Fürchte das Melodramatische' (interview with W. G. Sebald), *Der Spiegel*, 11–12 March 2001; <http://www.spiegel.de/spiegel/0,1518,123049,00.html> (accessed 28 July 2004). I am grateful to Eva Paus for assistance with translation.
[7] James Wood, 'An Interview with W. G. Sebald', *Brick*, 59 (1998): 29.
[8] Wood, 'Interview', 29; Sebald, *TE*, 166.
[9] Mark M. Anderson, 'The Edge of Darkness: On W. G. Sebald', *October*, 106 (2003): 105–6.

a movement *towards*. To leave one's country, any point of departure, is always to return by way of contemplating its implications, to see its resonances elsewhere. Indeed, it is to see the resonance, the connection, the afterlife *everywhere*.

Towards the end of *The Emigrants*, S recalls some pictures he had seen in Frankfurt the year before, of the Litzmannstadt ghetto established in 1940 in Lodz, a town that had once been called the *polski Manczester*—another shadowing or echo. The photographs had been taken by a book-keeper and financial expert named Genewein, who, like the accountant Marlow meets in *Heart of Darkness*, was probably untroubled by atrocity in recording the industry he saw around him. One of the pictures shows three women at a loom, and as in Conrad they remind S of the fates who run and terminate the thread of life. But equally telling is that the patterns of the carpet they are weaving remind S 'of the settee in our living room at home' (*TE*, 237). The threads across space and time are inescapable. For Sebald there is a sense in which the Lodz ghetto is always 'in our living room at home'. Atrocity—its past, its aftershadow, is where we live, in our most intimate spaces, and the even greater horror is that we live not despite it but *because* of it. It is imprinted in the very way we live.

This is a reality that was undoubtedly evident to Ferber, who had been drawn to Manchester as a young man, and who, once he arrived, never left. But then he had never really 'left' Germany either. 'When I think of Germany,' he had told S, 'it feels as if there were some kind of insanity lodged in my head' (*TE*, 181). When he handed S his mother's memoirs, he indicated why Manchester originally seemed like home to him. It had been a city with a strong German and Jewish influence and, as he put it, 'I am here, as they used to say, to serve under the chimney' (*TE*, 192). This was the last thing Ferber told S, and there is no doubt which chimneys his further silence invoked by way of connection and complicity.

And of course there is another side to the living room. In German, it is *Wohnzimmer*, one kind of literal translation.[10] But then there

---

[10] This is exactly the phrasing of the German original in *Die Ausgewandetern* (Frankfurt: S. Fischer Verlag, 1994), where Sebald writes of 'unseres Wohnzimmersofas zu Hause' (355). Of course the other, reverse translation suggested in my discussion is 'accidental', contingent, but given Sebald's sense of uncanny transitivity, might be one he would have recognized if not initiated overtly.

is also *Lebensraum*. Through the shadowed transitions of language—partly contingent, partly inevitable—this becomes almost a prophecy for Sebald. The world through which he moves, and which he writes, becomes the history of this 'living room'. His obligation is to find another way of living in it, writing it through such forms as this. That is why it takes the shape of a journey, searching out these connections. Biography (as its etymology suggests) turns into nothing less than a life-writing, a form of navigation allowing these enmeshings to surface.

## *VERTIGO*, OR THE UNCANNY

What it means to be in this kind of movement—which for Sebald is an intrinsic part of the transnational—is suggested in the title of his first prose work, *Vertigo*, a book that also begins to characterize the condition more fully.

The title in the original German was '*Schwindel. Gefühle*', a disarticulation and recombination of the usual form, '*Schwindelgefühle*'.[11] Instead of one word, we have a kind of syntax stretched across a gap—where the period marks both the boundary and the space of crossing. Here meaning multiplies—'*schwindel*' suggesting dizziness, giddiness, or vertigo but also swindle and deception, and all of these in relation to 'feelings'/*gefühle*. But why this collocation, the phenomenology of vertigo in the first place? Dizziness and deception: the journey is doubled, haunted by its own undertakings. This is borne out in the second section of *Vertigo*, a section aptly titled '*All'estero*' ('to the foreign country') which describes two journeys undertaken by S in 1980 and 1987 through Austria and northern Italy—the first the record of a personal crisis, the second a recapitulation involving (in every sense of the word) 'research'. Every journey is a retracing, the foreign is the shadowed, the self at the edges of its boundaries. Here are Sebald's characteristic obsessions, where, if features or events are not doubled, then doubled or tripled attachments come to them. So, Klosterneuberg is where S visits the poet Ernst Herbeck at a pensioners' home; but also (we learn later)

---

[11] W. G. Sebald, *Vertigo*, trans. Michael Hulse (New York: New Directions, 2000). Henceforth referenced as *V*. On the German title, see Mark R. McCulloh, *Understanding W. G. Sebald* (Columbia, SC: University of South Carolina Press, 2003), 87–8.

where S's wife Clara attended school, and where her mother lived in an old-age home. It is also the site of Kafka's last journey in 1924, when he was admitted into a nursing home to die. Through it all, not only the observed but the observer comes under inspection. 'Not until I am on the train to Milan do I become visible again to my mind's eye,' S remarks (*V*, 103). Here the self is the self both then and now, the same, yet shifted, obscurely narrating itself, emerging only in certain quanta of visibility, certain dislocations and superpositions, following its journey through forms of hiddenness, compulsion, and intuition: a syntactic, navigatory self across gaps in time as well as space.

If every feature in *Vertigo* seems doubled, its most haunting presence is that of Kafka, whose presentiment of what was to come in Europe had a spectral illumination of its own. This is the research S undertakes on his second expedition, retracing Kafka's journey to the region in 1913. (In much of Sebald's writing 1913 is a marked year, a pause in the boundary of time prior to the coming destruction.) Following Kafka more than seventy years later, S himself feels both tracker and tracked, as hints and signs crop up everywhere. Some of them reveal the comedy of obsession. In the railway station of Desenzano, S visits the *pissoir* and sees the graffito '*il cacciatore*' (the hunter), to which he adds '*nella selva nera*' (of the black forest). The reference is to the Hunter Gracchus in Kafka's story of the same name, who comes from the Black Forest. Later, on the bus to Riva, S sees a pair of twins who look strangely like Kafka; when he approaches them for a photograph, their parents turn him away as a disturbed pederast. But this is part of the condition of vertigo, where the line between mania and intuition may be all but indistinct. S also follows Kafka (called 'Dr K' in this section) from life into his fiction and back again—a form of navigation that mirrors every kind of crossing in Sebald's work. Here, through versions of detection and interpretive reconstruction, it is the story 'The Hunter Gracchus' which S explores, the germ of which came to Kafka in Riva on Lake Garda in 1913.[12] We see Dr K in letters to Felice Bauer, in relation to a young woman he meets at Riva, in a moment of homoerotic desire, and then transformed through autobiographical displacements

---

[12] For the 1913 origins of the story, see Franz Kafka, *The Diaries 1910–1923*, ed. Max Brod, trans. Joseph Kresh, Martin Greenberg, and Hannah Arendt (New York: Schocken, 1948, 1949), 234, and n. 61.

in the story.[13] There the Hunter Gracchus cannot live and cannot die, and touches for an instant the knee of the town's mayor—named Salvatore, 'saviour'—who hears his account before Gracchus must sail on in a world that can neither release nor accept him. Gracchus himself is a mythic foreshadowing—for Kafka, for S, for who else?—journeying without visible end towards no possible redemption or resolution.

The notion of the accidental in Sebald's work is something of a suspended category, since by definition any phenomenon is connected through underlying transitions and shifts with an unending chain of others.[14] From that point of view, there is a second presence haunting *Vertigo*, though embedded conceptually as much as in person. At a certain point in the Dr K section, S refers to a tarot reader who had interpreted the cards for both Dr K and the young woman at Riva. In Dr K's case, we are told, she had found almost nothing of significance, and he had to acknowledge that such cards were 'as far as possible removed from his person, to the very limits of the game, so to speak' (*V*, 160–1). Here the reference may be to Wittgenstein, who in his exposition of language in the *Philosophical Investigations* wrote of games: 'board-games, card-games, ball-games, Olympic games, and so on'. One cannot say of all these games, remarks Wittgenstein, that there is 'something common to all', but rather there is 'a complicated network of similarities overlapping and criss-crossing: sometimes overall similarities, sometimes similarities of detail'.[15] This is the foundation for Wittgenstein's concept of 'family resemblance', where meaning involves neither essence nor singularity

---

[13] On the moment of desire, see the letter to Felice Bauer, 21–22 February 1913, in Franz Kafka, *Letters to Felice*, ed. Erich Heller and Jürgen Born, trans. James Stern and Elisabeth Duckworth (New York: Schocken, 1973), 203–4. For Kafka in the period that interests Sebald, see the *Letters* c. pp. 317–26. Michael Hulse's translation of Kafka's 'lust' letter appears superior to the English translation in the *Letters*; for the original see Franz Kafka, *Briefe 1913–März 1914*, ed. Hans-Gerd Koch (Frankfurt am Main: S. Fischer Verlag, 1999), 108.

[14] One of the temptations of reading Sebald is that we find and follow connections everywhere, both within and beyond the text. So, *graculus* (half-homophone or quasi-diminutive for *gracchus*) in Latin is a jackdaw; a jackdaw in Czech is *kavka*; and the *kavky* in Prague when Kafka grew up there were prostitutes. See Jiří Gruša, *Franz Kafka of Prague*, trans. Eric Mosbacher (London: Secker & Warburg, 1983), 18, 39. On the 'Gracchus'/*graculus*/*kavka* connection, McCulloh, *W. G. Sebald*, p. 100, is not quite correct.

[15] Ludwig Wittgenstein, *Philosophical Investigations*, trans. G. E. M. Anscombe, 3rd edn (New York: Macmillan, 1958), 31e–32e, paras 65–7. Also see n. 53 below.

but a spectrum of continuities and transitions—a syntactic version, in some form. There are at least two resonances here for Sebald's work, for a 'complicated network of similarities overlapping and criss-crossing' is *exactly* what he explores in his writing. The second resonance derives from Kafka as much as it does Wittgenstein, that there is *no outside* to such investigations, whether of self or world. Exploring the game one is *within* the game, even to its 'very limits'. This is foundational for a grammar of identity and location: there are unending chains of connection, but no outside from which to locate self, meaning, or place. As in Conrad, our navigations have to take place within and not beyond our horizons in a world without end.

Elsewhere, Wittgenstein is a persistent figure in Sebald's work. We have already seen him in Palatine Road in *Vertigo*. In *The Emigrants*, besides the Max Ferber story, there is Paul Bereyter, S's old schoolmaster, who, like both Wittgenstein and Sebald, teaches in a remote mountain village.[16] Wittgenstein also appears in *Austerlitz*, not so much as a character but through a metonymic appendage—Austerlitz's rucksack, which, like the rucksack Wittgenstein carried everywhere, becomes his very sign. It is even the form, as we shall see, through which Austerlitz recognizes *himself*—a remarkable moment. In *Austerlitz* there is a photograph of the rucksack, and S comments on how it connected the two individuals in his mind: 'now, whenever I see a photograph of Wittgenstein somewhere or other, I feel more and more as if Austerlitz were gazing at me out of it, and when I look at Austerlitz it is as if I see in him the disconsolate philosopher...'.[17] Early on in *Austerlitz* there is a set of photographs of two pairs of eyes. At the Nocturama (a night-time zoo) in Antwerp, S has seen animals with large, intent eyes that remind him of 'the fixed, inquiring gaze found in certain painters and philosophers who seek to penetrate the darkness which surrounds us' (*A*, 5). The lower set of eyes belongs to Wittgenstein.[18]

---

[16] Wood, 'Interview', 29. It is clear that Sebald was not sentimental about Wittgenstein, speaking of the time Wittgenstein spent 'in his misguided idealism... as a primary school teacher in this beastly village in upper Austria'. There are also many differences between Bereyter and Wittgenstein.

[17] W. G. Sebald, *Austerlitz*, trans. Anthea Bell (New York: Random House, 2001), 41. Henceforth referenced as *A*.

[18] See the photograph of Wittgenstein in Swansea, in Ray Monk, *Ludwig Wittgenstein: The Duty of Genius* (Harmondsworth: Penguin, 1991), 494–5. Once one starts on this trail, connections appear everywhere. In the summer of 1920 Wittgenstein

Hauntings, retracings, the re-emergence of the lost; metonymy as a connection resurrecting unknown or otherwise concealed links; a 'complicated network of similarities overlapping and criss-crossing'. One word for all this is the uncanny, and writers on Sebald have been correct to see it in his work.[19] If S, travelling on a bus, sees twins who look like Kafka, that may seem like the uncanny. If he sees in a graffito a half-link to one of Kafka's stories, then that only adds to the sensation, especially when S completes the allusion. But—and this might clarify things a little more—if Austerlitz, travelling to Prague in search of his own identity, feels as if he has been there before, it is uncanny because *in fact he has been there before* and did not know it until he sees the location unfolding before him as he arrives. The connection, in other words, was always there, but suppressed. This is one of the great implications of Sebald's writing—that the prior history of everything we see is inscribed within, if only we have the persistence and commitment to discern it. Much of his work is a search for and through this prior history.

But beyond persistence and commitment, there may be other dimensions to this compulsion, other stories it has to tell. Here we should return to the authority on such matters, Freud, who in his essay on 'The Uncanny' gave the phenomenon its classic description—a description which has specific applications for Sebald's writing, not least its national and transnational aspects. In his essay, Freud defines the uncanny as a 'class of the frightening that leads back to what is known of old and unfamiliar'. He indicates that it often (though not always) involves doubling; and while the uncanny sometimes marks the resurfacing of 'old beliefs' in the magical or numinous, it generally 'proceeds from something familiar which has been repressed'. A suggestive note adds that the line between consciousness and the unconscious works something like a national boundary, policed by 'a damned toll-collector—excise man—deputy-chief customs officer, who has set up his infamous bureau in our top storey'.[20] The key insight, however, is a linguistic

---

worked as a gardener at the Klosterneuburg Monastery in Vienna (Monk, *Wittgenstein*, 191); the same Klosterneuburg that in *TE* links Ernst Herbeck, S's wife Clara and her grandmother, and Kafka.

[19] See, for instance, McCulloh, *W. G. Sebald*, 3–5.

[20] For these quotes and observations, see Sigmund Freud, 'The "Uncanny"', in *The Standard Edition of the Complete Psychological Works of Sigmund Freud*, vol. 17, ed. James Strachey (London: Hogarth Press, 1955), 220, 234, 247. The note, a comment on

one: the uncanny (the *unheimlich,* or unhomely in German) is linked
to its opposite, the *heimlich* (or homely), and they can in effect come
to mean the same thing. Indeed, a syntagmatic chain connects the two
words: 'Thus *heimlich* is a word the meaning of which develops in the
direction of ambivalence, until it finally coincides with its opposite,
*unheimlich.*'[21] The reason Freud proposes for this is crucial: underlying
and linking the two terms is the idea of the *geheim* or secret, for secrets
are both kept at home and characterize the half-known, half-familiar
world of the uncanny. We can take this in a direct way: not only is the
secret in the home, but the home is in the secret. Literally, the *heim* is
in the *geheim,* down to its very presence in the word.

The significance for Sebald's work is immense. Freud quotes Schelling
on the *unheimlich*: ' "Unheimlich" is the name for everything that ought
to have remained . . . secret and hidden but has come to light.'[22] Sebald's
impulse, however, reverses the dictum: the uncanny is the name for
*everything that should have come to light but has remained secret and
hidden.* Moreover, it has remained secret and hidden not only because it
originated in the home but because the home still cannot fully confront
or fathom it. In the case of Germany—particularly for someone of
Sebald's generation—it is evident what this secret is. It is the original
crime of the Holocaust, everywhere present, everywhere absent. Nor
should it ever be fully fathomed, because it is in every meaningful
way unfathomable. What does it involve then? Search, perpetual and
unending; responsibility, perpetual and unending.[23] It involves tracing
and retracing, a series of implications that neither fully appear nor will
ever disappear. Its compulsion and its method therefore *have* to be the
uncanny: an horizon always receding, signs and intimations everywhere.
Moreover, because the secret is in the home, you have to go through
and beyond the home to find it. As Freud suggests, the national is the

Hoffmann's *Die Elixire des Teufels,* is adduced by Freud's editors from a different source,
pp. 233–4.

[21] Freud, 'The "Uncanny" ', 226. Azade Seyhan, *Writing Outside the Nation*
(Princeton and Oxford: Princeton University Press, 2001), 25–6, also considers the
etymology of the *heimlich/unheimlich* duality. And see my discussion on *Jane Eyre*
in Chapter 4.

[22] Freud, 'The "Uncanny" ', 224.

[23] See Ernestine Schlant on the impossibility of the end of mourning in Sebald's work,
in *The Language of Silence: West German Literature and the Holocaust* (New York and
London: Routledge, 1999), 233–4.

boundary that holds off the unconscious of its own reality. Therefore, the search must intrinsically become *transnational*: both within and beyond, in transit across the boundaries of the national.

We might speak of a transnational uncanny. We see its roots in an early work such as *Vertigo*, but thereafter Sebald recognizes its fuller implications. The journey across borders begins because of the secrets of the 'living room', so to speak. This is the origin of Sebald's transnational form, the underlying compulsion of his writing life and journey. And, though the Holocaust is often held to be a 'singularity', we can take it as emblematic of a wider pattern. Where the national has emerged through a history of crime and trauma, the transnational will be experienced, and may be intimated, as a form of the uncanny. It is part of the grammar of the world we inhabit, part of our mapping.

## ETHICS OF APPROACH

How then should this territory be approached? Sebald may have felt answerable to special circumstances, but let us consider three moments in his writing, all from *The Emigrants*. They are small moments, but characteristic; characteristic because they show how even the small can have quite large dimensions.

When Ferber hands his mother's letters and photos to S, he says (in S's revoicing), 'I would rather you took the package' (*TE*, 193). Here are the letters, documents, parcel of meanings handed over as journey; here is weight, trust, care, loss, all the delicacy of the subjunctive voicing (already layered, already handed over), 'I would rather . . .'. All that is now taken on by S; there is profound *space* in such a moment—the space of crossing, this responsibility.

When S looks at the photos of Lodz taken by Genewein, of the three women knotting the carpet at the loom, he not only looks at them but feels their look returned. 'I sense that all three of them are looking across at me, since I am standing on the very spot where Genewein the accountant stood with his camera' (*TE*, 237). The viewer, even in the afterlife of the photograph, is implicated in its taking. This is the 'very spot'—but not the very spot: there is a metonymy of implication, carrying over. Genewein was the accountant, but S stands in the continuing trajectory of his place, connected with it. He too is an 'accountant': the one who must give account, recite, tell—in every sense of the word be 'accountable'.

Then, from the Paul Bereyter story, a question of trespass. Bereyter was a schoolteacher, banned from his work by the Nazis because of his partly Jewish heritage, yet who also, strangely, served in the German army during the Second World War. When S hears of his suicide on the railway tracks near his home, he imagines the circumstances of Bereyter's death—then withdraws, because imagining brings only brief emotional moments that seem presumptuous. S remarks, 'It is in order to avoid this sort of wrongful trespass that I have written down what I know of Paul Bereyter' (*TE*, 29). Paradoxically, writing is a way of avoiding trespass, but then it must be a different kind of writing. It is a writing of 'knowing' rather than imagining, must find its depth and resonance that way; but it also knows the limits of such knowledge, the dangers of trespass on experience not one's own.

What connects all three of these moments is the question of the boundary. This is the boundary as divide, the boundary as crossing, the boundary as the very image of the transitive, with all its implications and accountabilities, protocols that must be observed and taken on. In short, in Sebald's work the boundary is the place where the nature of transmission is the very problem to be engaged. In the wake of trauma, in the wake of crime, what does it mean to encounter this boundary? What can legitimately carry over, and how?

Eric Santner defines trauma as an event that is not yet past, and considers its relevance for the Holocaust: 'The uncanny sense that the Holocaust is not yet past, that it persists as a haunting proximity, means that it has, in a certain sense, not yet "taken place".' This is not a matter of Holocaust denial, but as Santner indicates, has everything to do with a resonance that cannot be grasped, cannot end: 'In response to each account our feeling is: this is not *it*.'[24] From a different direction, this is part of the significance of Primo Levi's reflection, a reflection which (as we saw in the Introduction) proposes a kind of maximum boundary. Levi had been inside what he called the *unicum*—the singularity of

[24] This and the preceding quotation: Eric Santner, 'Freud's *Moses* and the Ethics of Nomotropic Desire', *October*, 88 (Spring 1999): 36. I was led to Santner's article by Julia Hell, 'Eyes Wide Shut: German Post-Holocaust Authorship', *New German Critique: An Interdisciplinary Journal of German Studies*, 88 (2003): 15. On a related theme see Adam Phillips, 'Close-Ups', *History Workshop Journal*, 57 (2004): 142–9.

the concentration camp at Auschwitz—and there had seen all kinds of confusion, border crossings in notions of identity and self which he was quite prepared to discuss. Yet regarding those who remarked to him afterwards that in his place they 'would not have lasted a single day', his response was simple: 'This statement does not have a precise meaning: one is never in another's place.'[25]

This is the maximum boundary indeed, and it provides a generative grammar in the ethics of Sebald's writing. Given the circumstances, Sebald is always on the outside of the *unicum*, and must remain so. Because of the nature of *this* boundary, he cannot cross over, must not trespass, grasp, or intrude. Yet also because of the boundary he must continually approach the place of transmission where, if nothing else, the nature of the boundary is encountered—and perhaps something of a story be transmitted.

Sebald remarked, 'I don't think one can write from a compromised moral position.'[26] The boundary does not stop the journey, it is why the journey continues. It is a place one always approaches, it always recedes as you come near. Transmission is of the essence, the essentials cannot be transmitted. The boundary is the place of navigation, but to cross it would be to recommit the crime. Here, at this boundary, what matters is the *form* of the approach.

## TRANSFICTION

The ethic becomes an aesthetic. At every stage the underlying compulsions of Sebald's work become the inner gestures of his writing, and through the aesthetic we discover the particular balances of his transnational form.

Take, for instance, one of its defining characteristics, the way in which every detail in Sebald's work becomes resonant in its linkages and uncanny meanings. In *Vertigo*, S stands before a fifteenth-century fresco

---

[25] Primo Levi, *The Drowned and The Saved*, trans. Raymond Rosenthal (New York: Vintage, 1989), 60. Here was Levi's sense of the confused boundaries of identity: 'the "we" lost its limits, the contenders were not two, one could not discern a single frontier but rather many confused, perhaps innumerable frontiers, which stretched between each of us' (38).

[26] Jaggi, 'Recovered Memories'.

by Pisanello in Verona, pondering the artist's remarkable method—
which, with one important difference, could be a description of his own:

What appealed to me was not only the highly developed realism of his art,
extraordinary for the time, but also the way in which he succeeded in creating
the effect of the real, without suggesting a depth dimension, upon an essentially
flat surface, in which every feature, the principals and the extras alike, the birds
in the sky, the green forest and every single leaf of it, are all granted an equal
and undiminished right to exist.   (*V*, 72–3)

The important difference is that for an artist such as Pisanello the
unseen hand of creation which gives everything its equal and undiminished right to exist is that of God; for Sebald it is the history and
prehistory of destruction which leaves its imprint in every last detail
of the visible. The method may be similar, then, but its implications
are diametrically opposed. The Holocaust is not everything for Sebald,
but in this respect it is both originary and emblematic. Like some
equivalent of the Big Bang, it can be witnessed—must be witnessed—
everywhere in its traces. In seeing it, one travels backward in time
without leaving the present; in travelling into the past one can see it
coming forward, evident in its precursors, always coming towards us
because it is everywhere. The cosmological analogy is compelling: there
is no centre, no edge; the whole is in the part, the part in the whole.
Of course it is curved, but it *feels* flat, like the proverbial ant on the
surface of the expanding balloon.[27] Hence the 'flat panel' of Sebald's
own work, which goes right up to the edges—and *off* the edges—
of his world. Here if depth is created it is only out of linkage, out of
flatness, out of the uncanny sense of the trace. All this keeps on going,
in the same way Ferber, or Paul Bereyter, or Austerlitz, seem to go on
for ever.

There is another reason for the flat panel of Sebald's work, simply
that he distrusts any easy vantage point of height. As always he provides
the rationale for his own practice, as on one occasion in *The Rings
of Saturn* when S visits the commemorative Waterloo Panorama in
Belgium, with its reconstruction of the monumental battle, seen from a
viewing platform in the middle:

---

[27] This is a standard analogy for our impressions of the curvature of an infinite and
expanding universe. It is not a comment on the projected rates of expansion in models
of the universe described as 'open', 'closed', or 'flat'.

This, then, I thought, as I looked round about me, is the representation of history. It requires a falsification of perspective. We, the survivors, see everything from above, see everything at once, and still we do not know how it was.[28]

As Faulkner said, the past is not dead; it is not even past. We cannot be above our history because we are still *in* it, still making our way through its effects and its meanings. There is no location above, only in the *trans*—the travelling in, and through, the syntax and navigations of our journeys, discerning depth only in the traces and echoes of our encounters. On one of the few occasions when Sebald does take on height—S is flying from Holland to England over the North Sea—it is mainly to contemplate the mysterious comings and goings of human beings on the surface of the earth below, busy 'extending their dominion by the hour', and to consider 'how little we know about our species, our purpose, and our end' (*ROS*, 91–2).

This 'flatness' (which is not the opposite of the search for a different kind of depth) is the natural corollary and cause of the feature at the heart of Sebald's work: how the self is always a *migrant-I*, always journeying in body and mind, always seeking further across the expansive surface of its travels. This is navigation in the life, in the writing, the 'I' always in the transitive, the self in what James Clifford might call 'pilgrimage' across the nodal points and stations of its routes— in this case a pilgrimage whose purpose is not a destination but the contemplations of the journey.[29] (It is no accident that *The Rings of Saturn* was subtitled in the German original *Eine Englischer Wallfahrt*, an English 'pilgrimage'.) At these nodal points there is something between the hope and burden of transmission—a parcel of letters, a recognition, an intimation of absence or loss or understanding somehow transported, held in the moment of transportation. In this sense, both in its travels and contemplations (only a different kind of travel after all), Sebald's is quite profoundly a *philosophy of contiguity*—where the contiguous is at once the method and the problem to be examined,

---

[28] W. G. Sebald, *The Rings of Saturn*, trans. Michael Hulse (New York: New Directions, 1998), 125. Henceforth referenced as *ROS*.
[29] For Clifford on pilgrimage, see 'Traveling Cultures', in *Cultural Studies*, ed. Lawrence Grossberg, Cary Nelson, and Paula A. Treichler (New York and London: Routledge, 1992), 110.

a syntax of transmission the recurring and recursive proposal of his form.

In this regard the *migrant-I* is nothing less than a *metonymic-I*, comprised of its contingencies and transitions. It is constituted neither by S himself nor by the phenomena or people he encounters, but by what is transmitted between them at the point of connection. Time and again Sebald stages this in his work, so that it becomes almost a literal reality in formal terms. Consider another moment—small, large—from *The Emigrants* when Max Ferber tells S of a dream that he was opening the great art exhibition of 1867 in London (together with Queen Victoria, as it happens). There he found a man called Frohmann from Drohobyzc who had been travelling from ghetto to ghetto exhibiting a model of the Temple of Solomon which he had built from biblical descriptions. That Temple recurs in Sebald's writing—in *The Rings of Saturn* (though constructed by someone else)—and Drohobyzc was the town of Bruno Schulz, the Polish-Jewish writer killed by a Gestapo officer: all this, in and beyond the text of the story, is involved in the echoing navigations of Sebald's work. But one key element is how the paragraph continues in a typical, almost provocatively laconic way:

And I, said Ferber, bent down over the diminutive temple and realized, for the first time in my life, what a true work of art looks like. I had been in Manchester for the best part of three years when, having completed my research, I left the city in the summer of 1969 to follow a plan I had long had of becoming a schoolteacher in Switzerland. (*TE*, 176)

The point here—evident after a short moment of confusion—is that the second 'I' refers to S, not Ferber; but then S has voiced Ferber's 'I' as well, in his narration. What the writing stages is the *boundary* between one 'I' and another—the place of connection, the place of transition, the place in some manner of transmission. This is the metonymic-I.

Examples abound in Sebald's work. In *The Rings of Saturn* S talks of Mrs Ashbury, whom he meets in her sadly forlorn house in Ireland: 'At that time, said Mrs Ashbury, she had not the slightest notion of Ireland's Troubles, and to this day they remained alien to her. I remember waking the first night in this house, feeling I was completely out of this world' (*ROS*, 214). The 'I' there is Mrs Ashbury, not S; there is a *handing-off* from one form of the 'I' to another, from third person to first—and again it is the boundary that is at stake, the self as a syntax of transition. Or—also from *The Rings of Saturn*—Thomas Abrams (who built the other Temple of Solomon) is talking to S: 'That is how it has been for as long as I can remember. As I took my leave and mentioned that I had walked...' (*ROS*, 248). There the second 'I' is S, not Abrams; for a moment the 'I's' overlap, even as they separate and diverge. Or, Chateaubriand wonders how 'it would have been if he had undergone the transformation and led the life of a gentleman chasseur in that remote English county. It is probable I should never have written a single word' (*ROS*, 253). Again there is a handing off, or taking on. The question of transmission is everything in these versions of a navigational, migrant, metonymic-I.

One thing these moments stage is the problem of the edge. As one 'I' crosses into another, or takes on another form of itself, either there is no edge, or the edge is all. The seam is the point of the join; the join concerns the nature of the boundary. It is as if a paradox of Zeno's were being enacted: one cannot move beyond one's space and time; and yet suddenly something has moved. But there is also a paradox that goes deeper than the purely physical conundrum. Consider it this way: in the encounters of this travelling-I, who creates whom? Are the figures S encounters his 'creations'? Or do they in some sense create him— who is nothing less than the sum of his trajectories? We know Sebald's 'characters'—Ferber, Bereyter—are in some sense 'real', but also they have been altered (as has been S, as a figuration of Sebald). In the descriptions there is an extraordinary precision—but also a methodical withholding. When S is talking of Paul Bereyter, or to Max Ferber, or Austerlitz, even when he 'voices' them, the seam makes it clear that he cannot speak for them. Through S's metonymic provocations, readers themselves have to work at the implications of the seam; there is transmission, yet also a difference in 'height' and experience, what can be spoken of, spoken for. For Sebald, then, if the 'I' is at the point of transition, the other is a point both of arrival and departure: what can and must be told, what would constitute trespass. He is in the unusual position of writing characters whose inner experience he will relay but in some respects refuse to tell. This is not the usual fictional mode—one reason to consider it *transfiction*: a writing whose every contemplation is the nature of the transitive, of the boundary, of its protocols and obligations.

It is transfiction also in its modalities. For instance, when S tells of Ferber's dream, and then simply records how he went to Switzerland, the moment stages not only the question of the edge but also the question of the *frame*. There is no frame around one story before another begins. The same thing happens in *The Rings of Saturn* when the absorbing memoir of Chateaubriand suddenly stops as S continues his walking tour in another direction. There is no frame in the writing because there is no frame in our experience. Frames mark edges; they lend perspective; they tell us how to see the picture. No such luck here, and if anything is emblematic in this regard, it is the actual pictures—the photographs—scattered through Sebald's works. The photographs are literally *unframed*: they leak into and out of the text around them in ways that vary from the direct to the exceedingly enigmatic and obscure. Often the photos are grainy, spectral, unclear; they speak to us out of a past that cannot be reclaimed or fully addressed, and even when they are direct, their resonance seems to continue for ever.[30] S discusses the atrocities of the Croation Ustasha during the war, and there is a murky photograph of Jews, Bosnians, and Serbs hanged 'in rows like crows or magpies' (*ROS*, 97). At least that is what the text says, but the text is not a caption, and the picture says something of its own in a horrifically graphic way whose significance cannot be framed. Again the book becomes *transfiction*, and not only because it intersperses image and text: it is so because its dynamic is in the transitive, the crossflow between the forms.

Sebald complicates these questions even more in that some of his photographs, as he has said, are real, some found objects, some taken deliberately.[31] Even without knowing this, we would have questions. The picture that opens *The Rings of Saturn*—ostensibly of the window in S's hospital room: is that *really* the window? In *The Emigrants*, a photograph of a book-burning in Würzburg in 1933 turns out to have been faked by the Nazis, though the event really happened; reproduced

---

[30] I owe part of this awareness to a thought suggested long ago by James Simpson. On a different tack, it is true that in the German editions of Sebald's books the photographs are clearer; but then the shift in texture of the 'same' photographs is another way of making the points raised in this discussion.

[31] See Sebald, 'Ich Fürchte', where he also aligns taking notes in words and images: 'When I am on the road, naturally I write down what I see, and also take notes with my camera.'

in the book, it then documents its own forgery.[32] Paradoxically, the photographs—on one level the form that emblematizes the very possibility of documentary—raise the question of verisimilitude in relation to veracity. In Sebald's hands, however, this is not so much to discount the possibility of truth but to complicate the journey towards it, in some way to withhold the destination of meaning, which also means a form of ending. Concerning a traumatic history the point is an acute one. In *On The Natural History of Destruction*, which explores the bombings of Germany during the war, Sebald raises doubts about both documentary and fiction in attempting to fathom its realities. Fiction dramatizes— which intrinsically means overdramatizes; documentary assumes the real, or may simply resort to convention when it comes to reciting disaster.[33] By contrast, in Sebald's own hard-won practice, there is the *transfictional* whose every gesture is to make meaning only the endless transitive, a search.

This then is surely the rationale of Sebald's mixed modes—not only image and text, but even within the text the combination of history, memoir, fiction, journal, travelogue, catalogue, research—every available form. When Sebald was asked why he did not call *Austerlitz* (the most 'fictional' of his works) a novel, he declared it was 'a prose work of an undefined nature'.[34] James Wood, commenting on Sebald, rightly draws on Benjamin's observation regarding Proust, that 'all great works of literature establish a genre or dissolve one'.[35] There is a genius in Sebald's form which is astonishing. It is itself a migrant form— a transfiction—where one genre meets another at its edges, just as S himself encounters others and the world around him in his own travels.

---

[32]  See *TE*, 183–4. Sebald comments on this in Wood, 'Interview', 27.

[33]  Sebald remarks that 'the construction of aesthetic or pseudo-aesthetic effects from the ruins of an annihilated world is a process depriving literature of its right to exist': *On The Natural History of Destruction*, trans. Anthea Bell (New York: Random House, 2003), 53. For some of the complexities of documentary, see the same volume, 24–6. For the deliberate suspension of realism in Sebald's work, see Wood, 'Interview', 27.

[34]  'Es ist ein Prosabuch unbestimmter Art', Sebald, in 'Ich Fürchte'.

[35]  James Wood, 'W. G. Sebald's Uncertainty', in *The Broken Estate: Essays on Literature and Belief* (New York: Random House, 1999), 232. For the original, see 'On the Image of Proust', in Walter Benjamin, *Selected Writings*, vol. 2: *1927–1934*, ed. Michael W. Jennings, Howard Eiland, and Gary Smith, trans. Rodney Livingstone *et al.* (Cambridge, MA and London: Belknap Press, 1999), 237. Benjamin's essay evokes many analogies for Sebald: on Proust's 'syntax of boundless sentences' (237); on the intrinsic link between memory and forgetting (238); on the Latin *textum* as 'web' (238).

It is a syntactic form, a metonymic form, a navigational form. No one genre or mode is capable of capturing the truth; together they comprise a journey in modality as well as content. In every way transmission is its inner proposal and contemplation.

Transfiction: we might reflect on the term. S is 'transfixed' by his characters, as we are, but always there is a moving—moving towards, moving on. 'Fiction' itself comes from the Latin *fingere*, to fashion, mould, imagine, invent. So, there is a fashioning, imagining across. Sebald writes the text of the boundary, always in motion, always the condition and context of crossing. The transfiction is transnational not only because of S's travels but because the transitive is its very condition and modality, the ground and space of its being and approach.

## WORLD WITHOUT END: *THE RINGS OF SATURN*

Just how far Sebald can go with this practice is suggested in *The Rings of Saturn*. Here Sebald's roots become routes—the *rupta via* in a particular form as the punctuated journey—where each station of the pilgrimage becomes the occasion for further travel: travel through contemplation, through contiguity, through the space and time of history.

Part of Sebald's inspiration in this is explicitly—and intriguingly— Conradian.[36] The epigraph to the book comes from one of Conrad's letters to his 'Aunt' Marguerite Poradowska in March 1890, where he speaks of the need to forgive 'the unhappy souls who have elected to make the pilgrimage on foot, who skirt the shore and look uncomprehendingly upon the horror of the struggle, the joy of victory, the profound hopelessness of the vanquished'.[37] This is precisely S's experience walking along the shore of the south-east coast of England, retracing (in part) Conrad's steps in both actual and other ways. So, S spends some

---

[36] Conrad is an implicit presence in Sebald's other works as well. One need think only of S's Uncle Kasimir's remarks in *TE*: 'This is the edge of darkness. . . . I often come out here . . . it makes me feel that I am a long way away, though I never quite know from where' (88–9).

[37] For the full text of the letter, see Frederick R. Karl and Laurence Davies, eds, *The Collected Letters of Joseph Conrad*, vol. 1 (Cambridge: Cambridge University Press, 1983), 42–4.

time in Lowestoft, where Conrad first came to England in June 1878.[38] But he also follows him textually. Conrad's letter to his 'Aunt' was written from Kazimierówka, where he had returned for the first time in sixteen years to visit his Uncle Tadeusz, and *The Rings of Saturn* presents an astonishing description of the last stage of his journey, drawn partly (but not entirely) from *A Personal Record*, which established Conrad's associative method in the form of memoir.[39] We see Conrad in his encounters with Roger Casement, and also his other (and more famous) letter to Marguerite Poradowska from the Congo, where he declared everyone 'repellent' to him and himself equally repellent to all—in the original French (*ROS*, 121). Here there are profound metonymic slidings in the 'I' of the text, where the historical Korzeniowski modulates into the speaking voice of Marlow delivering his Conradian descriptions right from the heart of *Heart of Darkness*, yet where S also adds detail *not* in the novel, emerging from Marlow's account (*ROS*, 119–20).[40] Most profoundly, there is the Conradian ethos, of a spectral gloom, of a haunting reality and disaster whose traces are to be found everywhere. When S visits the abandoned military installations of the promontory of Orfordness, 'which seemed to have an extraterritorial quality about it', he sees the abandoned 'remains of our own civilization'. Transported back by his ferryman (direct resonances from the domain of the dead) he sees the roofs and towers of Orford and thinks 'There . . . I was once at home' (*ROS*, 233–7). This is the Conradian *disposition* in the doubled sense: the brooding reality of displacement, no matter where in the world you may be.

[38] Zdzisław Najder, *Joseph Conrad: A Chronicle* (New Brunswick: Rutgers University Press, 1983), 55, 58.

[39] Compare *ROS*, 114–16, and Joseph Conrad, *A Personal Record and The Mirror of the Sea*, ed. Mara Kalnins (Harmondsworth: Penguin, 1998), 33–4. S, whose description is fuller, remarks that Conrad had recorded his visit in 'a note' written very much later; Najder, who has chronicled Conrad's every move, indicates (*Conrad*, 119) that his only surviving account is in *A Personal Record*; so it appears that S may have imagined himself (brilliantly) into Conrad's journey. Also, S says that it was Conrad's first return in fifteen years; Najder and other Conrad sources say sixteen.

[40] The metonymic boundary, for instance, occurs across the following two sentences, the first Marlow's voice from *Heart of Darkness*, the second belonging to S: 'The black bones reclined at full length with one shoulder against the tree, and slowly the eyelids rose and the sunken eyes looked up at me, enormous and vacant, a kind of blind, white flicker in the depths of the orbs, which died out slowly. And as this man, scarcely more than a boy, breathed his last, those who were not yet worn out were carrying hundred-weight sacks of provisions . . . ' (*ROS*, 120).

If Conrad helped establish the associative method, here Sebald turns the form into the very content of his book—and takes it further. The opening of *The Rings of Saturn* sets the scene: a walking tour of Suffolk—with S carrying his own rucksack. He records how he felt carefree walking for hours each day, but in retrospect became preoccupied with 'the paralysing horror that had come over me at various times when confronted with the traces of destruction, reaching far back into the past, that were evident even in that remote place' (*ROS*, 3).[41] We then proceed from his hospitalization in Norwich, staring out of the window like Kafka's Gregor Samsa, to the figure of Thomas Browne, who lived in Norwich in the seventeenth century, and who wrote *Urn Burial*, itself a consideration of the traces of the past, of uncertainty and mortality. Browne was in Holland in 1632, at the same time as one Adriaan Adriaanszoon (alias Aris Kindt, who had recently been hanged) was dissected by Dr Nicolaas Tulp. This was a scene painted by Rembrandt as *The Anatomy Lesson*, itself subjected by S to extensive visual dissection for its anatomical peculiarities, which, he proposes, were deliberately introduced by Rembrandt to reflect the violence done to Kindt in the name of knowledge. Rembrandt's painting hangs in the Mauritshuis in The Hague, and other associations take the story further. Governor Johann Maurits, whose home became the museum, spent seven years in Brazil, and had fitted out his 'cosmographic residence' in keeping with his motto, 'Even unto the limits of our world' (*ROS*, 83). The Mauritshuis had been endowed as an art museum by a sugar dynasty whose wealth had come from the slave trade, just as the Tate Gallery was in London; moreover, the capital accumulated during that trade still circulates today, still bearing interest (*ROS*, 194). 'Even unto the limits of our world' indeed.

These then are the doubled and tripled movements of the book: association; migration; transmission from one nodal point to another, from implication to variation; recursion is built in, as one story punctuates or feeds into the next. This becomes the generative grammar of the text—a syntactic, combinatory, navigational grammar whose movements are embedded in the most ordinary of places and the most unlikely of motifs. One of them is herring, long fished off the coast of England, and

---

[41]  Despite the inference in the book, Sebald did not suffer any mental breakdown, but was taken to hospital with a shattered disk in his spine. See Jaggi, 'Recovered Memories'. Once again we need to distinguish between Sebald and the narrative figure I am calling S.

processed in places like Lowestoft. Here a rather brutal history—which S recounts succinctly—culminates in a film made in Germany in 1936, which S saw at school in the 1950s. According to the booklet which accompanied the film, it showed how 'railway goods wagons take in this restless wanderer of the seas and transport it to those places where its fate on this earth will at last be fulfilled' (*ROS*, 54). Each of these terms— 'railway goods wagons', 'restless wanderer', 'transport', 'fate on this earth'—seems like a harbinger, at once uncanny and prophetic, of what was to come in Germany just a few years after the documentary was made. In this resonant universe, culmination precedes the cause—it is almost the *cause* of the cause—and nothing is lost in a history of human depredation. Nor is the connection between the human depredation of nature—a 'natural history of destruction'—and the depredation of other humans.

So too with silk, which becomes the metonymic thread of the book. Thomas Browne, for instance, was the son of a silk merchant. 'That purple piece of silk he refers to, then, in the urn of Patroclus,' S asks of Browne's *Urn Burial*, 'what does it mean?' (*ROS*, 26). The rest of *The Rings Of Saturn* provides something of an answer through a transitive history. We learn of Tz'u-hsi, Dowager Empress of China, who in the great drought of 1876–9 oversaw the death of between seven and twenty million people, yet offered a daily blood sacrifice in her temple to the gods of silk, 'lest the silkworms want for fresh green leaves' (*ROS*, 151). S traces the migration of silk from the Chinese Empire into the West, and its spread via the Huguenot communities of France, who became the master-weavers of Norwich. Contemplating the silk looms of the nineteenth century, he comments on the similarity between weavers, writers, and scholars who sit bent over, day after day 'engrossed in their intricate designs ... pursued, into their dreams, by the feeling that they have got hold of the wrong thread' (*ROS*, 283). S also considers sericulture in Germany, where a master dyer by the quasi-eponymous name of Seybolt was Keeper of the Silkworms in Bavaria in the early nineteenth century. And then we go forward, to the revival of silk culture under the Nazis, where its importance is revealed as S, searching for the 1936 documentary on herring he had seen in the 1950s, comes across a film on silk made for the same series. Silkworms were perfect for illustrating not only insect anatomy and domestication but also 'the essential measures which are taken by breeders to monitor productivity and selection, including extermination to preempt racial degeneration' (*ROS*, 294). The film shows the hatching, feeding, spinning, and finally the killing, as cocoons are suspended over a boiling cauldron: 'when a batch is done it is the next one's turn, and so on until the entire business is completed' (*ROS*, 294).

In all these ways, on a self-contained walking tour of Suffolk, the reach of the book is seemingly unending; and if the Holocaust is not at its centre, its presence is dispersed throughout the observable universe. The degree to which this is literally true is revealed in Chapter 4 in one of the most haunting sections of the book. S, in Southwold, enters into a series of reveries and reminiscences (including his flight home from Holland, with the surface of sea and earth laid out below him) that leads to the Sailors' Reading Room. Here he finds a photographic history of the First World War which opens with images of Princip's assassination of Archduke Franz Ferdinand in Sarajevo. That night, as if by uncanny connection, S reads an article in a newspaper of the atrocities carried out fifty years before in Bosnia by the Croat Ustasha forces, in league with the Austrians and Germans. There are graphic descriptions and images, of a head being sawed off, of instruments of execution that included sabres, axes, and hammers—and this is where we have the photograph of the rudimentary gallows where Jews, Serbs, and Bosnians were hanged like rows of magpies. The archive which houses these records, S discovers, in 1942 served as the headquarters of the Heeresgruppe E intelligence division, one of whose members, Kurt Waldheim—for it was no less than he—administered the transportations and 'resettlements' of the period and later became Secretary General of the United Nations. And it is his voice recorded on tape, reports S, that represents us in space on board the Voyager II, approaching the limits of the solar system, so that any extraterrestrials who find the craft, along with its other human memorabilia, will know what we are like on earth.

We remember that Conradian image of 'the ship, a fragment detached from the earth...lonely and swift like a small planet', and Sebald's narrative makes the comparison a breathtaking reality. If space surrounds the earth as the sea surrounds the land, then it has already been contaminated by our touch. And if space contains us, then it also contains Kurt Waldheim, just as his voice, in space, 'contains' us, represents us, is our metonymic record and trace. There is no centre, periphery, or definitive boundary. We are *in* the boundary, the inside is outside, there is no beyond to which we can go. Like the house of Governor Maurits, we live in a 'cosmographic residence', and we have become its writing, a matter of awe and dread. Like Grandville's bridge extending along its piers from the Earth to Saturn, noted by Walter Benjamin in his essay 'The Ring of Saturn', the reach of the book is vast—and vastly chilling as well.[42]

## SYNTAX OF LOSS: *AUSTERLITZ*

If, as Sebald suggested, one cannot write from 'a compromised moral position', then some time after the publication of *Austerlitz* it appeared he may have fallen short of his own principles. What were these? Among other things, his concern neither to appropriate the experience of others nor trespass on their experience. Yet a woman named Susi Bechhöfer claimed the experience of Jacques Austerlitz in his book was hers, and that it had been appropriated. She, similarly to Austerlitz, had been taken out of Europe on one of the *Kindertransporten*. She, like Austerlitz, had been resettled in Wales, adopted by a Minister and his wife—in her case an even more abusive father than Austerlitz's. Unlike Austerlitz, she had a twin sister who suffered more from that abuse than she did; like Austerlitz, she had the first inkling of her history when, arriving at school for an exam, she was told to write under a name that seemed wholly alien to her. Her own book tells her story—of how through extraordinary persistence, the help of others, and some good fortune she recovered the truth of her past.[43] But when she read *Austerlitz*, she remarked, it felt that 'once more...my identity had been usurped'.[44]

[42] For Benjamin's essay, see 'The Ring of Saturn, or Some Remarks on Iron Construction', in *The Arcades Project*, trans. Howard Eiland and Kevin McLaughlin (Cambridge, MA: Belknap, 1999), 885–7.

[43] Jeremy Josephs and Susi Bechhöfer, *Rosa's Child* (London and New York: I. B. Tauris, 1996).

[44] Susi Bechhöfer, 'Stripped of my Tragic Past by a Bestselling Author', *Sunday Times* (London), 30 June 2002; LexisNexis Academic, University of Massachusetts, Amherst, <http://www.lexisnexis.com/> (accessed 1 July 2004). My other main sources for this affair are Jaggi, 'The Last Word'; and Jaggi, 'Recovered Memories'. For an important commentary, see Rebekka Göpfert, 'Susi Bechhöfer Fragt Zurück: W. G. Sebald Lieh Sich für "Austerlitz" ihre Biographie', *Frankfurter Rundschau*, 15 March 2003; Lexis-Nexis Academic, University of Massachusetts, Amherst, <http://www.lexisnexis.com/> (accessed 9 July 2004).

Sebald had read her book, and had seen a television production featuring her story, and it appeared had used the facts of her life. She wanted formal acknowledgement from him in future editions of the book; but then in December 2001 Sebald was killed in a motor-car accident, and his publishers refused her request.

This sequence of events illustrates, if anything, the extraordinary complexity involved in this kind of writing. Who defines appropriation? To what extent is experience inviolable? What, in particular, are the obligations and liabilities of a German writer in taking on—even by way of search and deferral—something as monumental in its implications as the Holocaust, and the experience of its victims? More generally, what are the implications and risks of a transnational perspective *at* the boundary of experience, where the question of 'height' can make all the difference? We have seen how, habitually, Sebald was meticulous in the face of these issues. He was deeply aware of the potential abuse of Jewish experience in his writing.[45] He also claimed that 'as a matter of principle' he always asked permission of people to use their stories.[46] Yet Susi Bechhöfer felt he had not done so in her case.

The issues are far-reaching, and cannot be dismissed, and nor can the reality of Susi Bechhöfer's anguish. In the midst of this, there are signs that Sebald made some distinctions of his own—for instance between stories he had heard privately, where he did ask permission, and published accounts, which he may have felt he could draw on for his fugitive, allusive forms.[47] Beyond that, while in interviews he acknowledged both Bechhöfer's book and the television production, he almost certainly felt he did not exactly reproduce her experience.[48]

---

[45] Sebald remarked in 'Ich Fürchte': 'One is on thin ice when one speaks extensively with [Holocaust] survivors, and lets them tell you their stories. One must acknowledge the fact that there are definite limits to such encounters, that discussion is limited, that one must return, that one must earn the trust of these individuals. And trust must go so far that ultimately the text measures up for these people. Whether I have succeeded in each case, naturally I cannot judge.'

[46] Sebald, 'Ich Fürchte'.

[47] See Jaggi, 'Recovered Memories', where Sebald comments that he felt a right to base Max Ferber in *TE* partly on Frank Auerbach 'because the information on his manner of work is from a published source'. Yet this did not entirely change the issues. Auerbach refused to allow his paintings to be used in the English edition, and Sebald changed his name from Aurach in the German to Ferber: 'I withdraw if I get any sense of the person's discomfort.'

[48] Regarding Bechhöfer's story, Sebald commented that 'the details of [her] life . . . are far more horrific than anything in *Austerlitz*. But I didn't want to make use of it because

Aspects of Bechhöfer's story (for instance, the sexual abuse of her sister) do not apply to Austerlitz, and there are many aspects of his life that do not apply to her. Sebald also evidently used other sources, both major and minor, for the figure of Jacques Austerlitz—not only an academic colleague whose specialty was architectural history, but also Fred Astaire, whose original name was Austerlitz, as well as the obscure fact that Kafka's nephew was circumcised by a *mohel* named Austerlitz.[49] This is the characteristic mix in Sebald's work, therefore, and ultimately its own implicit test may rest on other grounds: as he suggested in *On The Natural History of Destruction* and elsewhere, the degree to which it measures up to the nature of the experience in the *writing*. In this regard, though Sebald could have—perhaps should have—acknowledged Susi Bechhöfer's story more openly, if the story has been taken from her, it may be returned in another way. Sebald's book does not *substitute* for Bechhöfer's story; nor does it claim to represent it. In a sense it leads both *from* and *towards* it on the very edge of transmission, where the experience it approaches is evoked at the most profound and moving levels of contemplation.

We can put it this way. What happens to a man who finds himself on a journey without destination, looking for meanings that are everywhere present and yet everywhere recede, hints and echoes that intimate a history of horror and shadow, constructing a spiralling vertigo of suggestion in every place he encounters? For such a person, every place is a presentiment, because the presentiment lies within him. In effect, the history of what lies outside the self is the secret history *of* the self. This is the reality, the *unheimlich* of Jacques Austerlitz. For him the journey forward must be a journey into the past. By definition, because of the nature of that past, it is a voyage into the transnational— but only in uncanny forms. And the journey towards the self is also a journey deep into the blocked syntax of the self, because this syntax is what has been disrupted. Here it is nothing less than the mangled

I haven't the right. I try to keep at a distance and never invade.' Jaggi, 'Recovered Memories'.

[49] 'Ich Fürchte'. This information is also repeated in *Austerlitz*, 67–8, in the voice of Austerlitz, where, immediately after mentioning the exam incident, he proceeds by associative deflection away from the emotion of the moment to recall discovering these other 'Austerlitzes'. The Austerlitz who attended to Kafka's nephew had '2,800 circumcisions behind him'; see Kafka, *Diaries*, 147.

capacity for navigation that must be used to navigate. We are in the space identified by Walter Benjamin where the wakeful state approaches the dreamworld, where reality seems not identical with, but only similar to, itself.[50]

It is no surprise, then, that the book opens in the Nocturama in Antwerp, for peering into the dark—of the self, of the past, of a history of damage—is what confronts Austerlitz, and, through him, S. The Nocturama is overlaid in S's mind with the evocatively named *Salle des pas perdus* in the main concourse of Antwerp's Centraal Station. Constructed under the patronage of Leopold II, private 'owner' of the Congo Free State (all the Conradian associations), this is where S first finds Austerlitz, whose interest in architectural history through much of the book seems like a displacement of the more personal history he does not yet know he needs to find. Like Stevens in Ishiguro's *The Remains of the Day*, Austerlitz's narrative is one in which the tape of memory is continually winding and rewinding, concealing as it reveals, revealing as it conceals, always standing aside from or next to the object it pursues, which is somehow both within and beyond him. Here the Freudian is the *pre-metonymic*: the connection which exists but cannot be found.

It is in another architectural site, the Great Eastern Hotel in London, that by chance S finds Austerlitz after a long absence. (Here, as in all Sebald's writing, narrative and analysis—story and analysis—cannot be separated.) S has travelled to the city to have his eyes examined because of a partial loss of vision, in a setting that seems like an inverse of the Nocturama. There, instead of S peering into the dark, the specialist shoots light into his wide-open eyes, and later that day, waiting in the hotel for the train home from Liverpool Street Station, he comes across Austerlitz, who tells him, 'I have never known who I really was' (*A*, 44). This marks the beginning of Austerlitz's real account, an account in which his very name is metonymic, dispersing him, so to speak, across the history and geography of Europe. Napoleon's victory at the battle of Austerlitz is somewhere in the background.[51] In Austerlitz's

[50] Benjamin, 'On the Image of Proust', 239.
[51] This is an echo augmented by the fact that in all Sebald's work Napoleon is a precursor of Hitler. As he put it, 'Napoleon and everything Napoleonic appears in nearly all of my books as an historical paradigm that has something to do with the idea of Europe, exercised at that time through force. What interests me in turn is the fact that the same thing was then attempted again in Germany around 130 years later, using even more brutal methods...' (Sebald, 'Ich Fürchte').

namesake railway station in Paris, the Gare d'Austerlitz, there is a transport network linked to the whole of Europe—and to Austerlitz's hidden life. He was taken out of Europe as a child by train; trains from the Gare d'Austerlitz took French Jews—including very possibly Austerlitz's father—to the concentration camps. Austerlitz/Auschwitz: the names are quasi-homophonic; one was a point of departure, the other a horrific destination.[52] In this regard railway stations are emblematic of Austerlitz's sense of self and location. It is no accident that he confesses to an 'early fascination with the idea of a network such as that of the entire railway system'; later he tells S he has 'a sense of disjunction, of having no ground beneath my feet' (*A*, 33, 109). The very modes of origin, connection, and transit that link Europe are Austerlitz's grammar of loss.[53]

There is a paradox worth mentioning here. On the one hand, it is *as* a transnational figure that Austerlitz has suffered his sense of dissociation. This, in a way, would seem to be the opposite of the transnational as connective, as metonymic, as navigational. But this is the history from which Austerlitz has emerged. For the Nazis, Jews were cosmopolitan, transnational in a 'bad' sense, and so they turned that definition into a practice. Where Jews were not exterminated or enslaved, they were deported, exiled, exported—exactly Austerlitz's fate. Yet it is in this 'transnational' limbo that the search Austerlitz barely even knows about is under way—the search for the connective, the syntactic, the very means of navigation. That is our version of the transnational, represented here in extreme form, but emblematic in wider circumstances. Out of a larger world history of trauma inflicted by exclusive versions of the national comes the search for we barely know what—in one aspect, a different version of the transnational. That, to some extent, is the nature of our boundary.

---

[52] I am grateful to Lawrence Douglas for suggesting this thought.

[53] For a useful discussion of the significance of railways in *Austerlitz*, see Amir Eshel, 'Against the Power of Time: The Poetics of Suspension in W. G. Sebald's Austerlitz', *New German Critique: An Interdisciplinary Journal of German Studies*, 88 (2003): 84–6. Eshel notes that Austerlitz's fixation on railways is based on the concept of 'family resemblances', clearly indicated in the original German text as Wittgenstein's *Familienähnlichkeiten* rather than Bell's English translation 'family likeness' (*A*, 33). But, in typical Sebaldian fashion, the term comes up in the book in relation to *buildings* in a discussion *adjacent* to S's account of Austerlitz's railway fixation.

It is fitting then that Austerlitz undergoes his first epic moment of memory retrieval in a railway station, after a period of breakdown. To be precise, this is after a period of *syntactic breakdown*—deeply fascinating in an analysis of the 'grammar' of identity. For Austerlitz has found himself utterly incapable in language, completely traumatic for someone who has made his life through scholarship and writing. He tells S what it was like: 'The entire structure of language, the syntactical arrangement of parts of speech, punctuation, conjunctions, and finally even the nouns denoting ordinary objects were all enveloped in impenetrable fog.' In this state Austerlitz could see 'no connections anymore, the sentences resolved themselves into a series of separate words, the words into random sets of letters, the letters into disjointed signs...' (*A*, 124). The point is worth emphasizing: Austerlitz's generative grammar of self—of continuity, combination, transition, articulation—is utterly obliterated. He feels like a man who has been abroad for a long time and can no longer find his way at home; he has quite simply lost his place. Austerlitz has an impulse to throw himself over the third-floor stairwell of a building (echoes of Primo Levi's mysterious death); then he begins to wander the streets of London at night, in a form of Nocturama, seeing nothing but faces half-familiar, half-foreign, spectres speaking a language that sounds Lithuanian or Hungarian, something 'with a very alien note' (*A*, 127). Syntax is now only an uncanny and terrifying haunting.

This is where Austerlitz finds himself drawn to Liverpool Street Station, built on the site of the original Bedlam, where excavations in the 1980s revealed hundreds of skeletons, and where Austerlitz feels the dead are returning from exile.[54] It is in the station one Sunday that, for some reason he does not understand, Austerlitz follows a porter through a doorway he had not seen before, to find himself in the disused Ladies Waiting Room. It is the doorway and waiting room of memory, and Austerlitz's slippage past the barrier through an opening he did not know existed can be read not only in a Freudian frame of repression but almost literally, as a physical and bodily shift. Here the place of his arrival becomes a place of departure. For that is where, in the vision that comes to him, Austerlitz sees a man and a woman and the boy they

---

[54] With fitting resonance, Bedlam later moved to the site now occupied by the Imperial War Museum.

had come to meet. It is himself, and that is where he recognizes himself by his rucksack—his metonymic self-recognition. That was when he had arrived in England more than fifty years before, to be met by his adoptive parents, and this is his first inkling of a personal history that had been hidden ever since. His entry into the alien language of English at that time meant that the language of his pre-existence, like an unconscious, was broken and severed within him. It is this unconscious he must now—can only—journey to find.

And it becomes the logic of his journey. One day, in an antiquarian bookshop, Austerlitz overhears a radio programme. Two women are discussing their experiences on the *Kindertransporten* of 1939, and one of them mentions the ferry *Prague* that brought her to England. Without knowing why, he knows he must go to Prague. The outer journey becomes the expression of the inner; Austerlitz proceeds literally by word association, a matter both of syntactic and geographic navigation. This is where the journey forward is a journey into the past, a past whose announcements can only be shadowed and spectral. And this is when Austerlitz discovers that if Prague seems strangely familiar to him, *it is because in fact he has been there before and didn't know it*— the very definition of the uncanny in the Sebaldian sense. In Prague Austerlitz meets his former nurserymaid, Vera, who instantly produces in him the knowledge of Czech that he had lost for all those years: the unconscious *exactly* another language.[55] Syntax, like an archaeology, is being retrieved—a capacity buried in an individual life by the hugest of historical forces. But of course it is not the end of Austerlitz's pain; the *geheim* of the *heim* is a haunting and continuing secret.

The form of the book corresponds to these currents and flows. In a boundary-less world where the limits of association or destination are by definition uncertain, paragraphs have virtually no edges at all (there are only thirteen paragraphs in the book as a whole). When Vera is talking about Austerlitz's parents to Austerlitz talking to S, the metonymic-I, present at intervals throughout the book, becomes particularly pronounced: 'Maximilian, in spite of the cheerful disposition he shared with Agáta, had been convinced ever since I knew him, said Vera, so Austerlitz told me . . .' (*A*, 166). Equally, the recursive becomes

[55] The reference here is of course to Lacan: 'The unconscious is structured like a language.'

an intrinsic part of the narrative. One sentence, running in successive clause after clause for nine pages (*A*, 236–44), serves as the emotionally heightened vehicle for Austerlitz's discoveries (from H. G. Adler's 800-page book, which Austerlitz learned German by reading) regarding the inner workings of the Theresienstadt ghetto, where his mother Agáta probably died. The sentence is itself a combinatory revoicing and modulation of Adler fused through the anguish and memory of Austerlitz; and of course repeated by S in a further syntagmatic chain of transmission. In this regard, though Austerlitz is 'contained' within S's narration, he also stands *alongside* him as someone S cannot, in the precise sense, circumscribe. Again Sebald works a grammar of narration as much as identity: no one can stand in Austerlitz's place; but no one can stand wholly outside it or beyond it either. The transmission—contiguous, limited, interrupted, haunted, obligatory—is all.

Where place is problematic, so too inevitably is time. What else can it be when the journey forwards means going back? One definition of a particular kind of fate is to be doomed to that kind of journey: the fate of Austerlitz. Talking to S at Greenwich, the true–false 'origin' and measuring-point of time and space on earth (we remember the doomed Stevie, also asyntactic, at Greenwich), Austerlitz comments on the essential artificiality of time: 'if Newton really thought that time was a river like the Thames, then where is its source and into what sea does it finally flow?' (*A*, 100). Towards the end of the book he tells S he feels 'almost physically, the current of time slowing down in the gravitational field of oblivion', and wonders whether it might be the case that we have 'appointments to keep in the past' (*A*, 257–8). Austerlitz's experience of time too, therefore, is uncanny, non-homogeneous but without Benjamin's illumination of the 'now'. On the contrary, every 'now' for Austerlitz is a spectre intimating a past he can never recover. The most poignant rendition of this is literally a dissection of time, when Austerlitz finds a film made in Theresienstadt. It is a propaganda film produced by the Nazis, based on a documentary physics of illusion (*Der Führer schenkt den Juden eine Stadt*), in which Austerlitz thinks he might catch a glimpse of his mother. The version he sees is no more than a fourteen-minute patchwork of excerpts, with a running time-count on the screen. In the four-second segment from 10:53 to 10:57 a woman's face appears, while the hundredths of seconds on the screen flash by, discrete but too quick to register. If space-time really is composed of quantum 'grains', then there may be something irreducible about its fundamental units; but then equally, we may not be able to see inside them, or even know what they are.[56] The limits of time are the limits of navigation, and eventually it turns out that the woman in the film is not Austerlitz's mother.

Austerlitz ends his researches in the new Bibliothèque Nationale in Paris, built with its four towers (he remarks) something like a Babylonian ziggurat, designed primarily for the humiliation of the reader. The resonance is acute: this is the 'National Library', where repression is built into the very form in which information is stored—much as it is in Austerlitz's life. Here Austerlitz is frustrated in his search for any records of his father, who had managed to reach Paris from Prague but was probably rounded up before being deported to the East. In fact the library is built—we learn via S, via Austerlitz, via a library staff member named Henri Lemoine—on the grounds of what, during the war, was the German storage depot for seized Jewish goods. It was the Austerlitz–Tolbiac depot, known to the Jewish prisoners of the Drancy internment station as Les Galéries d'Austerlitz. Today the depot is buried beneath the foundations of a building which houses national memory, named (remarks Lemoine) after a pharaonic President. Again the resonances: the National Library is built on the ruins of atrocity; Austerlitz's own name is embedded—therefore lost, available only as a trace—in its very foundations. One cannot find the past in the national archive except in and through the forms of damage and repression.

At a certain point Austerlitz contrasts the new National Library with its prior incarnation, about which Alain Resnais had made a film entitled *Tout le mémoire du monde*. But can the National Library produce the memory of the world? Here Austerlitz would lose himself in research where books would lead to footnotes to further books to his own musings and notations. Yet even then he wasn't sure whether he was 'on the Islands of the Blest or . . . in a penal colony' (*A*, 261). The echo from Kafka—the script of the crime written on the backs of the prisoners— is exact.[57] Whether in its former or current incarnation, the National Library produces the limbo of a search that can neither be resolved nor

---

[56] For a theory of discontinuous spacetime, see Lee Smolin, 'Loop Quantum Gravity', *Scientific American*, 290/1 (January 2004): 66–75.

[57] Austerlitz's neighbouring reader in the library has been working for decades on an encyclopedia of church history, and has now reached the letter *K* (*A*, 261).

abandoned. The national is inscribed on the bodies as well as minds of those who seek to undo it. There are hints that Austerlitz must follow (or should have followed) another route: the novels of Balzac, stray photographs, the reading room in 'the little fortress of Terezín' (*A*, 283).

Austerlitz can find no Transnational Library to heal trauma and provide the resurrection of memory, whether his own or the world's. Earlier he had told S how, flying with his school-friend, Gerald Fitzpatrick, the two had gone on until 'the last gleam of light was extinguished on the horizons of the western world' (*A*, 114). That is how Austerlitz will continue. These are horizons that correspond to, and account for, the irredeemable loss at the core of his life: endless, without centre or circumference.

## FORT IX

Yet if Austerlitz can find no transitive grammar, such a possibility may— just—be glimpsed through the progressions and navigations of Sebald's book, a transfictional prose work of an undefined nature.

*Austerlitz* is much concerned with fortresses, such as the star-shaped versions of seventeenth-century Europe, which became linked together in constellations and chains of defence. One such is the fortress of Breendonk, outside Antwerp, maintained by the Germans as a penal camp during the Second World War. When S visits Breendonk, he finds in its half-familiar, half-nauseating paraphernalia a reminder of his childhood—the hidden 'secret' of the home. He recalls, too, his discovery that Breendonk was where the writer Jean Améry was imprisoned and tortured.[58] The idea of the fortress applies directly to Austerlitz, the equivalent of the barriers that confine him, the boundaries he cannot get beyond, emerging from a history of war. After Austerlitz's night of memory in Liverpool Street Station, he falls asleep for some two days, with feverish thoughts whirling through his head of being at 'the innermost heart of a star-shaped fortress, a dungeon entirely cut off

---

[58] For an extended consideration of Améry, see W. G. Sebald, 'Against the Irreversible', in *Natural History*. Levi also discusses Améry, in *Drowned*, ch. 6.

from the outside world' (*A*, 138–9). The brick walls around Terezín in the eighteenth century, where Austerlitz's mother died in the twentieth, had been built to 'a star-shaped ground plan' (*A*, 187). Austerlitz tells S how the self-administration office in Theresienstadt was housed in block BV, known as 'The Castle' (*A*, 237); again, the allusion to Kafka does not need to be stressed.

It is with these echoes in mind that, at the end of *Austerlitz*, S returns to Breendonk, bringing with him a copy of the book *Heshel's Kingdom*, written by Dan Jacobson, and given to him by Austerlitz. A form of transmission is under way. *Heshel's Kingdom* tells the story of Jacobson's search for the history of his grandfather, a rabbi from the district of Kaunas (or Kovno) in Lithuania, whose death soon after the First World War prompted his family to emigrate to South Africa—thereby allowing them to escape the mass exterminations of Jews in Lithuania some twenty years later.[59] S, following Jacobson, recounts how in the nineteenth century the Russians built a ring of twelve fortresses around Kaunas; in 1941 they fell into German hands, and 30,000 people were killed over the next three years in the most savage circumstances. In a dungeon at Fort IX, Jacobson had seen a message—which S relays in *Austerlitz*—written by the deportees who arrived there from Paris: *Nous sommes neuf cent Français*. We are given some of their inscribed names.[60]

Jacobson's book has other dimensions of the story not in Sebald's account. He tells of visiting the Jewish cemetery in Varniai, from which his mother's family came, where the last gravestones are marked no later than May 1941. Outside the town is the wood where the massacre of the town's Jewish population took place—people who had no formal burial place. A memorial stone is there, overseen by one of the last two Jewish residents in Varniai, a woman named Vera—the name given to Austerlitz's nurserymaid. Jacobson reflects on the significance of the memorial as 'a gravestone for nothing less than the cemetery itself'.[61]

S recalls how he read up to the end of Chapter 15 of Jacobson's book at Breendonk, before leaving. Then, as on so many previous occasions, he walks out of the picture of his own book, through the edge, out

---

[59] Dan Jacobson, *Heshel's Kingdom* (Evanston: Northwestern University Press, 1998).
[60] Jacobson, *Heshel's Kingdom*, 161–2. Sebald (*A*, 298) does not follow this exactly.
[61] Jacobson, *Heshel's Kingdom*, 189.

of the frame. Yet the book continues with us, as Jacobson's had with Sebald, and through him, S. This transfer, transmission of telling and retelling, is like S's earlier visit to the cemetery in Bad Kissingen. A stone, handed on, has been placed on the grave. Such stones do not make fortresses but only boundaries of memory. They are boundaries of telling, of journeying, boundaries we can pass through or along. They might be the boundaries of the transnational library.

# 6

## Village, Empire, Desert

### *J. M. Coetzee and Nadine Gordimer*

> A direct correspondence is established between the last traces of
> the camp and a text written upon the sand . . .
>
> Alain Badiou, *Handbook of Inaesthetics*.

'I live at 6,000 feet in a society whirling, stamping, swaying with the
force of revolutionary change. . . . The city is Johannesburg, the country South Africa, and the time the last years of the colonial era in
Africa.' Thus opened one of Nadine Gordimer's most notable essays,
'Living in the Interregnum', first published in 1983.[1] She wrote it in a
period when the signs in her country were extremely hard to read, their
potential outcomes difficult to foresee. The Soweto Revolt, which had
erupted with such intensity some seven years before, had now ebbed,
and though there was sustained, even rolling resistance throughout the
country under the umbrella leadership of the United Democratic Front,
the apartheid regime was embarked on the most barbaric phase of its
terror and suppression, the full enormity of which would be revealed
only some years later during the hearings of the Truth and Reconciliation Commission. (They were hearings that, if they had explored the
realms of fiction, might have examined the dealings of Colonel Joll,
chief antagonist of the Magistrate in J. M. Coetzee's *Waiting for the
Barbarians*; and perhaps the Magistrate as well.) Two successive states
of emergency lay ahead, and few would have predicted the way the

---

[1] 'Living in the Interregnum', repr. in Nadine Gordimer, *The Essential Gesture: Writing
Politics and Places*, ed. Stephen Clingman (New York: Knopf; London: Cape, 1988),
262. The essay was first presented as a lecture in 1982. It is notable that in Gordimer's
discussion of 'interregnum' in South Africa, she also comments on its features and
obligations in global terms.

political system of apartheid really did come to an end: with the release of the African National Congress leaders from prison in 1989 and 1990, and the unbanning of the ANC; in the constitutional negotiations of the early 1990s; in the first full, free, and democratic election of 1994, and the induction of Nelson Mandela as President of South Africa.

If Gordimer was right in her sense of momentous change, therefore, her understanding of the form it would take was necessarily unclear. Yet if we take her assessment further and question what she meant by 'revolutionary', it becomes apparent that what concerned her as much as the future was the present and in some respects the past. In her essay Gordimer goes on to describe her whirling, stamping world as follows: 'the past has begun rapidly to drop out of sight, even for those who would have liked to go on living in it. Historical co-ordinates don't fit life any longer; new ones, where they exist, have couplings not to the rulers, but to the ruled.'[2] And Gordimer continues: 'It is not for nothing that I chose as an epigraph for my novel *July's People* a quotation from Gramsci: "The old is dying, and the new cannot be born; in this inter-regnum there arises a great diversity of morbid symptoms." ' It is this interregnum, then, that concerns her: a space of transition, suspension, or displacement, where co-ordinates are dislodged, horizons uncertain, perception distorted in the very instruments it depends on. Gordimer talks of '[t]he successfully fitted device in the eye of the beholder' inducing such distortions even as people such as herself—members of the small segment of white society committed to participation in an alternative future in South Africa—have to believe in 'our ability to find new perceptions, and our ability to judge their truth'.[3] In these circumstances, she suggests, if there is to be a claim on the future, it can rest only on a specific and crucial foundation: 'how to offer *one's self*'.[4]

Interregnum and the self: these appear to be Gordimer's topics, and as we shall see they occupied her fully in her novel *July's People*, published in 1981. At about the same time as she was writing this work, her compatriot J. M. Coetzee was working on *Waiting for the Barbarians*, published in 1980. Yet where Gordimer was preoccupied with the

---

[2] This and the succeeding quotation: Gordimer, 'Living in the Interregnum', 262–3.
[3] Gordimer, 'Living in the Interregnum', 266.
[4] Gordimer, 'Living in the Interregnum', 264.

immediacy of revolution in South Africa, *Waiting for the Barbarians* was set in a timeless, placeless universe as Empire is drawing to a close: the South African topic in a way, but only distantly echoed. More particularly, while in an essay such as 'Living in the Interregnum' (and in many others, both before and after) Gordimer addressed the insistent complications of politics and subjectivity in South Africa, in Coetzee's non-fictional writing of the time he was absorbed with a very different set of concerns: in a word, with linguistics. Unexpected as this might have seemed, Coetzee had trained in linguistics, and during this period wrote three scholarly articles on questions of syntax and rhetoric. Later, in conversation with David Attwell, he resisted the idea that there was any direct link between these explorations and his novel—that, for example, the interest in 'passivization' or 'the agentless sentence' in his articles reflected a concern with vaguer or more amorphous kinds of agency to set against those of Empire in *Waiting for the Barbarians*, or its hypostatized notion of history.[5]

Yet the writer's currents move in mysterious ways, and notwithstanding Coetzee's objections we might reconstruct the question in a different form or at a different level. For instance, in his conversation with Attwell, Coetzee comments on the agentless sentence, 'A shot was fired.' Here, as he points out, 'either agency *is not thought*, or agency is thought, and then deleted.' Coetzee appears to be more interested in the challenge of the first possibility, for 'one can *say* act without agent, but can one *think* act without agent?' But the second option opens up equally testing challenges. For if, as Coetzee suggests, agency is thought and then deleted, 'where, so to speak, is it deleted *to?* Where is the unconscious of syntactic operations? Is it an unconscious whose contents can be recovered?'[6] Even if there is no intentional link between this and *Waiting for the Barbarians*, it provides an extraordinary pathway into the novel

[5] See 'Interview' (section on syntax) in J. M. Coetzee, *Doubling the Point: Essays and Interviews*, ed. David Attwell (Cambridge, MA: Harvard University Press, 1992). Coetzee offered his objections in a characteristic key: 'Should I be hospitable to every plausible idea I hear about myself, on the grounds that what has never occurred to me is likely to be what I am hiding from myself?' (144). Coetzee's three articles on linguistics from this period, included in *Doubling the Point*, are 'The Rhetoric of the Passive in English' (1980), 'The Agentless Sentence as Rhetorical Device' (1980), and 'Isaac Newton and the Ideal of a Transparent Scientific Language' (1982). He had spent 1979 on leave, working on both *Waiting for the Barbarians* and the essays.

[6] For this discussion, see 'Interview', in Coetzee, *Doubling*, 145.

and some of its underlying explorations. For the novel is concerned with the 'unconscious' of agency, not in a Freudian sense but in the sense that Coetzee has outlined: agency as the unconscious of a system, or of a form of expression. In the nearly totalized system of Empire invoked by the novel, what characterizes agency within it? Or, conversely, where has agency *outside* of Empire been deleted to? The Magistrate—chief character and narrator of *Waiting for the Barbarians*—is implicated in a universe in which any agency beyond Empire is also beyond *him*, and to that degree unconscious. He has, as it were, been 'passivized', but in a sense which goes far beyond questions of attitude. He is not able to recover any modality of agency because the syntax of Empire has placed this out of his realm. *Actions are taken in Empire*; that might be one way of putting it.

What is it then that links these two approaches, Gordimer's and Coetzee's, despite their different kinds of writing, their manifestly different concerns? Here is one suggestion: it is the question of *navigation*. In this study we have seen navigation as an underlying generative capacity that links questions of journey and search in the external world to linguistic and—most especially—syntactic structures and progressions. As different as these two writers are then, and as different as their novels may be, we can say that during this period they are each, in their different ways, concerned with the options and propositions of navigation. They may emphasize different aspects of that dimension—the syntactic, the question of search—but these aspects infuse one another, since navigation is a facility that incorporates them both; indeed, they are intrinsically connected in the novels. We can take the question even further by asking it this way: when the world is in crisis, when a period (apartheid, Empire) seems both to be ending and somehow endless, how is this conceived, and what transitive pathways remain open? It is a question that goes to the heart of this study, for the threshold is in some ways our own—our boundary, the one we are currently navigating. From the microcosm of South Africa in a very specific moment— heightened in Gordimer's novel, shifted in Coetzee's—these novels have something to tell us about navigations in the interregnums of a wider world.

Of course, the South African story did not close with the end of apartheid; that ending was transitive and transitional, not climactic— the product itself of quite serious political 'navigation', new forms of syntax. And though Empire may seem total, there is always a beyond, an 'after' in some sense. So it is important to carry the story forward. That is the aim in this chapter, to consider navigation in transitional times, whether the moment of crisis or its aftermath. The project is to do so by considering not two novels but three: Nadine Gordimer's *July's People* and *The Pickup*, and J. M. Coetzee's *Waiting for the Barbarians*. *The Pickup* was published some twenty years after the other two, in a post-apartheid era in which South Africa was entering a globalized world. There is a shift through the novels, therefore, from the intensely South African context in *July's People* to the concern with Empire in *Waiting for the Barbarians*, to the landscape of *The Pickup* which is much more overtly transnational—at least in its settings.

But that idea of setting gives us another reason to dwell on (and with, and in) these novels, for each of them is also an exercise in a specific kind of *spatial imagination*, working questions of syntax, navigation, and boundary. Each of them heightens a particular topographical location: in *July's People* it is the village; in *Waiting for the Barbarians*, Empire; in *The Pickup*, the desert. It is an intriguing fact that each of them also invokes—sometimes directly, sometimes loosely—the topography of the others, so that the key terms of the three novels apply variously to them all. In this regard there is an added dimension, for we can think of these topographies as *topologies*—an inner grammar of space. We can consider it this way: Austerlitz's fortress (present in another form in *Waiting for the Barbarians*), becomes the perimeter of Empire, becomes the sphere of the globe. Through these morphologies, what are our options for navigation? Topology, in this sense, constructs the nature of the boundary in a certain way; it constrains certain possibilities of transition, or invites others. What kinds of navigation are possible within and beyond our current settings, the boundaries we inhabit? Conversely, how might particular philosophies of navigation transform the nature of our boundaries, so that they become navigable in meaningful ways, constructing other 'grammars' of space?

Much of this comes into view in these three novels from South Africa. And there is progression of a kind. In *July's People* we see closure—and one version of opening—in a moment of national crisis. In *Waiting for the Barbarians* we see, with extraordinary power, the pathologies of the 'total' boundaries of Empire. And then, perhaps unexpectedly, it is *The Pickup* which gives us a glimpse of how, if the transnational has not been achieved, we might—even within the constraints of Empire—begin to envision its possibility.

Three novels; three accounts of the nature of the boundary; three grammars of identity and location. Village, Empire, desert: the underlying narrative of these novels.

## VILLAGE: *JULY'S PEOPLE*

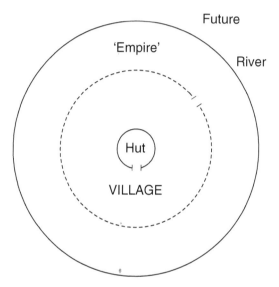

The novel begins with broken syntax, and a gap:

The knock on the door
no door, an aperture in thick mud walls ... [7]

The break in the sentence is the break in the walls, and is also the break in a life. The viewer here—the one who sees the aperture—is Maureen Smales, who has fled with her family in conditions of collapse in South

---

[7] Nadine Gordimer, *July's People* (London: Jonathan Cape, 1981), 1. Henceforth referenced as *JP*.

Africa to her servant July's village, where she finds herself waking in the morning after three feverish days of travel. If the hut presents the circle of the boundary—safe, imprisoning—it is a boundary that already has an opening, a space. In this way it anticipates the nature of Maureen's choice at the end of the novel: stay within the boundary of July's village—safe, imprisoning—or escape through the slightest hint of an opening. Here, in the hut, the space is one of uncertainty and vulnerability: the outside can come in through the opening, or the contours and definitions of the known leak out. The thick walls (relatively safe but apertured, open) exist within the circle of July's village; the boundaries of July's village (relatively safe but apertured, broken) exist within the larger context of apartheid. If apartheid is a fortress, its walls too are being breached in this imagined revolutionary moment. Everything is at stake here: whether there is an outside to the entrapments of apartheid and its internal mirror sites; whether the gap in the self can be the transitive space of a new kind of syntax; what grammar of identity can be formulated within—and beyond—these walls of self, hut, village, fortress.

These images came to Nadine Gordimer out of the intensities of the early 1980s in South Africa—the fictional counterpart of her musings in 'Living in the Interregnum'. Here, in a sense, imagination has been unleashed: the novel presents a setting of revolutionary breakdown as the very medium in which the future will emerge. Missiles have been fired at Johannesburg's airport, radio stations are going off the air, conditions of chaos and confusion prevail. In this regard, the scenarios depicted in the novel, if not the stuff of eventual reality, were in various quarters the matter of obscure imaginings: conditions of total war in South Africa with potentially terrifying outcomes. From that point of view the novel, while not wallowing in any conventional suggestions of horror, has allowed these presentiments to *condense*—to crystallize in this fictional form. We can think of *July's People* then as *symptomatic*, as an expression of its times. If that is true, however, it is so at a more profound level than simply the content of its imagined future. Rather, what matters is the *shape* in which that future appears: one of enclosure and concentration, boundaries closing in with only the slightest hints either of transformation or escape. There is little in the way of an imagined boundary to apartheid short of apocalypse—a particular kind of culmination, a topology in time as much as space.

And yet the village—July's village, to which the Smales family has fled—is not (or not yet) the place of apocalypse. Instead, it is the place of interregnum, between past and future, where the question of *navigation*, as an alternative to apocalypse, is paramount. Of course, Maureen and her family have, in one sense, 'navigated': with July's help, they have found their way to the village. This is the village as *destination*, but the more important question is whether it can be a place of *transition*. This has less to do with any actual or physical journey, and more with navigation as a mode of being, of disposition, of orientation. Having arrived in the village, can the family members, in these terms, *find their way*? Can they, in this setting of interregnum, see a way out of the past towards an alternative future? What of July, or the village's other inhabitants? Can the village help fashion a new outside from its present? These are some of the key and underlying questions of the novel.

In order to address them, it is worth taking a small detour through anthropological theory, for it allows much to come into focus. Here the relevant source (once again in this study) is James Clifford, who has rethought the site of the 'village' in ways that become resonant for the novel. Clifford notes how in Western anthropology, the village (as the pre-eminent locus of investigation) was traditionally regarded as bounded. Here the visiting ethnographer—the outsider coming in—would develop his or her knowledge through 'informants'. The informant would represent the village, and the village represent the culture as a whole—that representational form of metonymy lamented by Arjun Appadurai.[8] But it is the force of Clifford's argument that villages are not bounded or unchanging sites, and nor can they represent cultures 'as a whole'. Rather, in a world of movement, culture is something that travels in and *through* villages; movement not only makes boundaries permeable or changes the nature of a culture, but becomes part of the culture itself, always mediated, always part of that movement. In an important way, in our terms, this makes the village boundary not exclusive but *transitive*—on one level a positive aspect. But there is also a paradox we have to recognize, because, depending on circumstances, this transitivity can be bivalent. How this is so we can see from the novel.

---

[8] James Clifford, 'Traveling Cultures', in *Cultural Studies*, ed. Lawrence Grossberg, Cary Nelson, and Paula A. Treichler (New York and London: Routledge, 1992), 98, 100. Clifford, quite rightly, bristles at the term 'informants'.

For in this perspective, July's village is not separate from, or beyond the bounds of apartheid, because apartheid has always travelled through it. Nor is Maureen the equivalent of some 'outside' ethnographer coming in. Rather, the village is (and has always been) in apartheid, just as apartheid is (and has always been) in the village. And if Maureen is now in the village, so too—even before she arrived there—has the village always been 'in' her: because she too is in apartheid, because apartheid has been in her, not least because of her relationship with July. In that sense, the village is not 'alternative' ground at all.

If this allows us to see transitivity in a different light—to understand its potential liabilities—we can also see what makes the difference. What makes the difference is topology, specifically a topology of power and containment. The village is subject to apartheid, but the reverse is not the case. The seemingly closed circle is unbounded to the wider sphere of apartheid; its perimeter remains porous in the direction of the past—but has no access to the future. This then is a 'bad' kind of transitivity, and it is not clear how to fashion any other. Most of all, this affects Maureen, as the focal character of the novel. More than any of the others, she recognizes the essential continuity and asymmetry—that nothing, in the presiding terms of her present, can be free of the past and its residual power. She, more than anyone, is insistent that there can be no going 'back there'—by which she means Johannesburg, as well as a way of life: a temporal as well as spatial location, existential as much as historical. But it is by no means clear how to navigate forward into any other kind of reality, because the fact is that the village is still, in many of its dimensions, 'back there', as it always has been. This is how topology shapes the forms and possibilities of our navigations—something of great significance for any navigational theory.

It is in this location then, a location almost literally of *impasse*—morbid, residual—that everything comes under the microscope. Here, as everyone experiences what the novel refers to as 'an explosion of roles' (*JP*, 117), it is the past and present as much as the imagined future which falls apart.[9] The underlying beliefs, props, and habits of former lives disintegrate, yet there is nothing to replace them. This affects

---

[9] For a fuller discussion of the relation between present and future in the novel, see Stephen Clingman, *The Novels of Nadine Gordimer: History from the Inside*, 2nd edn (Amherst: University of Massachusetts Press, 1992; London: Bloomsbury, 1993), ch. 6.

Maureen and her husband, Bam, directly. What was it they believed in? The sacredness of human relations? Kindness and goodness towards others? But what, in effect, did these *mean* within the hall-of-mirrors world of apartheid, the enclosure of its Empire of lies? In such circumstances one's most generous impulses can be the most insidious because the most disguised; who knows what hidden mechanisms and motivations underlie them. In a chilling—and in some ways desperate—moment of recognition, Maureen understands how the sacred human relations she believed in, even between husband and wife, may be simply what one can afford. As for her own relationship with Bam, in these new conditions its old formulations crumble completely. He is still caught up within the logic of the past, fiddling with the radio for news, seeing out his identity as a white man with power, with the keys to the *bakkie* (pickup truck), with his hold on the gun, eventually stolen. To Bam's credit, as Maureen discovers a reduced and clarified modality of being, baring her breasts to her husband in a gesture that 'castrates his sexuality and hers' (*JP*, 90), to some extent he becomes domesticated, taking care of the children, his site the location of the hut. But it is clear that without the props and apparatus of the past, Bam and Maureen have become unmapped, strangers to one another, radically alien, simply 'he' and 'she': 'Her. Not "Maureen". Not "his wife"' to Bam (*JP*, 105); 'the blond man', as Maureen thinks of him (*JP*, 138). They are terms without relation or connection. The old syntax—metonymy—of a relationship has been destroyed because the context that underwrote it endures only as vestige, without validity.

This is the paradox, doubled and tripled. The past envelops the present; but it no longer has any legitimacy. Transitivity is a fact of existence in the village—but it is only of the 'bad' kind. Metonymy—attachment in its transitive form—becomes mainly ironic, because its grammar is still a grammar of the past, and there is no clear way of fashioning any other. We see this reflected in the novel's emblematic moments. So, when Bam and Maureen make love after the family has eaten a warthog he has shot, Bam wakes in the morning to find blood on his penis. He thinks for a moment it is the pig's, but it is Maureen's, for she has been menstruating. Metonymy makes the point: there is something predatory in the sexual identity of the male hunter, and of the system to which he (and Maureen too) belonged. Similarly, when the family are taken to see July's chief, the chief wants to learn how to use Bam's gun, to protect himself against the 'Russias' and the 'Cubas' if they come to his village. To this, Bam's response is that 'I don't shoot people', which brings a snort of derisive laughter from the chief (*JP*, 120). The fact is that Bam and Maureen were attached to a regime which did shoot people—the context, among other things, of the formerly 'absolute nature' of their intimate relations. Here the realities of metonymy as contiguity *and* representation cannot be separated—a shocking recognition. That is why Bam refuses to see himself as any kind of mercenary, but when he does so, it is his denial Maureen observes: 'She had been asked to note someone who had just arrived, but she saw the man who had been left behind' (*JP*, 126). Nor is it only the white couple whose residual linkages are problematic. The chief himself has been attached to the white government; this is why he fears the Russians and Cubans, not to mention the young fighters from Soweto who may overturn his authority. The point is worth emphasizing: it is not metonymy *as such* which is warped, but it is warped by the prevailing topology of apartheid and its residual power. The prevailing question in these circumstances is whether any alternative grammar of association is possible—whether the 'bad' transitive can be turned into 'good'.

It is a crucial aspect of the novel that it will not happen for Maureen and July through their relationship with one another. This, after all, might be the hope: that in the 'defamiliarized' setting of the village, the old relationships will transform, and July and Maureen find some altered basis of attachment and significance. But it is one of the thoroughgoing strengths of the novel that they cannot, for this relationship is also far too imbricated in the grammar of the past; and the village, as we have seen, is not really that kind of setting. July of course is more than a one-dimensional character. Even in the past, as a migrant working in Johannesburg, he was one of Clifford's 'travellers'—experience which separated him from others in his community, not least his wife. He also 'migrates' to some extent within the story; no longer simply a servant, he becomes a patron of sorts, a father figure to Maureen's children, a rival in authority to Bam. There is even a sexual dimension to this, evident at certain moments of intensity, and registered obliquely by Maureen. But, just like Bam, there is a part of July that has never left the world that is now 'behind'. Without someone to tell him to do so, July will not destroy his pass—the compromised symbol of his 'roots' as well as 'routes' under apartheid. That he too is caught up in the reverse syntax of the past is foregrounded in the key encounters between him and Maureen, all of which involve questions of language. Over the question of who should keep the keys to the *bakkie*, July will press Maureen on her 'trust' of him—'back there' as well as now in the village. He will insist on calling himself what Maureen always refused to: her 'boy'— the inner truth of the system of which they were both expressions. When Maureen tells him more about the fighting in Johannesburg, July remarks, 'We can only hope everything will come back all right' (*JP*, 95). That term, 'come back', is a signpost in Gordimer's writing, for it refers to the ANC slogan from the 1950s, *'Afrika! Mayibuye!'* ('Africa! May it come back!). Gordimer used it to moving effect at the end of *The Conservationist* (1974), a novel which anticipated the renewal of a black future in South Africa.[10] But here it is decidedly ambiguous. Either July intends the *'Mayibuye'* reference, or he does not and *would* like the past to 'come back'. That doubleness, that split, captures exactly the situation of July, caught betwixt and between in his own version of interregnum, unable to cross any boundary into a different future.

July's posture is not just a question (to adapt Homi Bhabha's phrase once again) of 'sly servility', but one in which 'slyness'—the maskings of deference—may double back and become *real* servility, just as Maureen knows she has been involved in forms of mastery towards July that have been both sly and real—perhaps never more real than when they were sly. Maureen's capacity for viciousness should not be underestimated: she holds out the threat of telling July's wife about his town woman (the sacred relations one can afford). In these passive–aggressive forms (so characteristic of master–servant relations in Gordimer's writing from the start), Maureen and July will nail each other to the crucifix of their doubleness. But when Maureen finally feels the full force of July's anger, she understands the lie at the heart of her own code. It is that the special consideration she had shown towards his dignity while he was by definition a servant 'would become his humiliation itself, the one thing there was to say between them that had any meaning' (*JP*, 98). Meaning is turned inside-out; all that is left is the broken syntax of the past, dislocated in Maureen's mind and across the gaps of the page:

---

[10]  Clingman, *Novels of Nadine Gordimer*, 141.

Fifteen years

       your boy

            you satisfy (*JP*, 98)

The syntax works both ways: who satisfies, who is satisfied? Maureen and July are one another's language, one another's form of expression. What we see then is not only symptom but pathology—and this is where Levinas's difference in 'height' makes a difference which cannot be resolved in the presiding terms of Maureen and July's relationship. Ultimately it is only when July berates Maureen in his own language, which she does *not* speak, that she understands 'everything' (*JP*, 152)— a negative syntax of a kind.

We see this form of fragmentation at every level in the village. So, Maureen is divided from July's wife and the other women—as is July, because of his past experience and the divided nature of his 'authority'. Only the children, members of a new generation, seem to modulate into the culture of their new surroundings—first Gina, the girl, with her friend Nyiko, and later the white boys, who slowly abandon the language and body-language of mastery. Here, in a more than literal sense, questions of 'height' do not matter, because the children have been less frozen by the topologies of the past. For those who have been 'passivized' by the world of apartheid, however, it appears no new kind of agency is possible, at least in any way that would allow a transition from past, to present, to future. It is in this context that in a radical form of divestiture at the end of the novel Maureen discards the very notion of attachment itself. An unmarked helicopter has come into land; Maureen abandons husband, children, and servant in running towards it. Gordimer calls her 'the enemy of all that would make claims of responsibility' (*JP*, 160); yet for someone who had not been 'in possession of any part of her life' (*JP*, 139), she follows the helicopter 'with a sense made up of all senses', running 'with all the suppressed trust of a lifetime' (*JP*, 159–60). A new physics of body and mind takes over. Maureen runs across open space and bush, through and across a river, and as she negotiates the river—the horizon tilts and then is righted again on the other side—it feels like a momentous crossing.

Yet what kind of navigation is it? The ending of the novel has generated debate: is Maureen running *from* or *towards*, should we see her response positively or negatively? To ask the question in these terms, however, may be misleading, for beyond simply 'positive' or 'negative' dimensions, the ending of the novel may be the product of a certain kind of *vision*—which, as such visions often do, comes with a sense of awe, dread, and radical ambiguity. Nicholas Visser reads the ending of *July's People* in relation to Yeats's 'Leda and the Swan', whose imagery it replicates: Maureen, as Leda drawn to the beating wings of the helicopter's Zeus, approaches annunciation, the beginning of a new era.[11] As Yeats reminds us, though, that annunciation set in motion developments that led variously to the broken walls of Ilium, and 'Agamemnon dead'. The future in that sense is unmarked: we do not know what it will bring. And this is perhaps why the visionary aspect is appropriate. As important as the future, at the end of the novel, is the *mode* in which it is addressed. The moment heralds a new time, but as Maureen crosses the river— baptism, redemption, hints of the 'promised land' with the fig tree on its bank—it seems she has also crossed into myth. The new time is *out of time*, apocalyptic and revelatory rather than 'real'. Crossing the river, Maureen has crossed from one form of reality to another, something not—or not yet—in the known world.

At the boundary of the village, this is a very different form of 'navigation'. If the hut has been open to the village, the village open to apartheid, this radical form of crossing seems to be the only way forward. We might put the question, then, in this way: what is the place of the woman who cannot remain within Empire—the Empire, loosely, of apartheid—but who cannot see a way towards any other future? In this moment of crossing it becomes apocalyptic, beyond, outside. Maureen is in a space and time of displacement, relocating not only herself but her 'self' in a time of interregnum. The grammar that achieves this, however, cannot be one of syntax, combination, or navigation in any of our usual senses. It is instead a grammar of *translation*. This in turn is not Walter Benjamin's version of translation, which proceeds by contiguity, the fragments which together make up a greater whole. Instead, we have that other meaning of translation— of 'carrying across', carrying beyond, the literal meaning of metaphor. Maureen is a translated figure at the end of the novel, just as time

---

[11] Nicholas Visser, 'Beyond the Interregnum: A Note on the Ending of *July's People*', in *Rendering Things Visible: Essays on South African Literary Culture*, ed. Martin Trump (Johannesburg: Ravan, 1990). I am also, to some extent, revising my own earlier readings of the novel here.

is translated from history to myth, just as she has been translated beyond contiguity. One time and place has been substituted for another. The novel has been translated beyond the grammar of metonymy itself.

In terms of topography, topology—the navigations they forbid and induce, the nature of the boundaries they invoke, the grammars of identity they constitute—the novel suggests its wider resonance. National closure, national crisis, produce apocalyptic modes. Similarly, when prevailing modes become apocalyptic, this is one measure of boundaries that have closed. *July's People*, with its vision of translation, is then the perfect symptom and emblem of its time. But its implicit question remains open: whether within the context of nation or Empire there is any form of navigation that would invoke not apocalypse but *transition*, transforming the nature of these boundaries.

## EMPIRE: *WAITING FOR THE BARBARIANS*

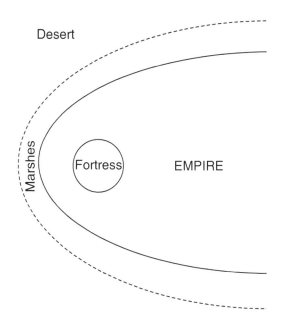

If so, we will not find it, exactly, in *Waiting for the Barbarians*, a novel which only heightens the sense of closure in *July's People*. But this, paradoxically, is among its many virtues, for the novel shows the pathologies of navigation under the virtually total conditions of Empire it not so much describes as *inhabits*. And while the novel is able to figure the possibility of an outside to Empire, consistent with its vision it also relinquishes the possibility of entering that space with any degree of claim, belonging, or habitation. For if by definition Empire is 'closed', how can we know, let alone claim or belong in that 'outside'? The novel, then, is profoundly concerned with the nature of the boundary under Empire—a boundary it does not assume to have found a way beyond. At the least, it is the kind of boundary we have to understand if we are ever to fathom alternative forms of navigation in its space.

The first thing to realize about the novel, against the backdrop of *July's People*, is that its topography is shifted. Here there is, strictly speaking, no 'village' (though there are the ruins of previous settlements, and the huts of the fisherfolk). Instead, the village has become the fortress— the fortress of Empire, of which it is the distant attachment but also the localized totality. Everything within the fortress is in the Empire, and the Magistrate's attempts at resistance notwithstanding, we might also say the reverse. So, village and Empire are in this sense—an even stricter sense than applies to *July's People*—coterminous. In this setting the Magistrate does become something of an ethnographer—he studies ruins, attempts to interpret runes—but realizes that he himself cannot be separated from his observation. Because he is both subject and object of Empire, his vision as well as his being lies (in every sense) within its circle—and this is one of the reasons he becomes an ethnographer too of his own subjectivity, as much as of the violence of Empire. There are gaps in the walls in the fortress—not openings of the kind Maureen found in her hut, but heavy doors with gates and locks—and the Magistrate can, to some extent, let himself outside its prisons, its walls. But the site which provides true opposition to Empire—into which the Magistrate ventures but where he cannot dwell—is the desert, home to the unsettled and nomadic barbarians. If this represents an 'outside' to Empire—something Maureen could not find except in apocalyptic terms—the Magistrate cannot find any footing in that outside at all.

How are we to read the novel's settings, against anything like the 'real' world? The South African echoes are there in Colonel Joll and the Third

Bureau (shades of South Africa's Bureau of State Security of the 1970s), as well as in the prisoner whose violent death is ascribed to an attack on his captors (the murder of Steve Biko, and all those deaths in South African interrogation rooms). Yet this could be the Roman Empire, the Gestapo, the Lubyanka Prison, or Abu Ghraib; unfortunately, the world keeps inventing new contexts for this novel. As to period, there are horse-drawn carriages and arrows, and Colonel Joll's sunglasses are a new invention, but there are also guns. The only hint of a setting is that spring comes in March, which means this is a northern Empire, but in other respects the novel's co-ordinates are fictional: Colonel Joll, inscribing the word 'enemy' on the backs of his prisoners, comes straight from Kafka's penal colony. In these ways, the novel takes on some of the attributes of a dream: its atmosphere is overwhelming, its details precise yet looming, its edges both marked and unclear. We have a word (or a set of words) for such features now in this study. The novel's setting is ghosted, spectral, uncanny, telling its secrets of the 'home'—of many homes, of the world as 'home' under Empire—with extraordinary power.

It is in this context that the Magistrate experiences the pathologies of navigation—patterns the novel suggests on every level, in every way. On the one hand, there is the world the Magistrate knows very well: he is the lazy official on the outpost of Empire, with his familiar routines. Yet there is always for him the sense of *another* time and space, without gradations, markers, or edge. The Magistrate feels 'the patter of sand driving from nowhere to nowhere across the wastes'. He remarks, 'Space is space, life is life, everywhere the same.'[12] He is an amateur archaeologist, but when he explores the ruins of previous settlements outside the battlements of the fort, time itself seems to have no sequence, or at most to be recursive in a self-referential way. Standing in the ruins, the Magistrate does not know whether he is stationed above the head of some former Magistrate like himself from a previous era. There is a paradox here which concerns the very nature of the boundary under Empire. When the Magistrate senses time and space as unmarked, this seems a trace—like some low hum in the cosmos—of the universe *outside* of Empire. But it is an outside the Magistrate cannot

[12] Both these quotations: J. M. Coetzee, *Waiting for the Barbarians* (New York: Penguin, 1999), 16. Henceforth referenced as *WFB*.

reach because, within Empire, something like those *same* conditions apply. Empire erects its ramparts against the endless horizontal, imposes its history on the featureless plane of time; its boundaries are severe, impermeable, and marked. But precisely *because* of that fact, the world within Empire is similarly undifferentiated. Empire does not permit any difference beyond the differences it constructs; it becomes a total environment, imposing its own version of the uniform. Its time and space are 'homogeneous, empty', and what it requires from its subjects is—in every sense of the word—'indifference'.

This is the Magistrate's problem: how *does* one establish 'difference' in such a setting? The Magistrate may imagine himself an alternative to Joll: kindly, ameliorative, well-intentioned. But under Empire what does this mean? Where Joll tortures stray captives, the Magistrate—the 'passivized' agent of Empire—is his witting and unwitting accomplice. Where the Colonel imposes his marks on the barbarian woman, half-blinding her and breaking her feet—the Magistrate is aware of his no less imperious desire to 'read' those marks and lay bare the woman's core. His inability to do so may mean only that he is a less successful reader than Joll is a writer, but this is in a way the point. Under Empire, the Magistrate cannot become an 'author': in his official capacity as agent he is, on the contrary, *authorized*—the exact equivalent of being 'passivized'. This, in part, underlies the Magistrate's recognition at the end of the novel, in relation to Joll: 'I was the lie that Empire tells itself when times are easy, he the truth that Empire tells when harsh winds blow' (*WFB*, 133). We are in familiar territory here, and it is akin to Marlow's at the end of *Heart of Darkness*. The truth maintained by the lie, the lie as a kind of truth, the fact that they are indissolubly connected and quite possibly indistinguishable under Empire: that is a horror of its own—a horror of meaning as much as of navigation.

For meaning and navigation are of course connected, and Empire neutralizes them both. The reason for this is intriguing. As we have seen a number of times, both meaning and navigation occur not despite but because of difference—the difference that makes transitivity possible. But in the realm of the homogeneous—*the regime of indifference*—the possibility of navigation is negated. What this means for the Magistrate is that he is precluded from navigation by the very conditions which prompt the need for it in the first place. Nowhere does he feel this more than in his relations with the barbarian woman. To the Magistrate, the woman remains a horizonless landscape, as if she had no interior, 'only a surface across which I hunt back and forth seeking entry' (*WFB*, 42). She is like the beyond of Empire: a landscape the Magistrate cannot fully enter into or understand. Navigation requires, in this sense, a 'navigable' boundary—one that in the form of gap and difference can become the space of transition. But in the land of the uniform there is only a *this* side and *that*, without any connection between them, so that both become distinctly unknowable—at least to the subject of Empire. That is why, for the Magistrate, any sense of journey or transition is closed; he can neither find the navigable boundary nor become a version of that boundary himself—a form of syntax between Empire and the woman, reconciling the distance between them.[13] Precisely *as* Magistrate he represents, in this sense, a different kind of 'law': the passivized law of navigation in Empire. The boundary under Empire is the space of a journey that is no journey, meaning that cannot generate meaning.

One sees this enacted in so many ways in the novel, not least in matters of language. 'Prisoners are prisoners,' remarks Joll (*WFB*, 21), or he educates the Magistrate on how pain will produce truth. Empire works through the indifference of tautology, or through equations of substitution (prisoners are guilty, prisoners are enemies, enemies are— or should be—prisoners). Yet, by way of contrast, there are the slips of wood the Magistrate finds in the ruins outside the fort. They are not called 'slips' for nothing, since their meaning is evasive. The Magistrate tries them in every combination, and—as there are 256 of them—they might even have mathematical combinations, but he can reconstruct nothing about them, neither lexeme, sequence, nor syntax. The only language that appears to escape the Empire of signs then is completely obscure—not one the Magistrate, 'by definition', can comprehend. Later, the Magistrate will turn this indeterminacy against Joll, inventing a kind of allegory of the slips. He tells Joll that the barbarian character for *war* can also mean *vengeance,* and inverted it stands for *justice* (*WFB*, 109). This is metonymy and menace of a different kind, and the Magistrate uses it to unsettle Joll. But Joll is not unsettled—at least not by this; he tells the Magistrate the slips are nothing more than gambling

---

[13] For an evocative account of the Magistrate's situation, where the barbarian woman herself is like the 'frontier', see Denis Hirson, *White Scars: On Reading and Rites of Passage* (Johannesburg: Jacana, 2006), 88.

sticks. And in a sense they are: the Magistrate has gambled on the *idea* of an alternative language, but within the passivized syntax of Empire, its difference is unavailable to him. He cannot connect *this* language with *his* language: a profound incapacity of navigation at the linguistic level itself, in the language of language. If there is a language outside Empire, the Magistrate cannot find the language to get there.

Intriguingly, these issues are also presented through an optical grammar in the novel. It begins with Colonel Joll, who arrives wearing two dark discs in front of his eyes, filters against the desert, truth, and reciprocity. Torturing the barbarian woman, he half blinds her with a fork-like instrument, so that she has only peripheral vision, and the rest is blurred. Her vision has been shifted metonymically: literally, she sees only contiguity, attached objects rather than the focus of any attention. It is no accident, then, that when the woman looks at the Magistrate her vision is oblique; she seems to be looking over his shoulder. And in a sense she is: she is looking at what he is contiguous to—the reality of Joll, to which he is attached. For his part, when the Magistrate looks at the woman, seeking connection, he finds only his own (doubled) reflection: 'I . . . stare into the dead centres of her eyes, from which twin reflections of myself stare solemnly back' (*WFB*, 40–1). This 'dead centre' is the centre of Empire, of Empire's damage to the woman, and the person reflected at its core is none other than the Magistrate. Here are further laws of Empire: Joll, representing the centre of power, can be seen in every aspect of its dispersal; the Magistrate, its oblique functionary, is reflected at the 'dead centre' of its effects. And there are other kinds of doubling. When the Magistrate tells the barbarian woman to look at him, she says 'I am looking. This is how I look' (*WFB*, 26). The bivalent verb—this is how I see/this is how I appear—becomes the optical equivalent of the passivized agency of Empire. Actions are taken in Empire; and this is how Empire 'looks'. Where Gordimer spoke of the 'successfully fitted device in the eye of the beholder', here the 'eye' is nothing less than the totality of Empire itself: its ways of constituting both the objects and subjects of perception. It is part of Empire's grammar of 'indifference', a kind of Imperial blindness.

Given all this—the impossibility of navigation, of transition, of meaning—it is no surprise that for sections of the novel the Magistrate adopts rituals he barely understands. With the barbarian woman he resorts to washing, first her feet and then her whole body. But is this expiation? An attempt to erase the marks of torture, make her feet whole? Is it a gesture of care, or another form of manipulation and abuse? It is an activity adjacent to sex, though it is not sex, just as it is adjacent to torture. Once again significance takes on metonymic form— linked and therefore, in this world, both evasive and complicitous. After these washings, the Magistrate falls into senseless sleep, where beyond the limits of consciousness he exists only in a state of unknowing. Sleep is the Magistrate's horizon, and perhaps this is where consciousness has been deleted to. Or, the only place he has an horizon is between consciousness and unknowing—the former compromised, the other inhabited by signs empty of meaning or syntax. At times the Magistrate has dreams which he recounts, vague images of children, a hooded girl with her back to him (connected with the barbarian woman perhaps), building a snowman, building a humanoid figure without arms or legs. But these are not Freudian dreams: there is no return from them with any repressed object of knowledge. These dreams take place not so much in the unconscious but in a parallel universe, adjacent, where knowledge is simply different, and therefore unknowable in waking life. For this reason, too, these dreams are not prophetic: there is nothing the Magistrate can see or learn here about himself, his Empire, or the future.[14] In the Magistrate's dreams, and in some sense throughout the novel, he experiences the displacements of a universe in which nothing answers back. Again, that means no meaningful journey. The syntax of the self is intrinsically incomplete, intransitive, a void without travel or return.

It is in these circumstances that the Magistrate adopts the only alternatives open to him: renunciation, refusal, and a degree of realignment—some attempt at reorientation within the limits of Empire. Renunciation, in one form, comes in his declaration to the torturer, Mandel, as culmination to his experiences: 'The crime that is latent in us we must inflict on ourselves. . . . Not on others' (*WFB*, 143). What the Magistrate renounces is the form of agency that might underlie Empire itself; a sacrificial logic of weakness in its very expression of power. Here the Magistrate draws on a principle that, almost like a trace from a language outside of Empire, may serve as a compass of a kind,

<hr>

[14] For a reading of the 'refusal' of these dreams 'to succumb completely to the interpretive drive', see Derek Attridge, *J. M. Coetzee & The Ethics of Reading: Literature in the Event* (Chicago and London: University of Chicago Press, 2004), 47. See in general his ch. 2, 'Against Allegory' for a discussion of *WFB*.

even if only in negative terms. Later, it is a similar gesture that stands behind the Magistrate's refusal. When Joll inscribes the word 'ENEMY' on the backs of the barbarian prisoners, and invites the inhabitants of the fortress to participate in their degradation, the Magistrate offers a monadic and monosyllabic response. He shouts '*No!*', and then '*No! No! No!*' (104). It is a primal moment, and a primal word of refusal—singular to Joll's singularity. But that is also part of the point, for the word is asyntactic—not a navigation, because it cannot be, but the essence of a moral absolute and injunction against the obscene. When the Magistrate does attempt the syntactic, he risks the florid and absurd—'We are the great miracle of creation!'—or else all he can manage are the bare fundamentals: 'Look!...How—!...Look at these men!...*Men!*' (105). There is much credit in his gestures, which seem to echo a universe both before and after Empire, or draw on moral reservoirs still available residually within it, but their non-limitation in that respect is still subject to Empire's neutralizing capacities.

From this point of view it is revealing that even in the Magistrate's refusal, the one word he cannot bring himself to mention is a different kind of absolute—a universal metonym with a syntax all of its own. As he remarks, '*Justice*: once that word is uttered, where will it all end?' (*WFB*, 106). The reason the Magistrate—always self-aware; he knows as much about himself as we do—cannot bring himself to utter the word 'justice' is because he knows it will come only with the end of Empire: 'for where can that argument lead but to laying down our arms and opening the gates of the town to the people whose land we have raped?' (*WFB*, 106). In this sense, the borders of justice cannot be contained; they cannot even be defined. They are illimitable borders to counter the limits of Empire, to undermine its own version of illimitability. But here the Magistrate will not choose justice, and it is part of the complexity of the novel that the reason why remains open. Is the Magistrate the servant of Empire because he refuses to choose its end? Or is there another possibility—certainly a non-trivial one—that under Empire *choice itself* has been 'passivized', so that what looks like free will is merely the structure of a certain kind of choice? The novel may not mean it exactly this way, but we can still ask the question: under Empire—the kind of Empire described in the novel—how many are free to 'choose' its end, with everything that may imply? Under these conditions, is it possible even to know what 'justice' means? Justice may be on the outside of Empire, beyond its space, before or after its time, but we cannot even know enough to ask what it may really signify or entail. In this regard, the Magistrate's choice—the nature of his navigation—may be emblematic rather than idiosyncratic.

It is within this logic, therefore, that if intimations of alterity come anywhere in the novel, they do so only in the desert—bordering on the outside of Empire—which the Magistrate journeys into with the barbarian woman. Here, in a mirroring landscape, as he and his band follow—or are followed by—the barbarians, are they agents or objects of agency? On native territory the woman regains some of her energy and animation, and there is even the beginning of a sexual relationship between her and the Magistrate. Yet their relationship—like that of Maureen and July in *July's People*—shows only a distorted form of reciprocity, a language they cannot mutually express or understand. When the Magistrate asks the woman to return with him to the world of Empire, it is she, like Maureen, who refuses to go 'back there'. There can be no free relationship on unfree ground, and the Magistrate is at least able to renounce possession and power in giving up the woman. But for the rest, there is only obscurity. There is an outside to the fortress and to Empire, in other words, and it may exist in the desert; the Magistrate can sense it, even enter it dimly on the edge of his world, but ultimately it represents a transition he cannot undertake. As in Coetzee's later novel *Foe*, where Friday's tongue has been cut out, there may be a different form of speech from that of Empire, but those within Empire cannot know or speak it.

In the end, when the barbarians lure Joll's expeditionary force to their doom in the desert, it seems the desert has the beating of Empire. It operates according to its own logic, and its version of time—allied to the seasonal cycles of the marshes, the birds—will overcome history: perhaps only for history to resume in a new cycle of Empire. In that sense archaeology is the best, and only, prophecy in *Waiting for the Barbarians*, even if its syntax is obscure. As for the Magistrate, he remains what he was at the beginning, the ameliorative functionary of Empire. He ends the novel 'feeling stupid, like a man who lost his way long ago but presses on along a road that may lead nowhere' (152). This is the journey without transition, the landscape of those who, even if they are not 'indifferent', cannot find meaningful difference. Navigation itself has been passivized.

Is this Empire the space of our world? The answer is both yes and no. It seems, at the least, to be a representation *of* our world, with its sense of the contained and unending, the limited and limitless— a different kind of interregnum. Coetzee's vision is one of totality, therefore—a horizonless world governed by Empire with no alternative that its inhabitants can claim or know. There is no translation here, no apocalypse, and most certainly no transition. Where might such a transition exist? If anywhere it is in the desert, on the 'outside' of Empire; but by definition this is space the Magistrate cannot grasp. In this regard, he remains enigmatic as well as emblematic: the self-consciousness of Empire, the representative of its passivized 'laws', its 'authorized' version, his resonance at the last both topographical and syntactic. For the Magistrate, mapped and unmapped by the topologies of Empire, the desert beckons, but it is space he cannot inhabit. It is the space to which, under Empire, an alternative grammar of identity has been deleted.

## DESERT: *THE PICKUP*

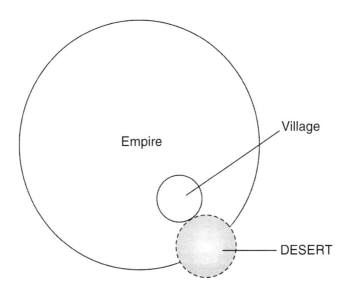

If Empire is the world that surrounds us, what options are there for navigation within its boundaries? This is one of the questions raised by Michael Hardt and Antonio Negri in their book *Empire*, which in its view of a total environment serves as something of an equivalent to the vision of *Waiting for the Barbarians*.[15] In this regard, according to Hardt and Negri, the world as we know it has undergone a paradigm shift. The old forms of Empire were the outward expressions of geographic control exercised by national powers, and they could, to some extent, be opposed through national resistance. But Empire itself is now different. In this new world, Hardt and Negri argue, 'Empire' belongs to no one, nor is it located 'anywhere'. Instead, it is an encompassing system, coterminous with the endless horizons of the globe itself, a new form of existence enmeshing all without escape. There is no 'outside' to Empire, no 'beyond' to which we might cross, no national location or principle that might oppose it. Empire has 'no limits'; it 'suspends history'; it 'creates the very world it inhabits.'[16] It is much like Empire in Coetzee's novel, in other words—or even, so much earlier, Conrad's vision in *Heart of Darkness*.

Yet this version of Empire poses a theoretical quandary. If Empire is so all-inclusive, if it creates the world it requires, what forms of resistance or alterity are possible? Much like the Magistrate in *Waiting for the Barbarians*, it would seem we are faced with a problem.[17] Here, however, Hardt and Negri convert the presiding strengths of Empire into a weakness, weakness into a kind of strength. If Empire is 'everywhere', that means 'anywhere' can be a point of resistance: 'If there is no longer a place that can be recognized as outside, we must be against in every place.'[18] Probably this will not happen in the old way: 'being-against' Empire will occur not through a direct opposition of forces but may be

---

[15] Michael Hardt and Antonio Negri, *Empire* (Cambridge, MA and London: Harvard University Press, 2000).

[16] Hardt and Negri, *Empire*, xiv–xv.

[17] It is intriguing that Hardt and Negri do not focus on *Waiting for the Barbarians*, perhaps because Coetzee's novel does not allow any forms of navigation 'internal' to Empire—precisely what Hardt and Negri attempt to develop. They do focus on *Life & Times of Michael K*, however, because Michael K is always in motion, preferring (like Bartleby in Melville's narrative) not to serve. For Hardt and Negri such refusals are the preface to new and more collective forms of navigation by a new social body. See *Empire*, 203–4.

[18] This and the following quotation: Hardt and Negri, *Empire*, 211, 212.

most effective 'in an oblique or diagonal stance'. It will come through the very patterns that Empire unleashes: migration which cannot be wholly policed; desire for wealth or the prospects offered by power; a 'new barbarism' prepared to start again in a depleted world; nomadism considered not so much as geographical movement but (in Deleuze and Guattari's sense) a refusal to be tamed by the co-ordinates of authority within one's very subjectivity. Hardt and Negri also mention terms that resonate for this chapter: 'exodus' and 'desertion' from assent to the very forms of being that Empire imposes on all its subjects.[19] From this point of view, though they understand both Empire and resistance in political and economic terms, Hardt and Negri's perspective meshes the existential with the material. The counter-Empire, they remark, must also be 'a new global vision, a new way of living in the world'.[20]

The book has proved controversial, and the criticisms are clear. Can any system be as maximal and inclusive as Hardt and Negri suggest? If so, can pure voluntarism undo it?[21] But we might still take something from the model. Let us grant for a moment that, whether or not we call it 'Empire', we inhabit a global system which seems interconnected and encompassing, with very few venues of meaningful opposition or escape. Let us also grant a conceptual distinction, between the 'global' per se— the system which encompasses—and the 'transnational' in the sense it has been used in this book, as a connective grammar of navigation which offers a different kind of mapping in the world. Where might such alternative begin? At the least it might be through a linkage between the material and the existential, in new forms of approach, new ways of being and seeing, of defining the self in relation to others, of the self in relation to the encompassing system—re-envisioning the nature

[19] Hardt and Negri, *Empire*, 212. In general for this discussion, see the 'Intermezzo' section, 205–18. Of Hardt and Negri's categories, the least persuasive seems to be that of the 'new barbarians', notwithstanding the resonance with Coetzee's novel. They take the concept from Walter Benjamin's 'Experience and Poverty', but fail to acknowledge what Benjamin also laments as a bankruptcy that has come with the poverty of experience. Hardt and Negri quote Nietzsche on the topic: 'Problem: where are the *barbarians* of the twentieth century?' (213). The answer, sadly, was *everywhere*.

[20] Hardt and Negri, *Empire*, 214.

[21] For a review which sees a 'theoretical ecstasy' in Hardt and Negri's approach, see Gopal Balakrishnan, 'Virgilian Visions', *New Left Review* 5 (2000): 142–8. For a ringing critique, see Timothy Brennan, 'The Empire's New Clothes', *Critical Inquiry*, 29/2 (2003): 337–67.

of the boundary to allow new forms of the transitive and transitional. If navigation encompasses movement, journey, and the formation of new meanings, such a reformulation might begin with carving out spaces *within* the system, or at its edges, where prevailing categories cannot completely hold sway. In other words, no matter where one is actually located, such spaces can be explored as a kind of conceptual topography, the possibility of a different kind of journey. This is exactly the approach embedded in Nadine Gordimer's *The Pickup*, and it turns out that the topography in question is the desert, set against—in a loose sense—the world of 'Empire'. And of course this means the topography is also a topology—a different way of conceiving the nature of the boundary.

*The Pickup* emerged in a South African universe in which much had changed—not least in terms of the local and the global. From the fiercely isolated national interregnum of *July's People*, South Africa had been through its 'miracle' and emerged on the other side—not through apocalypse, but through negotiation. This was not the promised land: HIV/Aids, unemployment, continuing social and economic disparities, crime, were all part of the post-apartheid landscape. And yet there seemed to be a way forward, defined by navigation itself, new forms of grammar and connection. In a wider context, South Africa had rejoined the global community, open to some of its opportunities and subject to its unevenness—the paradoxes and perils of the globalized system. What did South Africa have to say or offer in such circumstances? Perhaps it offered the idea of how space could be transformed, how a country could become another country, how, against the odds, an apparently closed system could change through a different approach. That idea—of 'another country'—is one *The Pickup* takes seriously, shifting it far beyond the South African setting.

It is worth reprising the basic developments of the novel. It opens in Johannesburg, where Julie Summers lives a pleasant though rather superficial life surrounded by an alternative family of friends of various colours and identities who habitually gather at their favourite café. The world of Johannesburg is cosmopolitan: the café, called the 'L.A.', is converted into the 'EL-AY', as if (with a suggestion of the novel's wider interests) a Middle Eastern presence in Africa. Africa itself is a cosmopolitan presence in Johannesburg, with people from all over the continent on its streets. Julie's father, Nigel Ackroyd Summers, is extremely wealthy, a member of the old/new South African elite; her mother (in another form of global reality) lives in California. One day, as Julie is on her way to the 'EL-AY', her car breaks down, and she takes it to a nearby garage, where she meets the mechanic who will fix it. She and he enter into a relationship, one of those chance meetings that change destinies. His name is Abdu, and it turns out he is an Arab from an unidentified Middle Eastern country, living under a false identity in South Africa, where he has already been ordered to leave. When the authorities catch up with him, he is given a final departure order. This is where the first twist comes, for Julie decides to leave with him. They are married, and go to Abdu's village, where Julie must learn the ways of his family and their culture. Abdu—now given his proper name, Ibrahim ibn Musa—is still desperate to leave his homeland, struggling to gain access to one first-world country after another: Australia, New Zealand, Canada. Eventually his papers come through for the United States, but here is the second twist: for Julie refuses to go with him. She will remain in the village and find her own meaning there, while he looks for prospects in the heart of 'Empire'.

The shifts in the novel carry their own significance. While Gordimer's novels have gone beyond a South African setting before, this marks a different kind of transition, into a more overtly transnational domain.[22] While there is always the possibility of coincidence, this particular move—the Middle Eastern setting—also bears a dimension of the uncanny, of fairly momentous proportions. For *The Pickup* was published in 2001—released in the United Kingdom just a week before the attacks on New York of September 11.[23] The novel of course does not address this dimension directly, and neither Ibrahim nor his friends are anything like Al Qaeda adherents. Yet as they discuss politics in a coffee house in their home country, their frustration and despair in both national and international contexts is evident—the kind that, in other circumstances, can turn towards apocalyptic solutions. In this regard, one might say, Gordimer sensed something seismic in the shape of the

---

[22] For two earlier novels which have 'travelled' (though in different ways), see Nadine Gordimer, *A Guest of Honour* (London: Cape, 1971), and *A Sport of Nature* (London: Cape, 1987). For commentary, see Clingman, *Novels of Nadine Gordimer*, ch. 4, and Prologue.

[23] Jonathan Steele, 'White Magic', *Guardian*, 27 October 2001; <http://books.guardian.co.uk/departments/generalfiction/story/0,,581532,00.html> (accessed 15 August 2007).

global itself, and turned towards it in her fiction. While it might have seemed a dramatic departure, however, it may have been only the latest in a long line of such moves, for Gordimer has always explored the edges of identity, where blacks and whites have interacted in a changing South African environment. Now the white South African Jewish writer enters a Muslim Arab Middle Eastern context: a metonymic progression in every way, exploring further dimensions of connection and navigation.

*The Pickup* gives a nuanced account of the varying effects of 'Empire' on its subjects, often centred on the possibilities of movement. The Nigel Ackroyd Summerses of the world are able to cross the globe freely, migrating as needed to Australia or New Zealand. The black lawyer Hamilton Motsamai (whom we last came across in Gordimer's previous novel, *The House Gun*), has 'migrated' out of his profession into a sphere of the corporate elite in South Africa. For such people, mobility defines freedom; to adopt James Clifford's terms, they are able to 'dwell' in every form of their 'travelling'. For Abdu/Ibrahim, on the other hand, both dwelling and travelling are fraught with difficulty. In his case, mobility from one country to another is nothing less than the *form* of his containment; the boundary is both hard and impermeable, and at the same time intangible and absent, an ever-receding horizon. In this context, identity for Ibrahim becomes a daily negotiation between self and performance—a bad version of displacement. Even between him and Julie, there are the problematics of 'height': the unevenness of their resources and experience. Their relationship is always marked by the faultline of this difference; even in the most intimate of settings, it is a fragmented space they have to navigate. Julie, even as a 'displaced person', has prospects Ibrahim will never have.

From that point of view, *The Pickup* puts much emphasis on questions of 'place'—a word which often appears in inverted commas in the novel. From the start this defines Abdu's predicament, whether as an illegal alien in South Africa or simply in terms of his living conditions in the decrepit room behind the garage where he works. In Julie's home the two find another kind of 'place', even if, as Gordimer writes, they come from different worlds, so that affluence can be 'as distant as space'.[24]

---

[24] Nadine Gordimer, *The Pickup* (New York: Farrar, Straus and Giroux, 2001), 8. Henceforth referenced as *TP*.

When the two fall in love, it is described as a metaphoric place of its own—'another country', in the words of William Plomer's poem that forms the epigraph to the novel. But when this 'other' country becomes real—when Ibrahim and Julie leave for his home—he is certain it is not a place for them. '[W]e do not live here,' he tells Julie (*TP*, 216). Instead it is the attraction of the West that draws him on, where access to resources, technology, a job, provides a 'placement' of its own. In America, Ibrahim tells Julie, 'people where I come from make it . . . they're in computers, in communications, that's where the world is!' (*TP*, 227). It is a conviction that echoes V. S. Naipaul's formulation in the opening sentence of *A Bend in the River*: 'The world is what it is; men who are nothing, who allow themselves to become nothing, have no place in it.'[25] At some level Ibrahim's fear is one of 'nothingness', and to avoid it there is only one place to be, at the heart of where the world is made and shaped: 'Empire', as we might call it. Empire in these terms is not only a *location*; it is a *condition*, and it is this condition in which Ibrahim would like to be located.

Living and doing, location and being: the novel makes their linkages clear, and in this global world of lure and surface, its aim is to deepen questions of agency and placement within the self. This is certainly an issue for Julie, who early on will respond to prompts about her work as a public relations officer by saying 'I don't know what I want to do, if that means what I want to be' (*TP*, 11). Gordimer makes her own concerns about this explicit in the novel: 'To discover the exact location of a "thing" ', she writes, 'is a simple matter of factual research. To discover the exact location of a person: where to locate the self?' (*TP*, 47). This is reminiscent of her formulation regarding the self in 'Living in the Interregnum', and Julie's answer to the question is to find her self in relation to Ibrahim. 'I'm here! . . . I'm with you' (*TP*, 110) is at the core of her address towards him. In this regard, her address is doubled: both a relation and a location. It is location as a form of being: being in relation to Ibrahim. As for Ibrahim, he too has his address, when he is present in himself to Julie: his silent words 'Here I am' (*TP*, 148, 168) announced not so much by his voice as by his body when he emerges from under her car in the workshop or lies in erotic half-sleep as she returns from an early morning walk into the desert. These are

---

[25] V. S. Naipaul, *A Bend in the River* (New York: Vintage, 1989), 3.

detailed features of the novel, and they are important, for Gordimer's formulations tell us where her focus lies. It dwells on place as a form of being, in response to the envelopment of Empire—whether the Empire of economics or signs.

And they take us in other, perhaps unexpected, directions. For 'Here I am' were the words uttered by Abraham in the Bible, when called upon by God—the God of nowhere, of the desert, of apparently empty space. Abraham was the common ancestor of Muslims and Jews, and Ibrahim bears the Arabic version of his name. The concept of the ancestor has been important to Gordimer before: in *The Conservationist*, a novel cast partly within the terms and forms of Zulu culture, the first attribute of an ancestor lies in claiming a place for his descendants.[26] That is in some respects the legacy of the biblical Abraham too, but Abraham's first response to the call of God is to *leave home*, become the nomad who finds God in *every* place, whether desert, path, or oasis. Abraham becomes 'located' (his 'here I am') in relation to the nowhere/everywhere of God, and for him the whole world is God's habitation. How then does Ibrahim's migrant nomadism in the novel compare? And where will he find meaning—only in America, working with computers, where 'the world is'? The logic of names in the novel goes further, for Ibrahim's colloquial name in South Africa is 'Abdu', short for 'Abdullah', meaning 'servant of God', and his full name is Ibrahim ibn Musa—or Abraham, son of Moses. Moses, that is, who delivered his people from servitude out of the Empire of Egypt, and took them on a nomadic exodus, guided by the God of the desert, towards the Promised Land (which, like a true nomad, he envisioned but did not enter). In these Arabic/Muslim/Jewish collocations—secreted in names, associations, stories of the journey and 'the way'—Gordimer explores metonymies of possibility which hold out hopes of a different form of location and being beyond the surface meanings of Empire or the fractured nature of the world.

And yet, such possibilities are not easy to find, and from this point of view we have to understand Ibrahim's situation. He is the kind of figure for whom the route *is* the *rupta via*, who faces policed realities where a stamp in a passport can be lifegiving, its absence an unmitigated disaster.

---

[26] See Nadine Gordimer, *The Conservationist* (Harmondsworth: Penguin, 1978); also Clingman, *Novels of Nadine Gordimer*, ch. 5.

He is not quite a refugee, as we might find in a novel by Caryl Phillips, for Ibrahim does have choices, and yet they are severely constrained. He has an economics degree from his university, but even—perhaps especially—in his 'home' country his prospects are stifled. In his village, the most he can hope for (and the job he rejects) is to be head of his uncle's car repair workshop: providing and salvaging vehicles for others, but only stasis for himself. What he wants is what others have: a form of place as *recognition*, the fulfilment of his desires and potential, the very possibility of 'dwelling' in the journey of his life, progress wherever he lives. This then provides his impetus to move, to find a place 'where the world is'. Yet we still have to ask, what shape will that finding take? Here the issue of names becomes relevant again. For in that 'other' world, Ibrahim is 'Abdu'—not Abdullah, 'servant of God', but merely 'servant', which is Ibrahim's perpetual role as itinerant.[27] In that sense his nomadism is a form of continual subjection to the very dictates of Empire he wishes both to evade and to join. His life, we are told, is '[l]ife in the meantime' (*TP*, 142), he is in search of '[p]ermanent residence' (*TP*, 186). It is easy for those who have permanent residence to decry its necessity, but there is a deeper matter here. For what, ultimately, can 'permanent' mean, in the context of life as we know it? It is an illusion of Empire itself to suggest permanence; and those who attempt to hold on to it—as we have seen in the extreme form of Colonel Joll—will end by subjecting others. Rather, the underlying question of *The Pickup* may be whether we can, in Pablo Neruda's phrase, make something different of 'residence on earth'.[28] And this in itself may be a matter of not of Empire or the global, but the transitive and transnational.

This may be the significance of the novel's other focus—its focus on Julie. For if Ibrahim understands the materialities of Empire, it is she who brings an existential quality to her response. From this point of view, there may be a way in which her version of translocation is ultimately more nomadic than Ibrahim's, despite the fact that she will remain behind in his village. Here we can understand the nomadic less as a matter of physical or literal journey, and more as a matter of approach. This is what we have to understand in Clifford's terms, 'traveling-in-dwelling, dwelling-in-traveling'; in the end, this is what

---

[27] For these perspectives on Abdu/Abdullah, I am grateful to Mazen Naous.
[28] The reference is to Neruda's *Residencia en la tierra*, first published in 1933 and expanded in 1935.

those terms must in part *mean*.[29] So we see it enacted in Julie's life. When she announces her decision not to travel with Ibrahim to the United States, he accuses her of wanting to return to South Africa. But, echoing Maureen's phrase in *July's People* (and the barbarian woman in *Waiting for the Barbarians*), Julie tells him that she will not go 'back there' (*TP*, 252)—back to a state of being as much as a location. She tells Ibrahim 'I don't belong there' (*TP*, 252), and says 'I'm staying here' (*TP*, 253), a place in the continuous present as well as a location in space. She says to Ibrahim, 'I'm in your home' (*TP*, 261)—an alternative, chiastic version of existence and location: *my* existence, *your* location. Being, location, approach: all are connected here.

But we have to ask the further question: which 'home' of Ibrahim's is it that Julie will inhabit? It cannot, in any significant sense, be his village. Like July's village in *July's People*, Ibrahim's village does not offer any form of binary opposition to 'Empire', for it does not exist beyond Empire's horizon. In more personal terms, it is clear that within the village Julie will also be 'subject'—to the patriarchal rules of Islam and local custom outside the home, and the matriarchal rule of Ibrahim's mother within it. On one level Julie does not mind this: this is the reality of her current 'location', a complication of where she happens to 'be'. But the village is not the space of some 'alternation' for her; instead, that space has to exist in another form, a form that offers her a different kind of vision. In *The Pickup* that space is the desert—the desert which borders on the village, into which Julie likes to walk. In the language of a previous generation of anthropologists, we might think of it as liminal space, where the self can withdraw, find its meanings, and then reintegrate, except that here reintegration into the known is not exactly what is at issue.[30] What matters, in some way, is the *deformation* of the known in a different kind of navigation. The desert neither belongs in Empire, nor does it exist in straightforward opposition. Rather, it is the place of non-definition where, precisely because it is unfixed and

---

[29] For Clifford's discussion see, 'Traveling Cultures', 108.

[30] For liminality, see Arnold van Gennep, *The Rites of Passage*, trans. Monika B. Vizedom and Gabrielle L. Caffee (Chicago and London: Phoenix, 1961), who refers to 'liminal rites' as 'rites of transition' (11), and also discusses the symbolic topography of 'neutral zones' (including deserts, marshes, and virgin forests), where individuals in transition 'waver...between two worlds' (18). Also, Victor W. Turner, *The Ritual Process: Structure and Anti-Structure* (Chicago: Aldine, 1969), ch. 3, 'Liminality and Communitas'. See too, on this matter, Hirson, *White Scars*, 89–90.

unmappable, the self can find other co-ordinates of existence. It is the place which, in every sense, matches Julie's *disposition*—her approach, orientation, displacement, renavigation.[31]

This is what Julie finds in the desert. There is 'no fixed object, no horizon to be made out' (*TP*, 167). She walks into the desert without wearing her watch; where Ibrahim has to live in the 'meantime' of Empire, here there is a different basis to time altogether. Julie walks out in the early mornings or evenings, when night shades into day, day into night—the very moments and passages of transition. Sometimes she is accompanied by a little girl, Leila—a child not her own, but an oblique kind of connection and continuity. In the desert Julie observes what appears to be a Bedouin woman tending her herd; but one day, when the woman comes close, Julie sees that she is a twelve-year-old girl. Perception is shifted, other relations of cognition established, visions that alter as soon as they appear. For Julie, then, the desert is less a territory than an itinerary, combining the material and immaterial, the space and non-space of habitation. Because desert and village flow at some undefined margin into one another, the very nature of the boundary here becomes different, not a border, but a space of realignment, where, without noticing, one finds oneself in a very different 'place'. Here, in the sands of the desert, where Empire folds into non-definition in a set of continually reshaping forms, Julie finds her own form of 'desertion', in the most positive sense. As she understands but cannot tell Ibrahim, the idea of staying behind—not following him into the heartland of Empire—has come from '[t]he desert' itself (*TP*, 262).

## COMING BACK

And so the novel ends in some tension and balance. On the one hand, there is Ibrahim's reality—the world he has to deal with as a matter of struggle and survival. There may be his implicit critique of Julie—the assumptions deriving from her privileged life that make her choice of the desert possible. And yet Julie has given up her resources and assumptions; the desert is now where she lives. On one level, in

---

[31] Again, for the doubleness of what Jean-Luc Nancy calls 'dis-position', see *Being Singular Plural*, trans. Robert D. Richardson and Anne E. O'Byrne (Stanford: Stanford University Press, 2000), 12, 96. Also see the Introduction to this book, pp. 24–5.

*The Pickup*, we can see a male story and a female story. The male story is to struggle with Empire, the female to develop a different vision of possibility. We do not have to see these as gendered in any strict biological sense, but they may stand for different versions of disposition, in the sense we have seen it. There are twinned realities in a globalized world: the compulsion to participate; the need to 'desert' according to Julie's model. In this form, if Julie's disposition is not in and of itself transnational, it may be an element of its *preface*; a way in which we can reconsider our mappings, the nature of our boundaries and affiliations, the forms of our identities and our navigations. If we have to bide time, as Julie does, to see it develop, then that too is part of our threshold, our interregnum.

Can these two stories come together? At the end of the novel, Julie's sister-in-law, Khadija, waiting for her own husband at work in the oilfields of a neighbouring country, tries to reassure her regarding Ibrahim. She tells Julie, 'He'll come back' (*TP*, 268). The phrase is exactly the same as in the ending of Gordimer's sixth novel, *The Conservationist*. There it concerns the body of a black man finally buried by the workers on a white South African farm. As Gordimer writes, 'They had put him away to rest, at last; he had come back. He took possession of this earth, theirs; one of them.'[32]

Coming back: perhaps Ibrahim will one day cease to be Abdu—a 'servant' to others. Perhaps like Moses/Musa his path will be one of freedom, an exodus not into but out of Empire. Perhaps he will become again an Ibrahim/Abraham who will find meaning in the 'nowhere' that Empire disdains, in the syntax it has deleted. Perhaps one day he will come back to reconnect with Julie's vision of a different kind of transition, not of possession but a different kind of boundary.

---

[32] Gordimer, *The Conservationist*, 267; again, for the full resonance of the 'he had come back' reference, see Clingman, *Novels of Nadine Gordimer*, 141. There are a number of echoes between *The Pickup* and *The Conservationist*, not least that it is open to early debate in the novel whether Abdu is 'one of them': the same phrase that is applied to the dead body in *The Conservationist*.

# Conclusion
## The Nature of the Boundary

> After all, counsel is less an answer to a question than a proposal concerning the continuation of a story which is in the process of unfolding.
>
> Walter Benjamin, 'The Storyteller'

What then has been the nature of the boundary in this study, and how is it connected with our underlying themes of self, location, the transitive, and transitional—the very issues of a grammar of identity? What follows here is not a summary, but a further set of explorations, based on what we have seen so far. The hope is that when this book closes, the navigations it has begun may continue.

So then. We have seen the boundary as a place; we have seen the boundary as a concept. Sometimes it is hard and 'real'; sometimes receding, absent, a space. We have seen it as fortress, the walls of a hut, the outline of a village; but it has also been a membrane, the shifting margins of the desert, the waterways of the earth. The boundary can surround us; it can also be very deeply inside. The boundary exists between countries and nations; it exists between one self and another; it can and does exist within the self. What matters is not whether the boundary exists but how we construct and conceive it. To conceive it is also to navigate it; to navigate it alters the nature of the boundary. Topology affects our navigations; our navigations affect our topologies.

This book has proposed the idea of the generative and transitive— that navigation, as a form of mobile, living syntax, emerges from both principles. Just as the structure of a landscape, metonymic in its essence, alters through its modulations, so the grammar of identity emerges from difference and distance—in space, in time, within and beyond the self. The grammar of identity is in that regard combinatory, not exclusive or substitutive, or surrounded by impermeable walls. But without such a grammar we *are* surrounded, by the limits of ourselves, what we call our identities, our locations. To engage this grammar we must travel— distances within the self which are no less vast for being 'contained', beyond ourselves to find that touch, contiguity with others, to make a larger syntax out of our differences. For navigation requires difference. Difference is not the barrier but the *prompt*, the very *ground* for transition and meaning.

The grammar of identity on the large scale is the transnational, where the transitive and combinatory become possible. The transnational, however, is not the same as the global—a world homogeneous, empty, not because it does not contain difference but because that difference is not the matter of transition. Transition turns the global into the transnational—in time, space, connective reality. This may be our way beyond the morbidities of our current interregnums, the nature of the boundary we have to navigate. Crossing this boundary makes new spaces within and beyond nation and Empire, a different kind of topology and therefore horizon. In this sense the generative grammar of space and time in our era of the global is the transnational, where varied realities are neither simply the same nor completely different, but must invoke the combinatory and transitive. Here too, difference is not the barrier but the space of crossing, where navigation is essential to the story we wish to become.

The problem of height remains an abiding reality, which is why our story cannot be simply one of celebration, of hybridity achieved, of the unlocated and transcendent. The fortress, the wall, Empire, the national—all exclude as well as incorporate. Our horizontal boundaries become vertical as we build them—the tower up to heaven, the ramparts, are matters of repression within the self, and hierarchy and oppression beyond. In that regard our navigations are not easy; our cartographies are in three dimensions, not two, and then there are others to add as well: time; inner space; culture; the psyche as well as the landscape. For some of these reasons the transnational exists as the uncanny of the national, of the global as empty, fractured, barred, uneven. That is why, through whatever journeys we make, there is always—and Sebald is the prime example—the suggestion of something deeper, something else. But these differences in height are not only our problem: in a grammar of navigation they are also our obligation. In the transnational setting as elsewhere, navigation is negated only by *indifference*; but difference is the very ground of its possibility and need.

These works of fiction have entered that territory, telling the story of who we are, who we might become. Though they have entered, they have not traversed—crossed the space of navigation to some other side. Rather, they are in the space of crossing, confronting its unevenness, its obstructions, its gaps; they themselves *become* the space of crossing. The grammar of fiction has in this sense—among many others—been a grammar of journey, finding a way to the transitive, transnational. In that sense the transnational has not been achieved, but is mapped out as a journey. The journey takes place in the space between inside and outside, the very boundary where fiction navigates; it is also a boundary in external space and time, not only in the lives of individuals, but in the world we inhabit, as we make our way uneasily from one era to another. To that extent all these novels are transfictions, even if they do not all match the term in a specific formal sense. They are transfictions because they have willingly and consciously entered a space where the grammar of navigation is what they are drawn to explore. The nature of their boundary is our boundary; the counsel of fiction becomes our counsel; the map of fiction our intrinsic cartography. What it tells us is by no means marginal to our times.

These writers have come from different places and directions. Some have written from within Empire, even as they explored its outposts; some have written from the midst of trauma or its aftermath, where navigation is among the most profound of problems. Some have written of refugees and exiles for whom migration is not a choice; some have written of those at the centre, or from the heart of the nation, where identity is still never quite what it seems. Whether on the waterways, or in the deserts, the chronotopes of trauma, the airwaves of All-India radio, the continuing journey of Othello, the ghost in the national machine, the angel with horns, the child rising from the ground, one thread that emerges is this: what divides us also connects us. We have to make that the project of our navigations, part of the grammar of our identities and time.

## THE SONGLINES

Two vignettes: one idealized, the other more minimal but also a guideline.

The first comes from Bruce Chatwin's *The Songlines*, a book that has been important in the genesis of this one. For one thing, it is a *transfiction*, both in its content and its form. *The Songlines* itself travels like a 'songline', from Australia to South Africa, North Africa to Afghanistan; it moves from prehistory to the present, and from genre to genre in a nodal, modal, juxtaposed, contiguous, and constellated way. Story alternates with travelogue, with notebooks. Anthropology, memoir, interview, digressions on 'gentlemen of the road' and Arctic terns cross into accounts of Bruce, Arkady, and Marian, and three dying men in the outback rejoining the Ancestors, 'going back' into the land at the end. It is a book whose anthropology may be questionable, but whose vision may still inspire.

For one thing, it is a book fiercely based on an idea of the nomadic as an essential ingredient of human history. This is true for Chatwin from the baby on her mother's back calmed by the rhythmic pace of her feet, to the 'feet' based on the rhythm of walking heard by Osip Mandelstam in Dante's *Inferno* and *Purgatorio*. Chatwin traces the nomadic in evolutionary history; he cites the Gautama Buddha: 'You cannot travel on the path before you have become the Path itself'; he quotes the palaeontologist Elizabeth Vrba: 'sedentary species, like sedentary genes, are terribly successful for a while, but in the end they are self-destructive'.[1] It is in this context that Chatwin turns to linguistics, in a primary, originary way. He pictures the first ancestor, Adam, calling out the names of everything in the Garden of Eden, just like an Aboriginal Ancestor in Australia: 'He puts a left foot forward and names a flower. He puts a right foot forward and names a stone. The verb carries him to the next stanza of the Song.' Chatwin continues: 'All animals, insects, birds, mammals, dolphins, fish and humpback whales have a navigation system we call "triangulation". The mysteries of Chomskyian innate sentence structure become very simple if they are thought of as human triangulation. Subject—Object—Verb' (*TS*, 282). This is the syntax of

---

[1] For these quotations, Bruce Chatwin, *The Songlines* (Harmondsworth: Penguin, 1988), 179, 249. Further references in the text to *TS*. Note that the page numbering in different editions of *The Songlines* varies.

the self in motion, the grammar of identity in transition—so long as we understand that, precisely because of transition, the subject itself does not remain unchanged.

It has consequences, for Chatwin, in the very concept of the map, founded on the Songlines. Chatwin gives his own account, drawn from Strehlow and other sources. The Songlines were sung originally in the Dreamtime by the Ancestors, who brought the land into being by calling out its features, so that the whole landscape of Australia is like a musical score. The Songline crosses space, and it also crosses time, because, following the Songline across the land, the Dreamtime is present again. There are no 'borders' in this sense: the 'score' of the song remains the same even as it passes across languages, from one community to the next. The Songlines even cross species, for the Ancestors *were* the different species, and each member of a family has a different totemic clan; therefore, territory is criss-crossed by allegiances that extend along the Songline and create other definitions of 'country'. To the extent there is 'ownership' of land, its implications have more to do with custodianship than possession. So, an 'owner' of an area of land (responsible for its upkeep) has a 'ritual manager'; they enjoy reciprocal rites in one another's territory, and work together to maintain them, which is a way of sustaining the land.

The key thing is this: in the Songline, the song and the map are the same; the language *is* the navigation. Here then is an image of the map according to this model:

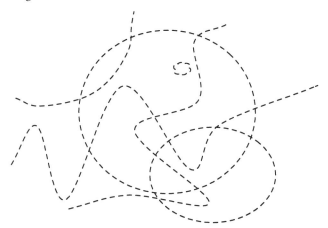

It looks like an Aboriginal painting, and with good reason. There are no 'hard' or exclusive boundaries; allegiances criss-cross; the map itself is a matter of perpetual and always re-created navigation. It remains an image—if not a reality then an ideal, even a kind of horizon to journey towards—of what navigation could mean in a world founded on a different grammar of identity.

## SACRIFICE

The second vignette comes from J. M. Coetzee's *Waiting for the Barbarians*.

It occurs fairly early in the novel, when the Magistrate goes out hunting. As he tells the story, he comes across a waterbuck, which he also calls a ram. When he trains his sights on the animal, for once vision in the novel is reciprocal: the ram gazes back at him, and eventually the Magistrate lets the gun slip from his shoulder. As he says, 'My pulse does not quicken: evidently, it is not important to me that the ram die.' The Magistrate feels the encounter may have deeper implications, that 'for the duration of this frozen moment the stars are locked in a configuration in which events are not themselves but stand for other things.' Yet, though the moment invites allegory, invites meaning, invites even— under the stars—constellation, for the life of him the Magistrate cannot tell what that meaning might be. As the ram skitters away, he trudges on through the marshes 'purposelessly'.[2]

If the event suggests any allusion, it may be to the sacrifice of Isaac. There God commanded Abraham to sacrifice his son to prove his loyalty; in the Muslim tradition, the son is Ishmael. In the story, God calls to Abraham, who gives his customary answer: 'Here I am'—the echo there in *The Pickup*.[3] The journey takes three days, and Abraham builds the altar, but just as his hand is raised to kill his son, a messenger calls out to him to sacrifice a ram instead, entangled in a nearby thicket

---

[2] For this episode: J. M. Coetzee, *Waiting for the Barbarians* (New York: Penguin, 1999), 38–9.

[3] Erich Auerbach has shown wonderfully how the story of Isaac is so powerful not only because of its intrinsic drama but also the spareness of its telling; he also points out how Abraham's 'Here I am' is a statement of self and location in relation to God. See Auerbach, *Mimesis: The Representation of Reality in Western Literature*, trans. Willard R. Trask (Princeton: Princeton University Press, 1968), ch. 1.

by its horns. It is a significant shift: the ram substitutes for Isaac, animal for human sacrifice. But substitution was built into the original commandment: the sacrifice of Isaac representing Abraham's loyalty to God. Somehow, the willingness to offer up a child is the probation of worthiness for patrimony. And this is what sacrifice seals: patrimony, identity, lineage, and location—even if it is the location of 'everywhere', the everywhere in relation to God.

In the Magistrate's version, however, even the ram is not sacrificed. Nothing substitutes for the Magistrate, nothing proves his loyalty or fealty, and nothing provides living proof of his patrimony. The episode may leave him without meaning, but at least it has not been important to him that the ram should die, and in that sense it too may be a preface. If the Magistrate is left to trudge through the marshes—a kind of wilderness—then he has abandoned the grammar of sacrifice: in his world, in our world, the grammar of singularity, of power, of lineage, of terror, of Empire.[4]

## BEFORE THE PROMISED LAND

The national always holds out the idea of the Promised Land. We may have escaped from the clutches of Empire, emerged from slavery in Egypt, but if we can hold onto our principles, then we tell ourselves we may reach the land and the perfect life we desire. The iconography is used by the powerful, just as it is used by the weak. What we need is our own place, our possession, and if we have to make sacrifices or sacrifice others, then this is the price to pay for our paradise on earth.

This book has proposed a different model—and it means a different view of the world as well as ourselves. Here identity is not exclusive, and nor is territory. Everything is in the navigation; the syntax is connective across both the waterways and landscapes of the earth. Even—perhaps

---

[4] There are any number of sources on what we might call the grammar of sacrifice. Without going into detail, here are some of them: René Girard, *Violence and the Sacred*, trans. Patrick Gregory (Baltimore: Johns Hopkins University Press, 1977); Giorgio Agamben, *Homo Sacer: Sovereign Power and Bare Life*, trans. Daniel Heller-Roazen (Stanford: Stanford University Press, 1998); Terry Eagleton, *Holy Terror* (Oxford and New York: Oxford University Press, 2005), ch. 6; Jacques Derrida, *The Gift of Death*, trans. David Wills (Chicago and London: University of Chicago Press, 1995), esp. ch. 3. Of course not all of these writers would agree with the views expressed here.

especially—those fighting for their liberation might accept these principles, for they more than anyone know what is at stake.

This book has not been an exercise in political philosophy, however; everything we have learned here has come from novels and some of the theory needed to read them. In foregrounding fiction in this way, there is an implicit claim: that literature—in its mysteries, in its indirections—can be a guide, can provide counsel for a story that is still in the process of unfolding. It is in this light, and in this spirit, that I would like to turn to another story: one that has both been—and not yet been—written. It is an alternative story, of Moses who led his people out of Empire, who wandered through the wilderness for forty years, and never entered the Promised Land.

His life is a fitting image of transition, of navigation, and I imagine him making a speech he never made. So there he is, on Mount Nebo, halfway between heaven and earth, gazing over a river, a translation he will never cross. At first—he says to those gathered around him—I was grieved that I would not enter the Promised Land. Now I know that it is my deepest lesson. You, he says, may cross into it; I shall never get there. But take my life as a measure. No one *ever* enters the Promised Land. When you think you are there you have left it. You have especially left it if anyone in that land is excluded or goes hungry. You cannot possess it. You cannot own it. You can build no fortress there, no ramparts, no wall that will not come down. It is not to be a place of sacrifice. It must be a place that people pass into, and through, and across. If you build the journey into the land, that will be your only and best form of dwelling. It is your only way. In every sense of the word, our place on earth can only be a place of *approach*.

# References

Achebe, Chinua, *Morning Yet on Creation Day* (Garden City: Anchor Press, 1975).

——, 'An Image of Africa', in Joseph Conrad, *Heart of Darkness*, ed. Robert Kimbrough, 3rd edn (New York: Norton, 1988), 251–62.

Agamben, Giorgio, *Homo Sacer: Sovereign Power and Bare Life*, trans. Daniel Heller-Roazen (Stanford: Stanford University Press, 1998).

Anderson, Benedict, *Imagined Communities: Reflections on the Origin and Spread of Nationalism*, rev. edn (London and New York: Verso, 1991).

Anderson, Mark M., 'The Edge of Darkness: On W. G. Sebald', *October*, 106 (2003): 102–21.

Angier, Carol, *Jean Rhys: Life and Work* (Boston: Little, Brown, 1990).

Appadurai, Arjun, 'Putting Hierarchy in its Place', *Cultural Anthropology*, 3/1 (1988): 36–49.

——, 'Global Ethnoscapes: Notes and Queries for a Transnational Anthropology', in Richard Fox, ed., *Recapturing Anthropology: Working in the Present* (Santa Fe: School of American Research Press, 1991), 191–210.

——, 'Sovereignty without Territoriality: Notes for a Postnational Geography', in Setha M. Low and Denise Lawrence-Zúñiga, eds, *The Anthropology of Space and Place* (Oxford: Blackwell, 2003), 337–49.

Appiah, Kwame Anthony, *The Ethics of Identity* (Princeton: Princeton University Press, 2005).

Armstrong, Andrew, 'BLOODY HISTORY! Exploring a Capacity for Revision. Restaging History in Wilson Harris's *Jonestown* and Caryl Phillips' *The Nature of Blood*', *Jouvert*, 6/3 (2002): 24 paragraphs; <http://social.chass.ncsu.edu/jouvert/v613/armstr.htm> (accessed 24 September 2004).

Attridge, Derek, *J. M. Coetzee & the Ethics of Reading* (Chicago and London: University of Chicago Press, 2004).

Auerbach, Erich, *Mimesis: The Representation of Reality in Western Literature*, trans. Willard R. Trask (Princeton: Princeton University Press, 1968).

Bakhtin, M. M., 'Forms of Time and of the Chronotope in the Novel', in Michael Holquist, ed., *The Dialogic Imagination* (Austin: University of Texas Press, 1981), 84–258.

Balakrishnan, Gopal, 'Virgilian Visions', *New Left Review*, 5 (2000): 142–8.

Bambini, Valentina, Claudio Gentili, and Pietro Pietrini, 'On Cultural Constraints on Pirahã Grammar', *Current Anthropology*, 47/1 (2006): 143–5.

Batchelor, John, *The Life of Joseph Conrad: A Critical Biography* (Oxford: Blackwell, 1994).

Baucom, Ian, 'Frantz Fanon's Radio: Solidarity, Diaspora, and the Tactics of Listening', *Contemporary Literature*, 42/1 (2001): 15–49.

Bechhöfer, Susi, 'Stripped of my Tragic Past by a Bestselling Author', *Sunday Times*, 30 June 2002, 6; LexisNexis Academic, <http://www.lexisnexis.com/> (accessed 1 July 2004).

Bell, C. Rosalind, 'Worlds Within: An Interview with Caryl Phillips', *Callaloo*,14/3 (1991): 578–606.

Benjamin, Walter, *Illuminations*, trans. Harry Zohn, ed. Hannah Arendt (Glasgow: Fontana, 1973).

——, *Selected Writings*, vol. 1: *1913–1926*, eds Marcus Bullock and Michael W. Jennings (Cambridge, MA and London: Belknap Press, 1996).

——, *The Arcades Project*, trans. Howard Eiland and Kevin McLaughlin (Cambridge, MA: Belknap Press, 1999).

——, *Selected Writings*, vol. 2: *1927–1934*, trans. Rodney Livingstone *et al.*, eds Michael W. Jennings, Howard Eiland, and Gary Smith (Cambridge, MA and London: Belknap Press, 1999).

——, *Selected Writings*, vol. 4: *1938–40*, trans. Edmund Jephcott *et al.*, eds Howard Eiland and Michael W. Jennings (Cambridge, MA and London: Belknap Press, 2006).

Bernabé, Jean, Patrick Chamoiseau, and Raphaël Confiant, *Éloge de la Créolité*, trans. M. B. Taleb-Khyar (Paris: Gallimard, 1993).

Bhabha, Homi, *The Location of Culture* (London and New York: Routledge, 1994).

Birbalsingh, Frank, ed., *Frontiers of Caribbean Literatures in English* (New York: St Martin's, 1996).

Booker, M. Keith, 'Beauty and the Beast: Dualism as Despotism in the Fiction of Salman Rushdie', in M. D. Fletcher, ed., *Reading Rushdie: Perspectives on the Fiction of Salman Rushdie* (Amsterdam and Atlanta: Rodopi, 1994), 237–54.

Bowker, John, ed., *The Concise Oxford Dictionary of World Religions* (Oxford: Oxford University Press, 2000), <http://www.oxfordreference.com> (accessed 21 December, 2004).

Brantlinger, Patrick, '*Heart of Darkness*: Anti-Imperialism, Racism or Impressionism?', in Joseph Conrad, *Heart of Darkness*, ed. Ross C. Murfin, 277–96 (Boston and New York: Bedford, 1996).

Brennan, Timothy, *Salman Rushdie and the Third World: Myths of the Nation* (New York: St Martin's, 1989).

——, 'The Empire's New Clothes', *Critical Inquiry*, 29/2 (2003): 337–67.

Brontë, Charlotte, *Jane Eyre*, ed. Richard J. Dunn, 3rd edn, Norton Critical Edition (New York: Norton, 2001).

Calvino, Italo, 'Ovid and Universal Contiguity', in *The Literature Machine* (London: Secker & Warburg, 1987).

Cameron, Edwin, *Witness to Aids* (Cape Town: Tafelberg, 2005).

Chatterjee, Partha, *Nationalist Thought and the Colonial World: A Derivative Discourse* (Minneapolis: University of Minnesota Press, 1986).

——, *The Nation and its Fragments: Colonial and Postcolonial Histories* (Princeton: Princeton University Press, 1993).

Chatwin, Bruce, *The Songlines* (Harmondsworth: Penguin, 1988).

Cheyfitz, Eric, *The Poetics of Imperialism: Translation and Colonization from The Tempest to Tarzan*, expanded edn (Philadelphia: University of Pennsylvania Press, 1997).

Chomsky, Noam, *Aspects of the Theory of Syntax* (Cambridge, MA: MIT Press, 1965).

——, *Syntactic Structures* (The Hague: Mouton, 1975).

——, 'Linguistics and Adjacent Fields: A Personal View', in Asa Kasher, ed., *The Chomskyan Turn* (Oxford and Cambridge, MA: Blackwell, 1991), 3–25.

——, 'Linguistics and Cognitive Science: Problems and Mysteries', in Asa Kasher, ed., *The Chomskyan Turn* (Oxford and Cambridge, MA: Blackwell, 1991), 26–53.

Clifford, James, 'Traveling Cultures', in Lawrence Grossberg, Cary Nelson, and Paula A. Treichler, eds, *Cultural Studies* (New York and London: Routledge, 1992), 96–112.

Clingman, Stephen, *The Novels of Nadine Gordimer: History from the Inside*, 2nd edn (Amherst: University of Massachusetts Press; London: Bloomsbury, 1992).

——, 'Other Voices: An Interview with Caryl Phillips', *Salmagundi*, 143 (2004): 113–40.

Coetzee, J. M., *Doubling the Point: Essays and Interviews*, ed. David Attwell (Cambridge, MA: Harvard University Press, 1992).

——, 'What We Like to Forget', *New York Review of Books*, 6 November 1997, 38–41.

——, *Waiting for the Barbarians* (New York: Penguin, 1999).

Conrad, Joseph, 'Geography and Some Explorers', in *Last Essays* (Garden City: Doubleday, Page and Co., 1926).

——, *The Secret Agent* (Harmondsworth: Penguin, 1963).

——, *Almayer's Folly* (Harmondsworth: Penguin, 1976).

——, *Congo Diary and Other Uncollected Pieces*, ed. Zdzisław Najder (Garden City, NY: Doubleday, 1978).

——, *Lord Jim*, eds Cedric Watts and Robert Hampson (Harmondsworth: Penguin, 1986).

——, *Heart of Darkness*, ed. Robert Kimbrough, 3rd edn, Norton Critical Edition (New York: Norton, 1988).

——, *The Mirror of the Sea and A Personal Record*, ed. Zdzisław Najder (Oxford: Oxford University Press, 1988).

——, *The Nigger of the 'Narcissus'*, ed. Cedric Watts (Harmondsworth: Penguin, 1988).

——, *Nostromo*, ed. Martin Seymour-Smith (London: Penguin, 1990).

——, *A Personal Record and The Mirror of the Sea*, ed. Mara Kalnins (Harmondsworth: Penguin, 1998).

Craps, Stef, 'Linking Legacies of Loss: Traumatic Histories and Cross-Cultural Empathy in Caryl Phillips's *Higher Ground* and *The Nature of Blood*', paper presented at the conference 'Caryl Phillips: Twenty-Five Years of Writing', University of Liège, Belgium 1–2 December 2006.

DeLoughrey, Elizabeth M., *Routes and Roots: Navigating Caribbean and Pacific Island Literatures* (Honolulu: University of Hawai'i Press, 2007).

Derrida, Jacques, 'Des Tours de Babel', in Joseph F. Graham, ed., *Difference in Translation* (Ithaca and London: Cornell University Press, 1985), 165–207.

——, *The Gift of Death*, trans. David Wills (Chicago and London: University of Chicago Press, 1995).

Desai, Anita, Caryl Phillips, and Ilan Stavans, 'The Other Voice', *Transition*, 64 (1994): 77–89.

Dimock, Wai Chee, 'Literature for the Planet', *PMLA*, 116/1 (2001): 173–88.

——, *Through Other Continents: American Literature Across Deep Time* (Princeton and Oxford: Princeton University Press, 2006).

Eagleton, Terry, *Exiles and Émigrés: Studies in Modern Literature* (London: Chatto & Windus, 1970).

——, *Literary Theory: An Introduction*, 2nd edn (Minneapolis: University of Minnesota Press, 1996).

——, *After Theory* (New York: Basic Books, 2003).

——, *Holy Terror* (Oxford and New York: Oxford University Press, 2005).

Edwards, Brent Hayes, *The Practice of Diaspora: Literature, Translation, and the Rise of Black Internationalism* (Cambridge, MA and London: Harvard University Press, 2003).

Eshel, Amir, 'Against the Power of Time: The Poetics of Suspension in W. G. Sebald's Austerlitz', *New German Critique: An Interdisciplinary Journal of German Studies*, 88 (2003): 71–96.

Esposito, John L., ed., *Oxford Dictionary of Islam* (Oxford: Oxford University Press, 2003); BLC University of Massachusetts, Amherst, <http://www.oxfordreference.com/> (accessed 11 February 2005).

Everett, Daniel L., 'Cultural Constraints on Grammar and Cognition in Pirahã', *Current Anthropology*, 46/ 4 (2005): 621–46.

Fanon, Frantz, *The Wretched of the Earth*, trans. Constance Farrington (Harmondsworth: Penguin, 1967).

Forster, E. M., *A Passage to India* (San Diego, New York and London: Harcourt, Brace, Jovanovich, 1924; repr. 1984).

Freud, Sigmund, *Totem and Taboo*, trans. James Strachey (New York and London: Norton, 1950).

——, 'The "Uncanny" ', in *The Standard Edition of the Complete Psychological Works of Sigmund Freud*, vol. 17, ed. James Strachey, 217–56 (London: Hogarth Press, 1955).

Friedman, Thomas L., *The World is Flat: A Brief History of the Twenty-First Century* (New York: Farrar, Straus, and Giroux, 2005).

Gane, Gillian, 'Migrancy, the Cosmopolitan Intellectual, and the Global City in *The Satanic Verses*', *Modern Fiction Studies*, 48/1 (2002): 18–49.

Gennep, Arnold van, *The Rites of Passage*, trans. Monika B. Vizedom and Gabrielle L. Caffee (Chicago and London: Phoenix, 1961).

Gibb, H. A. R. *et al.*, eds, *The Encyclopaedia of Islam*, vol. 4 (Leiden: Brill, 1978).

Gilbert, Sandra M. and Susan Gubar, *The Madwoman in the Attic: The Woman Writer and the Nineteenth-Century Literary Imagination*, 2nd edn (New Haven and London: Yale University Press, 2000).

Gilroy, Paul, *The Black Atlantic: Modernity and Double Consciousness* (Cambridge, MA: Harvard University Press, 1993).

Girard, René, *Violence and the Sacred*, trans. Patrick Gregory (Baltimore: Johns Hopkins University Press, 1977).

Göpfert, Rebekka, 'Susi Bechhöfer Fragt Zurück: W. G. Sebald Lieh Sich für "Austerlitz" ihre Biographie', *Frankfurter Rundschau*, 15 March 2003; LexisNexis Academic, BLC, University of Massachusetts, Amherst, <http://www.lexisnexis.com/> (accessed 9 July 2004).

Gordimer, Nadine, *A Guest of Honour*. (London: Jonathan Cape, 1971).

——, *The Conservationist* (Harmondsworth: Penguin, 1978).

——, *July's People* (London: Jonathan Cape, 1981).

——, *A Sport of Nature* (London: Jonathan Cape, 1987).

——, *The Essential Gesture: Writing Politics and Places*, ed. Stephen Clingman (New York: Knopf; London: Cape, 1988).

——, *The Pickup* (New York: Farrar, Straus and Giroux, 2001).

Gorra, Michael, *The Bells in Their Silence* (Princeton and Oxford: Princeton University Press, 2004).

Grusa, Jirí, *Franz Kafka of Prague*, trans. Eric Mosbacher (London: Secker & Warburg, 1983).

Hamilton, Ian, 'The First Life of Salman Rushdie', *The New Yorker*, 25 December and 1 January 1995, 1996, 90–113.

Hardt, Michael, and Antonio Negri, *Empire* (Cambridge, MA and London: Harvard University Press, 2000).

Hauser, Marc D., Noam Chomsky, and W. Tecumseh Fitch, 'The Faculty of Language: What Is It, Who Has It, and How Did It Evolve?', *Science*, 298 (2002): 1569–79.

Hawking, Stephen, *A Brief History of Time: From the Big Bang to Black Holes* (New York: Bantam, 1988).

Hell, Julia, 'Eyes Wide Shut: German Post-Holocaust Authorship', *New German Critique: An Interdisciplinary Journal of German Studies*, 88 (2003): 9–36.

Hirson, Denis, *White Scars: On Reading and Rites of Passage* (Johannesburg: Jacana, 2006).

Hochschild, Adam, *King Leopold's Ghost* (Boston: Houghton Mifflin, 1998).

Humboldt, Wilhelm von, *On Language*, trans. Peter Heath, ed. Michael Losonsky (Cambridge: Cambridge University Press, 1999).

Ishiguro, Kazuo, *The Remains of the Day* (New York: Vintage, 1993).

Jacobson, Dan, *Heshel's Kingdom* (Evanston: Northwestern University Press, 1998).

Jaggi, Maya, 'Recovered Memories', *Guardian*, 22 September 2001; <http://books.guardian.co.uk/departments/politicsphilosophyandsociety/story/0,,555839,00.html> (accessed 10 September 2004).

——, 'The Last Word', *Guardian*, 21 December 2001; <http://books.guardian.co.uk/departments/generalfiction/story/0,6000,624750,00.html> (accessed 1 July 2004).

Jakobson, Roman, 'Two Aspects of Language and Two Types of Aphasic Disturbances', in *Selected Writings*, vol. 2: *Word and Language* (The Hague and Paris: Mouton, 1971), 239–59.

——, 'Linguistics and Poetics', in *Selected Writings*, vol. 3: *Poetry of Grammar and Grammar of Poetry*, ed. Stephen Rudy (The Hague, Paris, New York: Mouton, 1981), 18–51.

Jameson, Frederic, *The Political Unconscious: Narrative as a Socially Symbolic Act* (London: Methuen, 1981).

Johnson, Barbara, 'Metaphor, Metonymy, and Voice in *Their Eyes Were Watching God*', in *A World of Difference* (Baltimore and London: Johns Hopkins University Press, 1987), 155–71.

Josephs, Jeremy and Susi Bechhöfer, *Rosa's Child* (London and New York: I. B.Tauris, 1996).

Kafka, Franz, *The Diaries 1910–1923*, trans. Joseph Kresh, Martin Greenberg, and Hannah Arendt, ed. Max Brod (New York: Schocken, 1948, 1949).

——, *Letters to Felice*, trans. James Stern and Elisabeth Duckworth, eds Erich Heller and Jürgen Born (New York: Schocken, 1973).

——, *Briefe 1913–März 1914*, ed. Hans-Gerd Koch (Frankfurt am Main: S. Fischer Verlag, 1999).

Karl, Frederick R. and Laurence Davies, eds, *The Collected Letters of Joseph Conrad*, vol. 1 (Cambridge: Cambridge University Press, 1983).

——, eds. *The Collected Letters of Joseph Conrad*, vol. 2 (Cambridge: Cambridge University Press, 1986).

Knowles, Owen and Gene M. Moore, *Oxford Reader's Companion to Conrad* (Oxford: Oxford University Press, 2000).

Lacan, Jacques, 'The Agency of the Letter in the Unconscious or Reason Since Freud', in *Écrits: A Selection* (New York and London: Norton, 1977), 146–78.

Lazarus, Neil, 'Transnationalism and the Alleged Death of the Nation State', in Keith Ansell-Pearson, Benita Parry, and Judith Squires, eds, *Cultural Readings of Imperialism: Edward Said and the Gravity of History* (New York: St Martin's, 1997), 28–48.

Ledent, Bénédicte, 'A Fictional and Cultural Labyrinth: Caryl Phillips's "The Nature of Blood" ', *ARIEL* 32/1 (2001): 185–95.

Levi, Primo, *The Drowned and the Saved*, trans. Raymond Rosenthal (New York: Vintage, 1989).

Levinas, Emmanuel, *The Levinas Reader*, ed. Seán Hand (Oxford: Blackwell, 1989).

——, *Basic Philosophical Writings*, eds Adriann T. Peperzak, Simon Critchley, and Robert Bernasconi (Bloomington: Indiana University Press, 1996).

Lewis, Charlton T. and Charles D. Short, *A Latin Dictionary* (Oxford: Clarendon Press, 1879); <http://www.perseus.tufts.edu> (accessed 14 January 2008).

Maguire, Eleanor A., David G. Gadian, Ingrid S. Johnsrude, Catriona D. Good, John Ashburner, Richard S. J. Frackowiak, and Christopher D. Frith, 'Navigation-Related Structural Change in the Hippocampi of Taxi Drivers', *Proceedings of the National Academy of Sciences, USA* 97, 8 (2000): 4398–403.

Mantel, Hilary, 'Black is not Jewish', *Literary Review*, February 1997, 39–40.

Mardorossian, Carine M., 'Shutting up the Subaltern: Silences, Stereotypes, and Double-Entendre in Jean Rhys's *Wide Sargasso Sea*', *Callaloo*, 22/4 (1999): 1071–90.

Matos, Nicole, 'Meiotic Fictions: Hybridity and the Reproduction of the New', *Rhizomes*, 9 (2004); <http://www.rhizomes.net/issue9/matos.htm> (accessed 12 January 2008).

——, ' "Join, Interchangeable Phantoms": From Metaphor to Metonymy in Walcott's *Omeros*', *Small Axe*, 10/2 (2006): 40–60.

McCulloh, Mark R., *Understanding W. G. Sebald* (Columbia: University of South Carolina Press, 2003).

Michaels, Anne, *Fugitive Pieces* (New York: Vintage, 1998).

Miller, J. Hillis, '*Heart of Darkness* Revisited', in Joseph Conrad, *Heart of Darkness*, ed. Ross C. Murfin (Boston and New York: Bedford, 1996), 206–20.

Monk, Ray, *Ludwig Wittgenstein: The Duty of Genius* (Harmondsworth: Penguin, 1991).

Morrison, Toni, *Beloved* (New York: Plume, 1988).

Mosse, George L., *Nationalism and Sexuality* (New York: H. Fertig, 1985).

Mufti, Aamir, 'Reading the Rushdie Affair: An Essay on Islam and Politics', *Social Text*, 29 (1991): 95–116.

Murdoch, H. Adlai, 'Rhys's Pieces: Unhomeliness as Arbiter of Caribbean Creolization', *Callaloo*, 26/1 (2003): 252–72.

Nadler, Steven, *Spinoza: A Life* (Cambridge: Cambridge University Press, 1999).

Naipaul, V. S., *The Enigma of Arrival* (New York: Vintage, 1988).

——, *A Bend in the River* (New York: Vintage, 1989).

Najder, Zdzisław, *Joseph Conrad: A Chronicle* (New Brunswick: Rutgers University Press, 1983).

Nancy, Jean-Luc, *Being Singular Plural*, trans. Robert D. Richardson and Anne E. O'Byrne (Stanford: Stanford University Press, 2000).

Ndebele, Njabulo, *South African Literature and Culture: Rediscovery of the Ordinary* (Manchester: Manchester University Press; New York: St Martin's, 1994).

Ngũgĩ wa Thiong'o, *Writers in Politics* (London: Heinemann, 1981).

Nietzsche, Friedrich, *Beyond Good and Evil: Prelude to a Philosophy of the Future*, trans. R. J. Hollingdale (Harmondsworth: Penguin, 1973).

Orwell, George, 'England Your England', in *A Collection of Essays* (New York: Harcourt Brace Jovanovich, 1981), 252–79.

Ovid, *Metamorphoses*, trans. A. D. Melville (Oxford, New York: Oxford University Press, 1998).

Parry, Benita, *Conrad and Imperialism: Ideological Boundaries and Visionary Frontiers* (London: Macmillan, 1983).

——, 'Problems in Current Theories of Colonial Discourse', *Oxford Literary Review*, 9/1–2 (1987): 27–58.

Phillips, Adam, 'Close-Ups', *History Workshop Journal*, 57 (2004): 142–9.

Phillips, Caryl, *The European Tribe* (New York: Farrar, Straus, Giroux, 1987).

——, *Higher Ground* (New York: Viking, 1989).

——, *Cambridge* (New York: Knopf, 1992).

——, *Crossing the River* (London: Bloomsbury, 1993).

——, 'Water', *Agni*, 94 (1994): 28–30.

——, *The Nature of Blood* (London: Faber, 1997).

——, 'On "The Nature of Blood" and the Ghost of Anne Frank', *Common Quest* (Summer 1998): 4–7.

——, 'Introduction', in Joseph Conrad, *Heart of Darkness and Selections from The Congo Diary* (New York: Random House, 1999), xi–xviii.

——, ed., *Extravagant Strangers* (New York: Vintage, 1999).

——, *The Atlantic Sound* (London: Faber, 2000).

——, *A New World Order: Essays* (London: Secker & Warburg, 2001).

——, 'Out of Africa', *Guardian*, 22 February 2003; <http://books.guardian.co.uk/departments/classics/story/0,,900335,00.html> (accessed 10 January 2004).

——, *A Distant Shore* (New York: Knopf, 2003).

——, Personal communication, 23 November 2004.

Pinker, Steven, *The Language Instinct: How The Mind Creates Language* (New York: Perennial Classics, 2000).

Pinker, Steven and Ray Jackendoff, 'The Faculty of Language: What's Special About It?' *Cognition*, 95/2 (2005): 201–36.

——, 'The Nature of the Language Faculty and its Implications for Evolution of Language (Reply to Fitch, Hauser, and Chomsky)', *Cognition*, 97/2 (2005): 211–25.

Piotrowska, Danuta, 'Biskupin 1933–1996: Archaeology, Politics and Nationalism', *Archaeologia Polona*, 35–6 (1997–98): 255–85.

Radhakrishnan, R., *Diasporic Mediations: Between Home and Location* (Minneapolis and London: University of Minnesota Press, 1996).

——, *Theory in an Uneven World* (Oxford: Blackwell, 2003).

Rege, Josna E., *Colonial Karma: Self, Action, and Nation in the Indian English Novel* (New York: Palgrave Macmillan, 2004).

Rhys, Jean, *Smile Please: An Unfinished Autobiography* (London: André Deutsch, 1979).

——, *Letters, 1931–1966*, eds Francis Wyndham and Diana Melly (London: André Deutsch, 1984).

——, *Wide Sargasso Sea*, ed. Judith L. Raiskin, Norton Critical Edition (New York and London: Norton, 1999).

Robinson, Gene, 'The Behavior of Genes', *New York Times*, 13 December 2004, 27.

Roeper, Tom, *The Prism of Grammar: How Child Language Illuminates Humanism* (Cambridge, MA: MIT Press, 2007).

Rushdie, Salman, *The Satanic Verses* (New York: Picador, 1988).

——, *Imaginary Homelands* (London: Granta, 1991).

——, *Midnight's Children* (Harmondsworth: Penguin, 2000).

Rushdie, Salman and Günter Grass, 'Fictions are Lies that Tell the Truth: Salman Rushdie and Günter Grass in Conversation', in Michael Reder, ed., *Conversations with Salman Rushdie* (Jackson: University Press of Mississippi, 2000), 72–8.

Said, Edward, *Beginnings: Intention and Method* (New York: Basic Books, 1975).

——, *Orientalism* (New York: Vintage, 1979).

Sanders, Mark, *Complicities: The Intellectual and Apartheid* (Durham, NC and London: Duke University Press, 2002).

Santner, Eric, 'Freud's *Moses* and the Ethics of Nomotropic Desire', *October*, 88 (1999): 3–41.

Sartre, Jean-Paul, *Anti-Semite and Jew*, trans. George J. Becker (New York: Schocken, 1995).

Schlant, Ernestine, *The Language of Silence: West German Literature and the Holocaust* (New York and London: Routledge, 1999).

Sebald, W. G., *Die Ausgewandertern* (Frankfurt: S. Fischer Verlag, 1994).

——, *The Emigrants*, trans. Michael Hulse (New York: New Directions, 1997).

——, *The Rings of Saturn*, trans. Michael Hulse (New York: New Directions, 1998).

——, *Vertigo*, trans. Michael Hulse (New York: New Directions, 2000).

——, *Austerlitz*, trans. Anthea Bell (New York: Random House, 2001).

——, *On The Natural History of Destruction*, trans. Anthea Bell (New York: Random House, 2003).

——, 'Ich Fürchte das Melodramatische', unsigned interview, *Der Spiegel*, 11–12 March 2001; <http://www.spiegel.de/spiegel/0,1518,123049,00.html> (accessed 28 July 2004).

Seyhan, Azade, *Writing Outside the Nation* (Princeton and Oxford: Princeton University Press, 2001).

Shakespeare, William, *The Tempest*, ed. Stephen Orgel (Oxford: Oxford University Press, 1987).

——, *The Tragedy of Othello the Moor of Venice*, ed. Russ McDonald (Harmondsworth: Penguin, 2001).

Singer, Peter, 'Reflection', in J. M. Coetzee, *The Lives of Animals*, ed. Amy Gutmann (Princeton: Princeton University Press, 1999), 85–91.

Smith, Johanna M., ' "Too Beautiful Altogether": Ideologies of Gender and Empire in *Heart of Darkness*', in Joseph Conrad, *Heart of Darkness*, ed. Ross C. Murfin (Boston and New York: Bedford, 1996), 169–84.

Smith, Zadie, *White Teeth* (New York: Vintage, 2001).

Smolin, Lee, 'Loop Quantum Gravity', *Scientific American*, 290/1 (January 2004), 66–75.

Spinoza, Baruch, *The Ethics; Treatise on the Emendation of the Intellect; Selected Letters*, trans. Samuel Shirley, ed. Seymour Feldman (Indianapolis: Hackett, 1992).

Spivak, Gayatri Chakravorty, 'Three Women's Texts and a Critique of Imperialism', *Critical Inquiry*, 12/1 (1985): 243–61.

Steele, Jonathan, 'White Magic', *Guardian*, 27 October 2001; <http://books.guardian.co.uk/departments/generalfiction/story/0,,581532,00.html> (accessed 15 August 2007).

Steiner, George, *After Babel: Aspects of Language and Translation*, 2nd edn (Oxford and New York: Oxford University Press, 1992).

Suleri, Sara, 'Contraband Histories: Salman Rushdie and the Embodiment of Blasphemy', in M. D. Fletcher, ed., *Reading Rushdie: Perspectives on the Fiction of Salman Rushdie* (Amsterdam and Atlanta: Rodopi, 1994), 221–36.

*The Oxford English Dictionary*, 2nd edn (Oxford: Oxford University Press, 1989); *Oxford English Dictionary Online*, University of Massachusetts, Amherst, <http://dictionary.oed.com> (accessed 30 November 2007).

Turner, Victor W., *The Ritual Process: Structure and Anti-Structure* (Chicago: Aldine, 1969).

Virgil, *The Aeneid*, trans. Robert Fitzgerald (New York: Vintage, 1990).

——, *Eclogues, Georgics, Aeneid 1–6*, trans. H. Rushton Fairclough and rev. G. P. Goold, ed. G. P. Goold, vol. 63, Loeb Classical Library (Cambridge, MA: Harvard University Press, 1999).

Visser, Nicholas, 'Beyond the Interregnum: A Note on the Ending of *July's People*', in Martin Trump, ed., *Rendering Things Visible: Essays on South African Literary Culture* (Johannesburg: Ravan, 1990), 61–7.

Warner, Marina, 'Its Own Dark Styx', review of *The Nature of Blood*, by Caryl Phillips, *London Review of Books*, 20 March 1997, 23–4.

Watt, Ian, 'Impressionism and Symbolism in *Heart of Darkness*', in Joseph Conrad, *Heart of Darkness*, ed. Robert Kimbrough, 3rd edn (New York: Norton, 1988), 311–36.

Wittgenstein, Ludwig, *Philosophical Investigations*, trans. G. E. M. Anscombe, 3rd edn (New York: Macmillan, 1958).

Wood, James, 'An Interview with W. G. Sebald', *Brick*, 59 (1998): 23–9.

——, *The Broken Estate: Essays on Literature and Belief* (New York: Random House, 1999).

Wright, Laura, *Writing 'Out of All the Camps': J. M. Coetzee's Narratives of Displacement* (New York, London: Routledge, 2006).

Zierler, Wendy, ' "My Holocaust Is Not Your Holocaust": "Facing" Black and Jewish Experience in *The Pawnbroker, Higher Ground,* and *The Nature of Blood*', *Holocaust and Genocide Studies*, 18/1 (2004): 46–67.

# Index

Printed and bound by CPI Group (UK) Ltd, Croydon, CR0 4YY